REIMAGINING PARLIAMENT

"The existential challenges that our democracies are currently facing require a deep transformation: this book reconceives parliamentary organisation, behaviours, roles and governance, to help to understand and lead this transformation."
Nicola Lupo, LUISS Guido Carli

"This innovative and insightful book is a must-have for anyone interested in the UK Parliament. Combining the views of academics, experts and practitioners who know Parliament inside and out, it gives a unique view of what is wrong with Westminster and how it can be reimagined."
Ben Worthy, Birkbeck, University of London

REIMAGINING PARLIAMENT

Edited by
David Judge and Cristina Leston-Bandeira

First published in Great Britain in 2024 by

Bristol University Press
University of Bristol
1–9 Old Park Hill
Bristol
BS2 8BB
UK
t: +44 (0)117 374 6645
e: bup-info@bristol.ac.uk

Details of international sales and distribution partners are available at bristoluniversitypress.co.uk

© Bristol University Press 2024

British Library Cataloguing in Publication Data
A catalogue record for this book is available from the British Library

ISBN 978-1-5292-2698-0 hardcover
ISBN 978-1-5292-2699-7 paperback
ISBN 978-1-5292-2700-0 ePub
ISBN 978-1-5292-2702-4 ePdf

The right of David Judge and Cristina Leston-Bandeira to be identified as editors of this work has been asserted by them in accordance with the Copyright, Designs and Patents Act 1988.

All rights reserved: no part of this publication may be reproduced, stored in a retrieval system, or transmitted in any form or by any means, electronic, mechanical, photocopying, recording, or otherwise without the prior permission of Bristol University Press.

Every reasonable effort has been made to obtain permission to reproduce copyrighted material. If, however, anyone knows of an oversight, please contact the publisher.

The statements and opinions contained within this publication are solely those of the editors and contributors and not of the University of Bristol or Bristol University Press. The University of Bristol and Bristol University Press disclaim responsibility for any injury to persons or property resulting from any material published in this publication.

Bristol University Press works to counter discrimination on grounds of gender, race, disability, age and sexuality.

Cover design: Nicky Boroweic
Front cover image: AdobeStock/Anderson
Bristol University Press uses environmentally responsible print partners.
Printed and bound in Great Britain by CPI Group (UK) Ltd, Croydon, CR0 4YY

Contents

Notes on Contributors		vi
Acknowledgements		viii
1	Introduction: What, Why and How of Reimagining *David Judge and Cristina Leston-Bandeira*	1
2	Reimagining Parliamentary Space *Alexandra Meakin*	16
3	Reimagining Rhythms, Rituals and Symbols *Emma Crewe*	32
4	Reimagining Parliamentary Representation *David Judge*	48
5	Reimagining Engagement between Citizens and Parliament *Cristina Leston-Bandeira, Didier Caluwaerts and Daan Vermassen*	65
6	Reimagining Working: Who Works and How? *Hannah White*	83
7	Reimagining Parliamentary Governance *Ben Yong*	98
8	Reimagining Scrutiny *Lucinda Maer*	112
9	Reimagining Parliamentary Procedure *Paul Evans*	126
10	Conclusion: Thinking Seriously about Starting Over *David Judge and Cristina Leston-Bandeira*	142
References		156
Index		173

Notes on Contributors

Didier Caluwaerts is Associate Professor of Political Science at the Vrije Universiteit Brussel. He was previously a Fulbright Democracy Fellow at the Harvard Ash Center for Democratic Governance and Innovation. His PhD (2011, Vrije Universiteit Brussel) was awarded the 2012 ECPR (European Consortium for Political Research) Jean Blondel PhD award. His research interests include democratic innovation, democratic long-termism and participatory democracy.

Emma Crewe is Research Professor and Co-Head of the Department of Anthropology and Sociology, SOAS University of London; Research Supervisor at the University of Hertfordshire; and Deputy Chair of the Study of Parliament Group. She has published ethnographies on the *House of Lords* and the *House of Commons*, and most recently the *Anthropology of Parliaments*. She is Director of the Global Research Network on Parliaments and People, coordinating a global coalition of researchers in Brazil, Ethiopia, Fiji, India, the UK and the US (European Research Council Advanced Grant).

Paul Evans worked in the House of Commons from 1981 to 2020. He has written extensively on parliament and in 2017 edited *Essays on the History of Parliamentary Procedure* (Hart). He has held visiting and honorary positions at University College London, King's College London, Birkbeck University of London and Lincoln University. He is a fellow of the Academy of Social Sciences and an associate of the Institute for Government.

David Judge is Emeritus Professor of Politics at the University of Strathclyde, Glasgow. His primary research interests are focused upon representative democracy, issues of democratic legitimacy and parliamentary institutions. He is the author/editor of 13 books including *The Politics of Parliamentary Reform* (Heinemann); *The Parliamentary State* (SAGE); *Political Institutions in the UK* (Oxford University Press); *Representation: Theory and Practice in Britain* (Routledge); and *Democratic Incongruities: Representative Democracy in Britain* (Palgrave Macmillan).

NOTES ON CONTRIBUTORS

Cristina Leston-Bandeira is Professor of Politics at the University of Leeds, Co-founder and Chair of the pioneering International Parliament Engagement Network. She has served as Chair of the UK Study of Parliament Group, Co-Convenor of the Political Studies Association Parliaments Specialist Group and Co-editor of *Parliamentary Affairs*. She has written extensively on the relationship between parliament and citizens.

Lucinda Maer is Deputy Principal Clerk in the House of Commons. She is currently the House of Commons Cultural Transformation Director. Her previous roles include Clerk of the Joint Committee on Human Rights, Clerk of the Liaison Committee, and Head of the Parliament and Constitution Centre in the Commons Library. She is an honorary researcher at the Constitution Unit, University College London, and member of the Study of Parliament Group.

Alexandra Meakin is Lecturer in British Politics and Programme Director of Politics and Parliamentary Studies at the University of Leeds. Her PhD thesis, *Understanding the Restoration and Renewal of the Palace of Westminster*, was awarded the 2020 Walter Bagehot Prize for best dissertation in the field of government and public administration by the UK's Political Studies Association. For over a decade she worked in the House of Commons for select committees and for MPs.

Daan Vermassen is a postdoctoral researcher at the Vrije Universiteit Brussel. His research interests cover democratic long-termism, democratic design and the representation of future generations.

Hannah White is Director of the non-partisan think tank the Institute for Government and a regular media commentator. After completing her PhD and a decade working in the House of Commons as a Parliamentary Clerk, she became Secretary to the Committee on Standards in Public Life. She joined the Institute for Government in 2014 and received an OBE in 2020 for services to the constitution. In April 2022 she published her first book, *Held in Contempt: What's Wrong with the House of Commons?* (Manchester University Press).

Ben Yong is Associate Professor of Public Law and Human Rights at Durham Law School. He has written on governance and parliamentary budgeting; and has had Leverhulme Trust funding to research legal advice to parliament and the accountability of parliamentary administration. He is the co-editor of the third edition of *Parliament and the Law* (Hart, 2022).

Acknowledgements

Why write a book like this? This is a question that has confronted the editors and contributors alike throughout the production of this book. At various stages the answers have undoubtedly been fraught with uncertainty as the schedules for writing chapters hit the buffers of far more pressing professional commitments, routines and rigours of daily life, and vagaries of time. Nonetheless, all contributors have shown commendable patience, perseverance and positivity in responding to the editors' numerous requests, suggestions and deadlines.

Despite these shared tribulations, the authors have also shared a fundamental motivation for writing this book: they care about parliament, they believe in its elemental importance within the UK's political system, yet their respective experiences as practitioners and academics leads them to perceive that now might well be the time 'to start thinking about starting over'. Indeed, this book would not have been written without the shared willingness of contributors to step outside of their professional and academic comfort zones and to embark on a process of reimagining. The editors hereby record their deepest gratitude.

Equally, this book would not have been written without the willingness of Stephen Wenham at Bristol University Press to take a punt on an idea that was, when first presented to him, big on ambition but not so big on the details of how that ambition was to be realised. Similarly, without the constant prodding and encouragement of Zoe Forbes at Bristol University Press the book would have taken even longer to produce than it eventually did. So, many thanks to Stephen, Zoe and the wider production team at Bristol University Press.

The production of this book might have been quicker if the expectations of the families Judge and Leston-Bandeira – for something resembling 'normal family life' – had not intervened. David knows that Lorraine, Ben and Hannah, as part of long family tradition, won't read this book, and still can't understand why he keeps wanting to write books. Nonetheless, he offers his thanks to Lorraine for her stoic forbearance. Cristina knows that her boys – James, Tomás, Rafael and Mário – will for ever find parliament boring, but also that they will always put up with her obsession with all parliamentary things. As always, she is very grateful for their patience with the time taken away from family time.

1

Introduction: What, Why and How of Reimagining

David Judge and Cristina Leston-Bandeira

Introduction

Few institutions, processes or practices – whether economic, social or political – have escaped a seeming imperative, in recent years, to 'think seriously about starting over' (Weiner quoted in KPMG, 2020: 1). Reimagining, in its literal meaning 'the action or an act of imagining something again, a reconstruction; a remake' (*Oxford English Dictionary*), captures this sentiment succinctly. It marks a critical juncture, when the constraints of past ideational and practical trajectories can be jumped and rerouted along different directional tracks. Reimagining does not predict the future but seeks to understand and identify possibilities for, and inhibitors of, alternative conceptions of the future. But reimagining is not simply wishful thinking, of identifying and hoping for a different future; it is also rooted in the present, in understandings and imaginings of current problems and pathologies. It is 'simultaneously about what does and does not yet exist, as it explores, but also at times troubles and explodes the border between the two' (Cooper, 2019: 2).

A book entitled *Reimagining Parliament*, therefore, is duty bound to explore and trouble (in the sense of challenging and disrupting) current imaginings of what parliament is and does. It should question long-held assumptions. It should seek to identify the elemental principles which underpin routines, organisation and operation, and project those principles into the future to rethink what parliament might be and might do. Consequently, a reimagining of parliament should extend beyond limited reform and simple improvement.

The aim of this introductory chapter is three-fold. First, to introduce the processes of reimagining by identifying what is to be reimagined, who is going to be doing the reimagining, and the approaches adopted in reimagining. Second, to provide a structural frame – constructed around notions of space, connectivity and interaction – within which key parliamentary activities can be reimagined. Third, to identify where we are starting from, if we are 'to think seriously about starting over'.

Processes of reimagining

While the aims and aspirations of reimagining are clear, the processes by which such rethinking can be prompted and achieved are more indeterminate. The first stage in these processes is to identify what is to be reimagined. In the case of this book the specific focus is the UK parliament. It is not about the genus of 'parliament', or of the general concept of 'parliament'. Instead, it is about the Westminster parliament with its own peculiar history, procedural idiosyncrasies, institutional proclivities, and encompassing social, cultural and political milieux. It is about a representative institution founded upon an electoral franchise rooted historically in geographical constituencies; with a majoritarian electoral system rooted in party competition; with a dynamic 'fused-powers' relationship between the executive (historically the 'crown') and parliament; with an asymmetrical bicameral system; with institutional claims to political sovereignty throughout the UK state; and with institutional capacity for 'shape-shifting' within the malleable frame of an uncodified constitution. In essence it is about a parliament firmly located within a 'Westminster system' of government (for the continuing relevance of this characterisation see Flinders et al, 2022: 357–60).

It is also a UK parliament firmly located in a post-Brexit, pluri-national, pluri-parliamentary state; in an increasingly multi-cultural, multi-ethnic, and multi-racial society. It is a polity increasingly aware of the intersectionality of representative processes; yet, nonetheless, a polity that manifests deep-rooted and continuing inequalities of class, gender, identity, race, ethnicity and (dis)ability as well as pronounced exclusionary political tendencies. Moreover, it is a polity in which there is widespread public dissatisfaction with the practice of UK politics, comparatively low levels of trust in parliament and even lower levels of trust in political parties (see Office for National Statistics, 2022; Policy Institute, 2023). Yet, paradoxically, belief in the *principle* of democracy has risen in recent decades, with the World Values Survey recording that 90 per cent of UK respondents in 2022 agreed that democracy was a 'good way of governing the country'.

This is the present (what currently exists). This provides the starting point for reimagining (what does not yet exist). Indeed, it is worth underlining at the outset that this future quest is bounded by the primary institutional focus of this exploration. It is not, therefore, a meta-reimagining of the UK's constitution, nor of the UK state and its wider system of governance, nor of it its broader polity, nor of wider UK society. It is a reimagining with a specific focus upon parliament as an institution. Nonetheless, it is an exploration and exposition of reimagining that is necessarily context-specific; and at various points the distinctive societal and political context of the UK will intrude into a reimagining of parliament.

The second stage of reimagining is to identify who is doing the reimagining. The selection criteria for contributors to this book were relatively simple. First, if the starting point of reimagining is to know what currently exists, then knowledge of what parliament does and how it does it, combined with the capacity both to analyse and evaluate its effectiveness in doing these things, is a basic requirement. A second requirement is that the collective knowledge of 'reimagineers' should draw upon both inside and outside perspectives: both the practical, professional experience of those who have worked in Westminster and the academic, research experience of those who have analysed parliament from a range of disciplines. Collectively the contributing authors to this volume combine the perspectives of both current and former senior parliamentary officials (clerks of the House of Commons) with the perspectives of researchers, academics and analysts who bring disciplinary expertise in social anthropology, constitutional law, policy analysis and political science. A third requirement is that, although contributors have extensive experience and knowledge of parliament, they should be willing to step outside their professional and academic comfort zones to be provoked into thinking afresh about how they might reimagine parliament (or more accurately, and specifically, the aspects of parliamentary organisation, behaviours, roles and governance that the editors asked each of them to consider). Spoiler alert: every contributor encountered difficulties in responding to this provocation.

A third stage is the 'how' of reimagining. While there are a great number of academic books and articles with the word 'reimagining' in their titles, there are relatively few that explain how to go about reimagining. Many works simply take 'reform' or 'improvement' as synonyms for 'reimagine'; leaving implicit or unstated the underpinning logic of such change – other than as a response to perceived current malaise. Certainly, the UK parliament throughout its history has been subject to reform, and to constant advocacy and agitation for reform. Reform carries connotations of improving what already exists, of rectification through putting something right, or of refinement through incremental change. In this sense parliamentary reform is restricted by pre-existing ideas of what the institution is, rather than of what the institution should be. The question of how a 'headshift' – in Keane's (2011: 218) sense of 'a break with conventional thinking' – can be achieved is rarely asked in relation to parliament.

Yet this was a question that was raised at a workshop for contributing authors convened at Leeds University in April 2022. To break with the orthodoxies of institutional perspectives – framed primarily in terms of parliamentary functions, powers and roles – authors were prompted to identify foundational principles that would drive the modelling *ab initio* of the parliamentary activity under consideration in their respective chapters; to explain why the identified principles were deemed to be foundational, and why they mattered. From the outset, intentionally so as not to restrict the scope of reimagining, no attempt was made to identify a set of cohesive, consistent or collectively agreed principles to guide the reimagining of the various dimensions of parliamentary space, connectivity and interaction covered in this book. In part, this was because of the wide span of possible 'spatial', 'cultural', 'political', 'process', 'governance' and 'people' principles to be considered across the chapters. In part, also, because of a recognition that 'foundational' principles are open to contestation and interpretation. Instead, each contributor was left free to identify and justify which principles provided the basis for their prospective reimagining.

Nonetheless, two broad categories of principles emerged from this identification process. In the first category are principles broadly reflective of current basic political tenets underpinning notions of liberal democracy in the UK, and those observable in a broader societal context in which the UK has become more diverse and more socially liberal: these include openness; engagement/connectedness; accessibility; inclusion; equality; fairness; responsiveness; and accountability. Principles in the second category are more closely delimited and are associated more with institutional and organisational norms and practices: these include wellness; ethical propriety; sustainability; organisational flexibility; and effective institutional governance. While this distinction is neither intended to connote a hierarchy of importance, nor are the categories mutually exclusive, nonetheless, it helps to explain why certain principles are of more direct relevance to some aspects of reimagining than others in the following chapters.

The present: the starting point of reimagining

The UK parliament serves as a unique focal point of UK governance. Its uniqueness stems from a distinctive historical lineage in the intertwining of processes of representational linkage with procedures of political responsibility and accountability, and with dynamic patterns of legitimation. Notions of space, connectivity and interaction help in defining its positioning and distinctiveness at the centre of UK politics. 'Space' focuses attention upon location, architectural space and purpose, and the symbols, performances and rituals of parliament. 'Connectivity' is concerned with the dynamics of representation, the identities of those to be brought together in parliament, and how citizens are included and engaged in parliamentary processes.

'Interaction' is multi-directional, both outward looking to inter-institutional connections and highly politicised processes of effecting government responsibility and accountability; and inward looking to intra-institutional modes of administration and regulation, demarcated by parliamentary procedures and processes of self-governance.

If ideas of space, connectivity and interaction help in theorising parliament's positioning and distinctiveness, they also serve as an ideational frame within which to structure an assessment of the contemporary significance of parliament. Parliament might well be central and distinctive in the UK's polity but is parliament still significant, is it effective, is it 'fit for purpose'? If not, then now would appear to be the time 'to think seriously about starting over'. But the prior question to address is where are we starting from: what is the condition of parliament now? The following sections – framed in terms of space, connectivity and interaction – seek, therefore, to provide brief overviews of where we are now, in anticipation that later chapters can provide more detailed answers to this question and 'explore and trouble' the boundary between current imaginings and potential reimaginings.

Where are we now?

Space

Physical space

Typically, parliaments are designed with what Parkinson (2012: 95) calls 'symbolic intent'. Their design provides architectural cues as to their political importance – as to what they are as institutions, and what their occupants claim to do in relation to citizens and the state. Yet, there are multiple ways of seeing and reading any given symbol. These ways may be influenced by changed historical, cultural, societal or political contexts which impact upon how citizens perceive parliamentary buildings. As a result, former monumental architectural styles 'may be respected, but not always identified with' (Therborn, 2014: 335). This has certainly been the case for the Westminster parliament. Throughout its history the symbolic intent of the Palace of Westminster has transmogrified from an architectural representation of monarchical power and authority in the 11th century; through 'profoundly conservative, hierarchical and anti-democratic intentions' (Parkinson, 2012: 98) of the designers of the rebuilt palace after the catastrophic fire of 1834; through to the strong conviction, expressed by MPs after the destruction of the Commons chamber by bombing in 1941, that retaining the basic shape, dimensions and Gothic form of the old chamber would now serve as 'the ultimate architectural manifestation of representative democracy' (Shenton, 2016: 4).

That was then: this is now. The Palace of Westminster is now a Grade 1 listed building and a designated United Nations Educational, Scientific and Cultural Organization World Heritage Site; yet, structurally, it is falling apart. Starkly stated, 'it is deteriorating faster than it can be repaired, increasing the risk of sudden and catastrophic failure' (Ellison et al, 2022: S69; see also Flinders et al, 2019; Meakin, 2019; White, 2022). So, the starting point for a reimagining of parliamentary architectural space is a decrepit building of exceptional architectural and historical importance, yet which is unsafe, unhealthy and unwelcoming for the people who work there or who have cause to visit. Westminster in the second decade of the 21st century hardly serves, therefore, as a symbol of 'the beating heart of a modern democracy' (Adonis, 2022). So, where we are now is that the necessity of major refurbishment of the parliamentary estate is beyond doubt (and has been formally evidenced in parliament's own Restoration and Renewal programme), yet there is an urgent need to transition away from mere respect for architectural heritage towards a more radical reimagining of space at Westminster.

The architectural fabric of Westminster, however, is only one element contributing to its designation as a World Heritage Site, included also are the Parliamentary Heritage Collections. These are some 26,000 'significant historical and contemporary artifacts' – including art works, sculptures, furniture, ceramics, panelling, wall paintings and other decorative arts – which are integral to 'the material culture of Parliament and part of the democratic process, both ceremonial and in daily use' (Ellison et al, 2022: S69). Historically, these artifacts, and the aesthetics of parliament's material culture, have symbolised social hierarchies; especially of gendered social order and power differentials associated with ethnicity and class (see Rai, 2017: 508; Verge, 2022: 1055). Where we are now, however, is that, in the context of rapid social and political change, previously unrepresented, or under-represented, groups have come to make demands that their identities should 'find spatial reflection within representative buildings' and gain 'visual representation through portraits and statues of different bodies' (Rai, 2015: 1184). In recognition of these demands, managers of the art collections in Westminster now identify one of their key aims as being to 'diversify the Collection and its interpretation to better reflect the diverse population of the UK' (House of Commons, 2022a).

Space: performance, interactions and rhythms

Beyond architectural conceptions of legislatures as physical spaces, they may also be viewed as 'public spaces' which provide venues – spaces – for the 'face-to-face performance of democratic roles' (Parkinson, 2013: 440; Prior and Sivashankar, 2023: 2–4). Shirin Rai (2015) has been particularly influential in developing a 'political performance framework' with parliament foregrounded as the institutional space where the performance of 'everyday politics', and political representation, 'goes on in symbolic and literal ways' (2015: 1180–1). In this view, space and performance are relational, and the nature of social interactions within parliamentary spaces are not pre-given. Performance in parliament is embedded within 'cultural histories, political economy, everyday norms and rituals', and broad social relations of class and gender, ethnicity and language are 'mediated through performance' (2015: 1182). As Puwar (2021: 253) points out: 'The architecture, timing, leisure activities, working procedures, political priorities, and bodily performances make each institution the type of gendered and racialized place it is.'

In the 21st century, the UK parliament is still 'the type of place' where rituals, rhythms and performances of everyday politics 'reflect, resist, and refurbish existing and shifting power relations' (Rai, 2015: 1181). Differences of class, gender, ethnicity and (dis)ability still mark some representatives, in a rhetorical sense, as 'space invaders' (Puwar, 2021: 254). Although participation in parliamentary rituals, performances and rhythms registers the insider status of members from these groups, the very same rituals, performances and rhythms also confirm, simultaneously, their outsider status. In this sense, members of minority and under-represented groups 'arrive and take up space, but their occupation of space is still contradictory and tenuous … they are thought to not quite belong' (2021: 254).

If this is where we are now, the challenge is to realign – to reimagine – parliamentary space and its symbols, rituals, performances and rhythms to foster an enhanced, expanded and inclusive sense of belonging.

Connectivity

In terms of parliament's connections with citizens, where we are now is not where we used to be. In the UK parliament's own story-telling: 'How Parliament works today is very different from how it worked when it began over 700 years ago. It has evolved so that everyone can have a say in how the UK is run and who runs it' (UK Parliament, 2023a). While the first sentence of this statement is incontestable; the second is deeply contentious in its depiction of the connections between citizens and parliamentarians in the contemporary UK.

In fact, throughout most of the UK parliament's history there has been no expectation or justification that 'everyone' could or should have a say in the exercise of government. For long periods the default setting was anti-democratic, with democracy treated as 'a problem' within British political culture (Wright, 1994: 9). Parliamentary government in the UK developed as a system that privileged government over parliament, and political representation over political participation. At the core of this system the principle of representation was fused with the principles of consent, legitimation and authorisation of executive actions. Its distinguishing feature was the transmission of opinion between representatives of the 'political nation' (variously reconstituted according to changes in the nature and scope of the electoral franchise) and 'government' (in its historical transmutation from monarchical to ministerial). Yet, paradoxically, as a peculiarly executive-centric form of government, UK governments had no independent source of legitimacy other than that derived from the legislature and its linkage with the 'political nation'. Significantly, as the social composition of that 'nation' changed, with extensions of the franchise in the 19th and 20th centuries, the older, narrower notion of 'representative government' became subsumed within the broader notion of 'representative democracy'. The transition to representative democracy also brought with it its own political paradox. The conjunction of 'representation' with 'democracy' brought into sharp focus the contradiction that political representation is as much about exclusion as inclusion, and that electoral processes simultaneously separate and link representatives from the represented (see Judge, 2014: 6–7, 25–7, 192–4).

Certainly, the membership of the House of Commons is now more representative of the UK citizenry than at any previous time in its history. Yet, still the discriminatory, exclusionary outcomes of UK elections are evident in the disproportionality of parliamentary representation in terms of gender, race, ethnicity, disability and social class. Indeed, recent social survey data indicates that people in the UK still feel distanced from their elected representatives, with significant proportions believing that politicians do not understand their lives (Patel and Quilter-Pinner, 2022: 20–1) and having little trust in parliament (Office for National Statistics, 2022: worksheet 1.4). Recent qualitative research has also revealed a pervasive and 'widespread belief that politicians do not inhabit the same experiential landscape as the people they speak for' (Coleman and Moss, 2022: 7).

Certainly, also, parliament is now more connected to the public in terms of its visibility and accessibility, and opportunities for the public to get involved beyond MP–constituent connections (Walker, 2012; Leston-Bandeira, 2016; Leston-Bandeira and Walker, 2018). This is reflected in a vast expansion over the last couple of decades of its usage of digital information communication technologies, its development of outreach, educational and visitor services, and its involvement of publics in the formulation, deliberation and scrutiny of public policies through, for example, e-petitions, deliberative workshops and 'lived experience' evidence utilised by committees, alongside digital engagement with individual MPs. Yet, despite this considerable expansion of parliament's public engagement activity, the effects and impact of this activity – the extent to which ordinary citizens can 'have a say' – remains indeterminate.

So, this is where we are now in terms of connectivity. The questions left unanswered, however, are: is this where we want to be or where we should be?

Interaction

Inter-institutional

When it comes to analysing parliament's interactions with the executive the adage 'where we are now is not where we used to be' has particular resonance. Historically, one of the main roles of the UK parliament has been 'to examine and challenge the work of the government' (UK Parliament, 2023b). This remains the case today. A functional scrutiny relationship is still at the heart of executive-legislative interactions whereby the activities of government are monitored, investigated, questioned and deliberated in the expectation that the government will publicly respond, explain and justify its policies and decisions to parliament. Underpinning this seemingly virtuous interaction are basic presumptions about 'willingness' and 'capacity': on the one side, that parliament is willing to scrutinise government and has the capacity to do so; and, on the other side, that government is willing to be scrutinised and will not seek to incapacitate parliamentary scrutiny processes. Through this interaction, the formal accountability of government to parliament is realised. What is distinctive about this formal relationship is that government is *required* to account for its actions to parliament – unlike other modes of external scrutiny centred upon the media (both mainstream and social), citizens' groups, informal monitoring agencies and audit bodies.

Certainly, the willingness of parliament to scrutinise government is manifest in the sheer time and effort devoted to its investigatory, questioning and deliberative activities (see HC 1, 2022; House of Lords, 2022). Equally there is little doubt that the scrutiny activity of parliament requires significant reciprocal executive activity – by ministers and officials from departments, agencies and other public bodies – in providing both information and evidence on the input side, and formal and substantive responses on the output side.

But willingness to scrutinise cannot be captured simply through quantification of activity levels at Westminster, it also requires qualitative assessment of the parliamentary processes and procedures designed to secure more effective executive transparency and accountability. In recent years parliament (or at least its non-executive members and House officers) has displayed a greater willingness to use existing procedures in a more creative manner to scrutinise ministerial actions (see, for example, House of Commons Library, 2023). Alongside this growing willingness to scrutinise has been an enhancement of the institutional capacity of parliament to scrutinise through the systematisation of select committees and the reconstitution of its legislative committees (see, for example, Thompson, 2015; Russell and Gover, 2017; Maer, 2019; Geddes, 2020a; Connolly et al, 2022).

Offsetting these advances – of increased willingness and improved institutional capacity of parliament to scrutinise the executive – is a profound unwillingness of government to be scrutinised and a strengthening of its political capacity to frustrate parliamentary scrutiny. This is nothing new, all post-war UK governments have displayed a basic reticence to have their activities exhaustively scrutinised in parliament. What is perhaps new, however, is that Conservative governments since 2015 have matched this unwillingness with intensification of executive capacity to frustrate scrutiny in Westminster (for details see Judge, 2021; Study of Parliament Group, 2021; White, 2022; Hansard Society, 2023; Russell and James, 2023). The truly exceptional, and eventually compounded, circumstances in this period – of Brexit and COVID-19 – might help to explain and justify the exceptional use of executive powers to minimise parliamentary scrutiny. But, as Hannah White (2022: 3) points out, 'these two crises … both highlighted and exacerbated worrying trends' and, in the case of the draconian policy responses of government to the COVID-19 pandemic, served to fuel these trends as if 'on steroids'.

Where we are now, therefore, is that parliament continues to expend most of its time on its investigatory, questioning and deliberative activities. Yet ministers have, at various times and on numerous occasions in recent years, shown both an increased unwillingness to assist parliament in its scrutiny of the policies, administration and expenditure of government departments, agencies and associated public bodies; while displaying a heightened propensity to subvert parliamentary scrutiny of their legislative programmes and proposals (through, for example, the fast-tracking of legislation, the introduction of greater numbers of framework/skeleton bills and the massive use of secondary legislation).

Intra-institutional

People

Whereas there is an institutionalised fissure in the interactions between parliament and government, the professional interactions of parliamentarians, as well as of those parliamentary personnel who provide elected members with support and assistance, might be anticipated to be less asymmetric. Nonetheless, there is an unbalanced relationship between MPs and all other personnel working at Westminster in associated parliamentary roles. MPs historically have claimed an ancient right to regulate their own affairs. Self-governance and self-regulation were grounded in privileges and protections afforded to MPs by the constitution but, as Hannah White (2022: 135–6) observes, 'the wish of parliamentarians to protect their right to manage their own affairs ... too often led to the preservation of inadequate administrative processes which ... facilitated bad behaviour'. The extent and reach of bad behaviour, in human resources (HR) terms, were exposed dramatically during the Johnson government, with mounting complaints against MPs for bullying, harassment or sexual misconduct, and growing concern at the absence of an independent rigorous and fair process in place to reach judgement on sanctioning such misconduct. In these circumstances even staunch defenders of 'the ancient responsibilities and rights of Parliament' recognised that self-regulation needed to be curbed as 'it is our fault that we have to do this and so it is right to change' (Jacob Rees-Mogg, HC Debates, 23 June 2020, col.1247).

But if that was then, what is the position now? Clearly parliament now is not where it was in terms of recognition of bullying, harassment or sexual misconduct, and in the deployment of significantly enhanced policies, procedures, guidelines, helplines, networks and HR teams to address these issues. Moreover, the UK parliament now has a formal commitment 'to ensuring everyone working [at Westminster] feels supported, safe and positive' (UK Parliament, 2023c). However, it is where it is largely because of external, public concern about its previously unregulated activities. In this reactive mode there is a danger, as Dávid-Barrett (2022: 11) points out, that '"fixing" the system for investigating and sanctioning misconduct may have crowded out a more constructive discussion about how individuals could do more to promote good behaviour'. Such constructive discussion would certainly seem to point towards the value of reimagining intra-institutional interactions at Westminster.

Internal governance

All organisations require some form of internal governance. Parliament is no exception. Yet, parliament is also held to be unique. The House of Commons has a 'singular character' insofar as it 'is run by its 650 Members, who have all been through the hard test of election'; is sovereign to the extent that it 'is constrained only by its own legislation which it may reverse' (HC 692, 2014: paras 12–13); and some of its members – holding government positions – exercise more influence in how the House is administered than others, despite all MPs being nominally equal. Adding to parliament's organisational distinctiveness is the fact that it is a bicameral institution with each House invested in protecting its own autonomy, status and privileges. The House of Lords has its own corporate leadership and administrative structures distinct from those of the Commons.

Yet institutional distinctiveness does not preclude good organisational governance – in terms of organisational efficiency, effectiveness, value for money and the upholding and monitoring of organisational performance and agreed standards – it just makes such governance far harder to effect. As the House of Commons Governance Committee observed in 2014:

> The governance arrangements for the House have developed over time often in response to particular issues or events. This has resulted in a situation where the complexities which are inherent in the character of the House as a legislature have been compounded by layers of interventions which have built on and adapted what went before rather than rationalising or restructuring it. (HC 692, 2014: para 26)

A history of governance at Westminster would chronicle, therefore: parliamentary officials performing, by default, day-to-day management; incremental change in governance until things went wrong – whether measured, for instance, by scandalous behaviour (expenses, sexual misconduct, bullying) or structural decay (restoration and renewal); and parliamentarians only becoming actively engaged in governance decision-making and implementation issues *in extremis* (see Yong, 2018: 90–1, 98–101). In more normal times, as Barrett (2022: 125) observes, 'the evidence does show that members collectively seem to go missing in action … [in] delivering effective governance and management'.

So where are we now? Certainly, both houses of parliament have in recent decades enhanced their formal governance mechanisms (see Kelly, 2023). Certainly, Penny Mordaunt, the Leader of the House of Commons in 2023, declared her intention of 'making our legislature the best in the world' by ensuring that 'the services it provides enable MPs to have the most agency and capacity … to be as effective as they possibly can be' (Mordaunt, 2023). To this end she maintained that the workplace of MPs 'needs to modernise'. Significantly, with an eye on the past, she was adamant that '"slow and dull" will no longer do'. This seemed like an invitation, whether intended or not, for a reimagining of House governance; and to encourage MPs no longer to 'go missing in action'.

Procedural

Parliamentary procedure provides the framework within which many of the inter-institutional and intra-institutional interactions, examined earlier, take place. In essence, procedure is the accumulation, chronicling and application of evolving practice, rules, standing orders and legislation governing the conduct of parliamentary business. It is often perceived to be boring in the sense of being 'arcane', 'complex', 'impenetrable' and 'incomprehensible' to all but the nerdiest of procedural experts, as well as being deemed to be largely beyond the comprehension of the public and even many MPs. Yet, in the words of one former Leader of the House of Commons: 'Procedure may be boring to some, but it is about the distribution and exercise of power. It really matters' (Straw, 2012, quoted in Besly and Goldsmith, 2019: 176; see also Norton, 2001: 30).

Parliamentary procedure, of necessity, is rooted in the past. Over a century ago Ilbert (1908: iv) observed that: 'Parliament strikes its roots so deep into the past that scarcely a single feature of its proceedings can be made intelligible without reference to history.' A century later Evans (2017: 18) noted that '[t]he same remark … could possibly be made today'. Indeed, the most authoritative publication on parliamentary procedure, Erskine May's *Treatise on the Law, Privileges, Proceedings and Usage of Parliament* (2019), not only documents the rules (both formal and informal) as to how parliament conducts its contemporary business, but also chronicles the historical adaptability of parliamentary rules and arrangements to changing political circumstances. What the historical record shows very clearly is the 'political nature' of parliamentary procedure (Redlich, 1908: xxxiii); it institutionalises 'dissensus' (Palonen, 2019: 46); it allows for profound disagreements to be deliberated and decided. In essence, it regulates who can speak and when; and who can decide and how. In other words, procedure reveals the power differentials in the control of parliamentary business and decision-making. These differentials were starkly exposed in the frequent and extensive rewriting of parliamentary rules in the late 19th and early 20th centuries, which secured the precedence of government business over the historic privileges and participatory rights of nominally equal representatives in the Commons.

In the 21st century, successive governments have been resistant to challenges to their precedence. Nonetheless, despite such resistance, recent decades have witnessed procedural challenges to executive dominance through the introduction of new standing orders, revisions to standing orders and the creative interpretation of standing orders by the Speaker. This has resulted in an incremental enhancement of the rights of non-executive legislators. More spectacularly, dramatic events in parliament – surrounding the Brexit process after the 2016 EU referendum – revealed the critical role of parliamentary procedures in how this process was structured, managed and regulated (for details see Russell and James, 2023). In elemental form, these procedures revealed – and in many instances stress-tested (almost to their furthest limits) – the organisational trade-offs to be made between upholding the equal rights of individual legislators and enabling their collective actions; conflicts over agenda-power and the control of parliamentary proceedings; and the mutability of procedures and organisational precepts that were conventionally held to be immutable. Significantly, however, this period did not mark an elemental shift in procedural development. At best, it witnessed short-lived informal procedural innovation alongside long-term procedural stability (Fleming, 2021: 959).

So, where are we now? Despite the Brexit process and its aftermath spotlighting the elemental importance of parliamentary procedure; procedural matters have – apart from the continued attention of a few think-tanks – largely receded back into the shadows of political attention. Now would be an appropriate time, therefore, to kickstart a more comprehensive and creative rethinking of the political nature of procedure and how it might be adapted to changing circumstances of the 21st-century parliament.

Conclusion

The starting point for 'thinking seriously about starting over' should ideally be some basic understanding of where we are starting from. The purpose of this chapter has been, therefore, to provide a sketch – in the literal sense of providing a preliminary, brief outline – of the present positioning of the UK parliament within an analytical frame constructed around notions of space, connectivity and interaction. This frame encompasses key dimensions of parliamentary presence and activity at the heart of the broader political system of parliamentary democracy. It provides an organising structure within which questions can be posed as to the integrity and symbolism of the architectural space of Westminster, and as to the 'type of place' that its rituals, performances and rhythms reveal about parliament as a 'public space'. It prompts consideration of how, and how well, parliament is connected – through processes of representation and opportunities for engagement – to the peoples of the UK. And it raises fundamental governance issues concerning the bidirectional institutional interactions between parliament and the political executive; issues of internal self-governance and how parliamentarians manage their own affairs; as well as issues associated with procedural interactions and the governance of parliamentary business.

From this brief sketch, deeper exploration of each of these dimensions and associated problematisations is undertaken in the following chapters. The present condition of parliament is thus an ever-present concern in each chapter, in the sense that all contributors recognise that parliamentary form and function are not immutable, that institutional change is endemic, and that where parliament is now – in terms of its culture, governance, and linkage with other state institutions and citizens – is not necessarily where it used to be at the start of the 21st century. But understanding where parliament is now is of importance not simply in a descriptive sense but also in a comparative sense: of the distance between the present and a future reimagined position. This is a distance between what is and what should be. The present serves as a touchstone against which a reimagined future can be tested and judged.

The authors of each chapter did not start from the premise that their individual reimaginings were part of a cohesive, collective, collaborative exercise. Instead, they were left to determine, individually, the extent and nature of reimagining required in their own designated chapter. Thus, how a 'headshift' was to be achieved, or even if such a cogitative state was achievable, was left to each contributor. But one commonality emerged: the search for new understandings would be principled – in the sense of being guided by foundational principles. Exactly which principles were chosen, why they were chosen, and the extent to which current imaginings and practices diverge from the envisaged principled future of parliament is revealed in the following chapters. Read on!

2

Reimagining Parliamentary Space

Alexandra Meakin

Introduction

Who and what are our legislative buildings for? Are they designed simply to facilitate the passage of parliamentary business? A workplace for parliamentarians and the essential staff supporting them? Or is their purpose broader? Should they act as a hub for engaging with politics, welcoming and inclusive of all citizens? How about broader still: as a global symbol of democracy? The buildings of the UK parliament must fulfil all of these purposes at different times and to different audiences, but – in their current state – risk fulfilling none. The 19th-century Palace of Westminster has been criticised since its very opening for its lack of suitability either as a modern legislature (for example, HC Debates, 2 August 1850, col.727) or as a public space (for example, HC Debates, 17 June 1997, cols.113–14), and now requires a major renovation due to long-standing neglect of its physical fabric and infrastructure.

If criticism of, and unease with, parliamentary buildings at Westminster is endemic, then why not simply reimagine them out of existence and build a new eco-friendly, open and inclusive estate? Obviously, such a radical option is attractive to some (for example, HC Debates, 31 January 2018, col.897); yet a case will be made in this chapter for a reimagining of existing parliamentary space. This case will be founded upon two intersecting observations. The first is that, despite mixed feelings held by the public, there is evidence, nonetheless, that 'people strongly value the Palace of Westminster and want it to be restored and protected for future generations' and that 'it should set an example, particularly in terms of accessibility and inclusion and sustainability' (UK Parliament, 2022). The second is the importance currently afforded to 'restorative architecture'. As one of the winners of the 2021 Pritzker architecture prize noted: 'Transformation is the opportunity of doing more and better with what is already existing' (Jean-Philippe Lacton, quoted in Ravenscroft, 2021).

Taking these two observations as its starting point this chapter seeks to move beyond the criticism of the current Palace of Westminster to think about how we can reimagine parliamentary spaces. It considers four spatial purposes in turn. We discuss parliamentary buildings first as a symbol of democracy; second as a legislative space; third as a working space; and, fourth, as a public democratic space. The first section asks us to consider, therefore, how we think about a parliamentary building, and the stories it tells, as well as those that are told about it. Then following sections consider who needs to be present within the legislative building, as a necessary precursor to considering what space should be provided and how this space should be configured.

Parliamentary buildings as a symbol of democracy

Perhaps the best starting point in a reimagining of parliamentary space is to consider the 'stories' told about the Palace of Westminster and about the foundational story of the UK parliament as 'a symbol of democracy'. This will serve to open the debate up to more voices, to more stories about what we want the parliamentary building to tell us, and to more questioning about whether these new stories can – and should – coexist with the stories told by the current Palace.

To explore this question, this section posits that the legislative building acts as a symbol for the institution and the nation. In her seminal work, Hanna Pitkin (1967: 92, 111) conceived of 'symbolic representation' as one of the four types of representation, and recognised that this 'representing can be by inanimate objects'. Legislative buildings offer an excellent example of this type of representation, with their own meaning and relationship with citizens in this concept (Manow, 2010; Rai, 2010). Saward (2010) built on Pitkin's work to conceive representation as 'a dynamic process of claim-making', and he highlighted 'the symbolic architecture of our political systems' as part of this process (Saward, 2010: 3, 90). Similarly, Parkinson (2012: 93) argued that parliamentary buildings 'embody claims about who the rightful decision-makers are'.

Yet, the claims made are often counterposed. On the one hand, for many parliamentarians the symbolic value of the current parliamentary building is powerful already. In 2019 the then prime minister, Theresa May, stated that 'obviously the Palace of Westminster is recognised all over the world as a symbol of democracy' (HC Debates, 8 May 2019, col.551). Conservative Peer, Lord Gardner of Kimble, argued that the Palace 'represents so much about Britain across the world', adding that 'it has been a symbol of freedom to the world through some of the darkest periods in history' (HL Debates,

26 November 2014, col.973). His colleague in the Commons, Sir Geoffrey Clifton-Brown, claimed that 'the Palace of Westminster is an iconic symbol of this nation. It is absolutely symbolic of everything the UK stands for' (HC Debates, 25 January 2017, col.108WH).

The symbolism of the building is offered as a key reason for why the Palace should remain in its current form. Tim Loughton MP, for example, opposed leaving the Palace because of the symbolism of the current building:

> It is not just a UNESCO world heritage site. Probably uniquely among UNESCO world heritage sites in this country, it is a working building where history is still being made. The history of the fabric of the building still has relevance to the ongoing organic development of our constitution and the way we govern this country. That is why it was so important that when people said, 'Why don't we just turn this into a museum and have Parliament move into a purpose-built building?', the point was made that that would completely ignore the importance of the heritage, history and cultural background of this place, which we could not repeat in a soulless, characterless, heritage-less, new, modern building. It would completely change the whole character of what we do here. (HC Debates, 19 June 2019, col.278)

On the other hand, the former MP, Laura Pidcock argued that: 'The Palace of Westminster is a beautiful, historic building. We have to recognise, however, that for many in this country it is also a symbol of corruption, power, dominance, greed and suffering' (Pidcock, quoted in Meakin, 2019: 27). This is not the symbol that all MPs would like their workplace to present, as shown by Green Party MP, Caroline Lucas: 'In the Netherlands the new Parliament building has glass walls so that the public can look in on their representatives – a symbolic way of reminding their MPs why they are there and who they are supposed to serve' (Lucas, 2015: 203).

There are multiple other examples of conscious decisions made for new or refurbished parliamentary buildings to offer a certain symbolic value. The refurbished Reichstag building in Berlin, for example, is topped by a glass dome, with the aim of symbolising transparency (Vale, 2008; Roberts, 2009; Jones, 2011; Waylen, 2014). In the UK, in Scotland, Judge and Leston-Bandeira (2018: 6) have noted how the Scottish Parliament building at Holyrood was 'designed with clear symbolic intent'. In Wales the chamber of the Senedd building in Cardiff is 'sunk below the public space'. This design feature reflects, in the words of one of its architects, Lord Rodgers of Riverside: 'The hierarchy – members below and the public above – deliberately reflects how politics should operate. ... Transparency, for passers-by and visitors, and for the people watching the democratic debates below, is the driving force' (Rogers, 2015: 13–14).

The strong feelings – both positive and negative – about the symbolism of the current Palace of Westminster, make the prospect of reimagining parliamentary space challenging. By its nature, reimagining means considering what could be different about the space, but the existence and consequent symbolism of the current building means we cannot start from a blank slate. A way forward may be to move away from the extremes of the debate where the only two options are a neo-Gothic Victorian masterpiece versus a purpose-built modern, glass legislative building.

In acknowledging that reimagining of parliamentary space is challenging and that its symbolic value is not always positive, we seek to move beyond blanket criticism of the current Palace of Westminster and to prompt innovative thinking about not only the symbolic role the building should portray, but also how space can be repurposed to better serve the very purposes for which parliament exists. The following sections consider these purposes in turn: parliamentary buildings as a legislative space; parliamentary buildings as a workplace; and parliamentary buildings as a public democratic space.

These sections consider who needs to be present within the legislative building, as a necessary precursor to considering what space should be provided and how this space should be configured.

Parliamentary buildings as a legislative space

This section seeks to reimagine how to design and create a legislative building to best facilitate the business of the legislature. In the UK context we start from the existing institutional structure of a bicameral parliament – but even working within these constraints, there is much that could be considered when reimagining parliamentary space.

Who needs to be present?

One answer to this question was provided in the response of parliament to the harrowing circumstances of the COVID-19 pandemic. Long-standing and seemingly fixed views about physical presence on the parliamentary estate were overturned during the pandemic (even if only reluctantly on the part of the then responsible minister, Jacob Rees-Mogg). The need for social distancing in April 2020 severely restricted the number of parliamentarians allowed to be present within the debating chambers – limited to 64 in the Commons and only 12 in the Lords – requiring the introduction of virtual participation for the first time. The institution officially encouraged MPs to work virtually and stressed that 'no preference is being shown to members whether they attend the Chamber virtually or in person' (UK Parliament, 2020). Electronic voting was introduced, allowing MPs to vote using mobile phones from any location. The measures would prove short-lived, reversed by the end of May 2020 by Rees-Mogg, a decision ratified by a physical vote of MPs for which those who were shielding were denied a say. Furious reactions on both sides of the debate highlighted the strong feelings on the issue of physical presence (see Jacob Rees-Mogg, HC Debates, 2 June 2020, col.726; David Davis, HC Debates, 2 September 2020, col.246; Sir Edward Leigh, HC Debates, 23 September 2020, col.1069). Robert Halfon MP, who lives with cerebral palsy and was shielding during the pandemic, argued: 'Is it really morally just to say in effect to MPs, because you are not Tarzan-like and able to swing through the chamber, beating your chest, shouting to your constituents, "Look I am here!" that you are effectively euthanised from the Commons?' (Merrick, 2020). As the controversy showed, the shift, however short-lived, to remote proceedings was a watershed moment for the UK parliament, as Procedure Committee Chair Karen Bradley described in the Commons:

> Since the 16th century, this Chamber and its predecessors have been the absolute focus of the House's life. Our procedures are founded on the principle that everything is done in the Chamber. That is a sound principle. Members rely on face-to-face communication. The word 'parliament' comes from the French 'parler'. The idea that the Chamber is now not available to many of us is a massive dislocation. (HC Debates, 2 June 2020, col.739)

There is a difference, however, between tradition and principle, and it could be considered that Bradley's statement conflated the two. Just because the business of the Commons has always been done in a certain way does not mean that this should take precedence over the rights of Members when the two are in conflict. To reimagine parliamentary space is indeed to take this debate back to the fundamental principles of representation. Why is physical presence necessary in the legislature? In the same debate on remote participation, Rees-Mogg argued that physical presence was not required for some elements of parliamentary business:

> [L]et me address the argument made by some Members that if a Member is not able to vote, they will be entirely disenfranchised. I do not accept that. There are many other ways in which MPs represent their constituents in Parliament, including through tabling written questions, writing correspondence, tabling amendments and attending hearings of Select Committees, which will continue. (HC Debates, 2 June 2020, col.733)

There is, of course, a value to 'being there' – the power to persuade through oratory as referenced earlier. But if we accept, as Rees-Mogg has, that representation can be delivered through written form in questions and virtual hearings for select committees, it opens up the opportunity to consider if virtual participation and voting can offer a different – but equal – level of representation. Instead of simply considering what is lost if you are not in the same room for a speech in the Commons chamber, we can ask what could be gained by opening up parliament to different voices and views from people who may not be able to be physically present. Baroness Campbell of Surbiton, who lives with spinal muscular atrophy, described the benefits of the continued use of remote participation by the House of Lords (long after the Commons had ceased this practice):

> It has helped not only those of us with a disability but also Members living far from London, carers or those with short-term health conditions. Early morning meetings, followed by late night voting, demanding one stays for many hours at a stretch is exhausting for me. But with virtual capacity I can attend to the business of the House any time of the day, contributing to Parliamentary activities with an alert mind and effectiveness more than ever before. (Campbell, 2021)

Crucially, Baroness Campbell has also described how she would be able to 'watch debates at home on my night-time ventilator and to vote' (HL Debates, 21 May 2021, col.725). This highlights the importance of the principle of inclusiveness when reimagining how parliament could work. Furthermore, the benefits of remote participation, Campbell added, went beyond allowing a more diverse range of voices, to also encouraging 'more focused and concise' contributions. This suggests there can be benefits not just in *who* gets to speak but also *what* they say (Campbell, 2021). This should not, Campbell argued, be used to deny the benefits of face-to-face meetings and informal discussions within Westminster, but that both could coexist. Crucially, to return to the principle of representation, it may ensure that people living with disabilities are given a voice within the legislature that otherwise they would be denied. Hannah White (2022) has noted that:

> [C]urrent MPs are, by definition, a cohort who have chosen to stand for election to the House of Commons as it is currently configured. ... Logically, there must also exist a cohort who would have made brilliant MPs but who have looked at the role of a member of parliament and decided it was not for them. Among many possible reasons, this might be because of what they could see about parliament's physical environment. ... It would not be surprising if an individual with a physical disability thought they would find the Palace of Westminster difficult to navigate. (White, 2022: 167)

The premise that remote contributions can complement rather than replace solely physical participation has significant repercussions for the use of parliamentary space. Famously, neither the chambers of the House of Lords or Commons have sufficient space for all the Members of each House to take a seat – as is clear on the busiest days of the Commons calendar, when the space around the bar of the House is crammed with those unable to squeeze onto the green benches. For the majority of the time, however, the chamber is much quieter, and a smaller space would suffice. Allowing some virtual participation would further enable a smaller plenary chamber or reconfiguration of space and, as discussed later, prompt exploration of ideas about how the space could be constituted. Electronic voting would further reduce the space required for a main debating chamber, allowing the limited capacity of the Palace of Westminster to be used to its greatest advantage.

Similarly, the question of who needs to be present could include opening up parliament to different groups of parliamentarians. In addition to the physical accessibility barriers noted, the style of the Palace has often been seen as being more suited to some parliamentarians than others – 'ex-public schoolboys, Oxbridge graduates and gentleman who frequent the august London clubs' – as ethnographer Emma Crewe (2005: 9) has pointed out. The depiction of women, people from minority Black and ethnic communities or from a working-class heritage within the artwork in parliament has been cited as a particular issue (Miller, 2021). These concerns go beyond décor, however, with the configuration of space being also a particular issue. Even where practical steps have been taken to make the building more suitable for MPs with families these have not always achieved the change envisaged. Urwin cited a female MP who attempted to use the Family Room created just off Central Lobby in the Palace: '[T]he first time she went in with her baby, five colleagues were having a meeting about Brexit. "They've not made much effort with the room", she adds. "It's got some shabby toys, like someone just dumped the detritus from their house there"' (Urwin, 2022). The next section seeks to consider how reimagining the parliamentary building could make a difference to the type and number of people required for the legislative space.

What space do you need and how should it be configured?

The scope for a fully reimagined parliamentary space is, by definition, considerable. Translating this scope into practical changes that can feasibly be introduced within the constraints of the current footprint of the parliamentary estate can be challenging, however. Sarah Childs' report *The Good Parliament* (2016) recommended flexible seating in the Commons chamber to allow the space to be used better for the non-set-piece events, as well as improved access for Members using wheelchairs. This would be an excellent starting point for using space in a different way. Other suggestions that could form part of a reimagined space have included 'glass-roofed atria' in the courtyards, little-used parts of the Palace, to make the building an 'exciting, more open place to eat, meet and welcome the public' (HL Debates, 6 February 2018, col.1954); or the repurposing of the Elizabeth Tower as a 'modern communication tower, with digital screens displaying news updates about what is going on inside Westminster' and correspondents reporting directly from inside (Block, 2019).

But reimagining parliamentary space could allow us to go even further: must debates and meetings be held in the same spaces they have always been? This section uses the introduction of Westminster Hall, in 1999, as an additional space for Commons debates, as a case study to illustrate the capacity to establish alternative spaces for parliamentary business within the existing footprint of the Westminster estate. As Cowley (2001: 816–17) noted, traditionalist MPs 'reserved especial scorn for the newly created parallel debating chamber'. Certainly, Cowley's own immediate verdict on the new space was lukewarm; yet over the course of the next two decades, the use of Westminster Hall came to be adjudged as providing vital additional space for backbench scrutiny of government (Rush and Giddings, 2011), with particular benefits for smaller parties (Thompson, 2020).

Crucially, however, the greatest benefit has been one which was not foreseen at the time: the use of the space by the revived Petitions Committee with a direct impact on public engagement with the institution (Walker et al, 2019). Westminster Hall has become the venue for debates on e-petitions which have received over 100,000 signatures and been selected for debate by the Petitions Committee. While ministers respond to these debates, no divisions can be held. But while this was initially considered to be a limitation, it may be a positive. Indeed, Westminster Hall debates feel very different in tone and content to those in the main chamber of the House of Commons: the tables are arranged in a horseshoe shape in contrast to the adversarial choirstalls and the public are seated just a few feet away from the MPs participating in the debate, with no security screen in between. The effect is powerful: petitioners are encouraged to attend in person and their presence is frequently referred to in the debate. For example, a debate on staff–child ratios in early years childcare settings was attended by the petitioners, Zoe and Lewis Steeper, who had tragically lost their son, Oliver, in a nursery accident. Their very presence highlighted the stakes of the debate and the human impact of the issues being discussed, with multiple MPs referring to them by name and praising their bravery in being present. The lead MP, Catherine McKinnell, Chair of the Petitions Committee, also used the opportunity to put a question from the grieving parents direct to the Minister: 'I want to put one final question to the Minister, which comes from Zoe and Lewis, Oliver's parents, who started the petition and are here with us today. It cuts to the chase: would Government Ministers be happy to put their two-year-old child in a 1:5 setting?' (HC Debates, 14 November 2022, col.180WH). McKinnell's closing comments highlighted the importance of the debate and the use of Westminster Hall in this way:

> I thank the Minister for that response. It did not necessarily answer the question, or give a firm response to the petitioners, but I am heartened to hear that there is a listening tone on this issue, because it is so important that it is looked at in the round. I thank everyone who contributed to the debate; I know it means a huge amount to those who signed the petition, and to Zoe and Lewis, that people have taken part. It is notable that there has been a huge amount of challenge and constructive feedback, in particular from Members on the Government Benches. (HC Debates, 14 November 2022, col.98WH)

Clips from McKinnell's speech, as is customary for Westminster Hall debates on petitions, were widely shared on social media, presenting a different image of parliamentary politics compared to events such as Prime Minister's Questions. The use of Westminster Hall for such debates – and how this would connect with the public – was not cited as an original intention for the space when the parallel chamber was established, demonstrating how spaces can evolve and offer benefits which may not be obvious or expected in advance.

The case study of Westminster Hall shows how parliamentary space can be repurposed. It also shows the interconnection between the design of parliamentary buildings as a legislative space and parliamentary buildings as a symbol, and parliamentary buildings as a public democratic space. Before we consider the latter, this chapter moves to consider how the parliamentary space can be reimagined for the largest group of users of the building: the staff working for parliament or the Members of either House.

Parliamentary buildings as a workplace

There are 18,000 passholders working within the Palace of Westminster and yet debates about the future of the building have tended to focus on a tiny majority of these: the 650 MPs that make up the House of Commons (evidence from John Benger, the then Clerk of the House, Public Accounts Committee [HC 1100, 2022]). There can be good reasons for this: the elected Members fulfil the primary purpose of the building's existence. Further, they are the most visible occupants of the building: the Commons chamber, Central Lobby, and, to a lesser extent, committee rooms, are the parts of the building featured on television. By its very nature the 'behind the scenes' work of the vast majority of those working within the

Palace is unseen by the public. The nature of work varies extensively: from committee clerks and librarians, to catering staff and cleaners, to researchers and secretaries, to locksmiths and engineers, and hairdressers to electricians. The one common factor for all these people is that they work within or around a listed building that forms part of a United Nations Educational, Scientific and Cultural Organization (UNESCO) World Heritage Site – an awe-inspiring royal palace which, nonetheless, often provides a challenging working environment. Staff face the same issues – the rattling windows, leaking sewage and mice – caused by the neglect of the physical fabric as Members do, and often additional challenges: from lack of space to working within the deepest recesses of the building. Indeed, there are several staff whose entire roles are trying to hold back the tide of building failure: fire wardens are required to patrol the building 24 hours a day.

Reimagining parliamentary space means more than just thinking about the public face of the buildings, but also about the space needed for the staff serving the legislature to work.

Who needs to be present?

A functioning parliamentary building will require fewer staff tasked simply with keeping the lights on (and putting fires out). There is also scope for reducing the number of staff required to be present at any time: remote working for some staff of the House of Commons was introduced during the COVID-19 pandemic and was only rescinded in 2022 following political pressure. Enabling some level of remote working on a consistent basis would reduce the size of the office space required, saving money for the taxpayer, and allowing more imaginative uses of the existing space. An increase in remote working for parliamentarians, as outlined here, would have a knock-on impact of requiring fewer staff present within the building: some of the catering facilities are predicated on the need for MPs to be able to access the Commons chamber within eight minutes to vote; remote voting would mean fewer people restricted to the parliamentary estate and its immediate environs for long stretches. If greater numbers of Members are permitted to work remotely, they may need fewer support staff physically located in the legislative building, similarly the growing priority placed on constituency work could lead to MPs prioritising staff locally, rather than in London.

What space do you need and how should it be configured?

The nature of an in-person legislature means some physical space will always be required for the people to keep the institution functioning. Security and police are essential to protect Members and the building itself, Clerks will need to help the Speaker keep order within the Commons and advise

Members of both Houses of procedure in committees or their chambers; it will always be necessary to have cleaners and maintenance staff, and it is likely that the quality of scrutiny and legislation would deteriorate exponentially without the baristas providing a steady stream of caffeine. All staff should be provided with sufficient space not only to carry out their duties, but also for breaks, comfort and hygiene, and to store their belongings.

Beyond the space requirements, accommodation for staff must also facilitate efficient ways of working – and obstruct the creation of difficult working environments. In 2019 an independent inquiry into bullying and harassment in the House of Lords concluded that 'the Palace of Westminster is not designed to accommodate, or inculcate, modern ways of working' (Ellenbogen, 2019: 84). It also emphasised that '[s]taff work in small rooms (often housing only two individuals) on long corridors and can be physically distant from their managers and other colleagues. Contributors told me that, in particular, when doors are closed, the environment can feel threatening and inappropriate behaviour can go unobserved by colleagues' (Ellenbogen, 2019: 84).

Greater use of open-plan office space is more likely to be considered as suitable for the staff of each House, rather than the staff working directly for Members of each House, who often work in small teams (or individually) supporting their parliamentarian. But the warning of the Ellenbogen report is equally valid for Members' staff, for whom bullying and harassment has often taken place unimpeded in small office spaces. A bold reimagining of the space required could work with the political parties to create more shared working areas for Members' staff, with private meeting rooms provided for sensitive discussions (such as casework). This could have widespread benefits, helping to facilitate more collaboration between MPs and, potentially, bicamerally, offering particularly useful spaces for the smaller parliamentary parties, allowing them to pool limited resources across both Houses. Shared workspaces could also help to break down barriers between the different groups of staff within parliament. For example, co-locating procedural, committee or public engagement House staff with Members' staff could increase mutual understanding and promote more effective working. The key principle should be designing the space to promote modern working practices, respecting the dignity of all employees inside efficient and effective workspaces. Crucially, the space should also be safe for staff: the former Leader of the House of Commons, David Lidington, tweeted about the current parliamentary building after leaving office: 'If it were any normal place of employment (several thousand ppl [*sic*] work at Palace of Westminster) or tourist venue it would almost certainly be closed on health and safety grounds' (Lidington, 2021). The duty to ensure a safe workplace for staff should be at the core of reimagining the parliamentary space.

Parliamentary buildings as a public democratic space

This chapter started by considering the stories the Palace tells as a symbol of democracy. It comes full circle by considering the practical element of the Palace as a democratic space. This is a perspective often lost in discussions around the legislative building. Hannah White (2022: 169), for instance, has cautioned that debates about the future of the Palace 'have focused almost entirely on the palace as the workplace of MPs and peers or as a heritage building to be protected, not as an institution belonging to the nation, to which citizens have a right of access'. Indeed, while the Palace is generally well-loved by the public, their experiences of visiting the physical building are more mixed, with many recording a sense that 'Parliament did not feel "open"', or that the buildings were 'intimidating in their splendour' (Walker, 2012: 274), or generated a 'sense of unease' for certain visitors (Puwar, 2004: 35).

How can this sense of exclusion be resolved, and parliamentary buildings reimagined as a public democratic space? Again, this requires reversion to foundational questions. If the legislature is a public space, public access should be the default, rather than a privilege. While it is technically possible for any member of the public to walk into Central Lobby and request to see their MP, in practice this access is restricted in multiple large and small ways. The first is a lack of knowledge that this access even exists. Indeed, the Restoration and Renewal programme (tasked with refurbishing the crumbling Palace), in its public engagement work proactively contacted 300 people from groups less likely to participate with parliament and found that:

> All groups were surprised by the current level of access and activities available to the public; they were unaware of the range of activities, including being able to get married there, free tours, the ability to watch debates live and accessibility to their MPs. There was a desire to make sure these opportunities were advertised more widely for people to increase engagement and participation. (Involve, 2022: 11)

Once the public are aware of their right to access the building, there are practical barriers. The queues for entry can be long and involve airport-style security checks, with armed police patrolling the visitor entrances. The Restoration and Renewal programme (2022) noted how participants in their public engagement work expressed concerns about how this impacts different groups:

> 'If you were a person who was autistic going through security – and I know it has to be done – you would be anxious in that area.' (Disabled People's/Workshop participant)

'When I came through the security area it was a bit embarrassing for me ... trying to keep my balance. I felt that it should have been more private. ... I dropped my stick. ... It wasn't a nice experience.' (Disabled People's Tour/Workshop participant)

'I believe the largest physical barrier into the Palace of Westminster is the police presence'. (Online Conversation participant)

'Security is very intimidating, especially for ethnic minority groups.' (Feedback via Community Conversation facilitator; Involve, 2022: 23)

Any prospective visitor is questioned as to whether they have an appointment and once inside they are limited to a small area of the Palace, with limited access to seating, refreshments and toilet facilities. While arrangements for the public have actually improved considerably over the last decade, it could be argued that in doing so, the role of the public has been confirmed as 'visitors' to the Palace, rather than an integral part of the democratic process. Part of this is the impact of hosting the legislature in a royal palace and listed building: the purpose of coming to Westminster can be – and is perhaps more likely to be – for heritage reasons rather than to engage with democracy. This is still a vital task, as Leston-Bandeira (2016) notes: 'A visit to parliament is therefore more than a leisurely activity – it is a vehicle for the expression of symbolic representation which officials hope to strengthen a sense of attachment to the institution' (Leston-Bandeira, 2016: 511). Reimagining the parliamentary space gives us the opportunity to go further, however, and consider the democratic function separate to the heritage of the Palace: what would the building look like if the public's access to democracy was the primary purpose for the design?

Who needs to be present?

This fundamental question becomes both less tangible and more important when considering the parliamentary space as a legislative building or as a workplace. If the central purpose of the building is as a public democratic space, then it follows that the space should be designed for mass access. This would still prioritise those able to participate in the democratic process through voting but would also recognise the benefits of including those who will in the future be granted the franchise, whether through age or achieving UK citizenship. The central purpose of the building becomes the facilitation of public access: does the space become open as default? Simply encouraging the public to enter the parliamentary building and engage with the democratic process could transform how the building functions. The practical implications of adopting this approach wholesale would be immense and insurmountable: obviously no legislative building would be able to accommodate tens of millions of people and there are valid reasons why access must be restricted in some areas (such as division lobbies). Further, a mindset change about the role of the public would not eliminate the need for security measures, given the context of terror attacks and threats both within Westminster and against parliamentarians.

There are also more conceptual questions: as the UK is a representative rather than direct democracy, what are the benefits of more direct access to the legislature? Would greater public access to the legislative building prioritise those living in London and the south-east of England, and with the financial means to travel to Westminster? Should we focus on physical access to the building rather than digital? Just as the Palace of Westminster when rebuilt after the 1834 was criticised as being designed for a legislature that no longer existed, does prioritising physical access in the 21st century risk a building more suited to the 20th century? Indeed, if there are fewer Members and staff working in-person on the parliamentary estate, as suggested earlier, this raises questions about the value of mass public access to the building. More fundamentally, does greater access or exposure to the legislature lead to greater understanding and subsequently increased trust and belief in the institution? This is certainly not automatic: the chaos of the Brexit Parliament between 2017 and 2019 led to both the highest viewing figures on record for BBC Parliament and record low levels of trust in the legislature (Hansard Society, 2019; King, 2019; Marshall et al, 2019). While these questions highlight important limitations to reimagining the parliamentary building to prioritise public access, this chapter posits that there could be a middle ground between the current situation, as outlined in the introduction, and the extremes discussed within this section; and that the benefits of a new approach make this middle way worth examining. The next section seeks to consider how this could be done.

What space do you need and how should it be configured?

How could we reimagine parliamentary space to place the public's role in the democratic process at its core? There are small steps that could be addressed (relatively) easily: ensuring the décor and artwork are inclusive and do not actively portray an elitist governing system; addressing the appalling access for people with disabilities (including hidden disabilities such as autism); providing more seating and facilities for the public in Central Lobby and Westminster Hall (with a particular recognition of the needs of older visitors); ensuring there are prayer rooms for religious observance and quieter spaces. More difficult but for greater benefit could be reconfiguring the space to provide far larger public galleries for the chambers of the two Houses (including the parallel debating chamber in Westminster Hall) perhaps, and greater public space in committee rooms; more spaces for MPs to meet with constituents; and replica legislative spaces to be used for educational purposes. But we could go even further still: could the democratic space be used to facilitate contact between groups of citizens, in addition to the constituent–MP relationship? Could the spaces of the parliamentary building be used for mass meetings and as a protest area? Would the public feel more connected with the democratic system if they were invited into the legislature to directly air their grievances? Again, the limitations of space and security, as noted earlier, cannot be ignored. But they could perhaps be managed. One possible solution could be to incorporate Parliament Square into the wider parliamentary estate, providing not only additional space but, crucially, a space long associated with protest (and offering a powerful symbolic message in the face of past controversies over the policing of the space). This is not a new idea: the Hansard Society in 2011 argued for this space, which it described as 'the constitutional heart of the UK', to be incorporated into a broader strategy for Westminster and its immediate environs. The prospects for Parliament Square in particular would offer a new democratic space within the broader legislative institution:

> The Square should be a forum for spontaneous and organised citizenship similar in style to a Speakers' Corner. It should be a place where the great thinkers, writers, and artists of the day can give talks and lectures and engage in discussion with the public about their ideas. The Square could also on occasion be a theatre for bringing alive our democratic history: a place where key moments in the development of British democracy are dramatised. (Hansard Society, 2011: 8)

By reimagining the legislative building as a democratic space, we can reframe the idea of citizenship and the relationship between the public and the institution of parliament.

Conclusion

Who and what are our legislative buildings for? This chapter has sought to explore four different purposes of the legislative building and how each one can be reimagined. It has shown how considering these different roles raises deep questions about the role of parliamentarians, the institution's duty to its staff, the nature of democracy and representation, and the symbolic importance of the legislative building. Reimagining the parliamentary building should include an exploration of these questions – ideally in the form of a public debate – in order to come to a consensus about who and what the legislative buildings are for. With this consensus achieved, a reimagined parliamentary building can be created: one which tells the story of a legislature that is inclusive, proud of its heritage but appropriate for the present, one in which the space is flexible and can be deployed in varying and evolving ways for different purposes, one which provides a working environment that encourages collaboration for staff and is open and welcoming to the public. The potential of a reimagined parliamentary building is thus vast: it could empower new ways of working for Members and staff, create new ways of connecting with the public, and provide a symbol of a legislature not just of the past but of the future.

3

Reimagining Rhythms, Rituals and Symbols

Emma Crewe

Introduction

Democracy is a work in progress around the world and one of the key sites offering opportunities for a transformation of our political processes can be found within parliaments. Focusing on one aspect of these processes, the organisation of political interaction at the heart of our democracies deserves our attention. Political work is made up of endless encounters between politicians, and between them and others in society, in both face-to-face and digital interaction, navigating both time and space. Some of these encounters are ritualised – replete with rules, symbols of power and performances that aim to demonstrate various formal and informal hierarchies – while others are informal and spontaneous. These include and exclude different groups in various ways depending on their rules, habits and rhythms. Some of the problems that emerge within these encounters, as seen from different perspectives, are discussed in this chapter and then suggestions made as to what we might do about them. Guided by the principles of recognising the complexity and value of different kinds of knowledge; promoting diversity, equity and inclusion; enhancing wellness; and restoring ethics and standards, the argument is advanced for rethinking the way interaction is organised in parliament. More specifically, recommendations are made for changing the rhythms, rituals and symbols as part of a reimagining of Westminster.

Challenges

The critiques of our parliamentary system tend to highlight constitutional, structural and individual problems, requiring an oscillation between abstract discussion and idiosyncratic situations that defy generalisation. In contrast, this chapter focuses more on challenges that arise out of four main social challenges: hierarchies of knowledge; inequality and exclusion; unwellness; and shallow ethics. These problems are clearly interrelated. The inequalities found in wider society unsurprisingly appear in parliament and one example of this is observed in attitudes to knowledge, evidence and testimony. After observing debates in Westminster since 1998, and tracking both the making of laws and select committee inquiries, I have observed various patterns in the way knowledge is treated. It tends to be the case that those professions that are seen as producing 'gold standard' evidence, especially scientists and lawyers, tend to get taken more seriously than those relying more on arts, humanities, social science and personal testimony. MPs and peers tend to make assumptions about 'evidence', rather than investigating how it was produced. As Latour (2010: 229–43) explains, lawyers and scientists produce evidence in completely different ways, through legal process on the one hand and experimentation on the other, so the rigour of their knowledge is not directly comparable. Social scientists conceive of rigour differently depending on whether they have been more influenced by science or humanities, relying differentially on imagination, comparative analysis, logic or replicable tests and surveys. Practitioners gather knowledge though their personal experience and whether this is taken seriously, and whether they are seen as 'experts' communicating expertise, depends on their status. Whether considering the interaction between MPs, or between parliamentarians and others in society, inequalities based on gender, class and race re-emerge with depressing regularity.

Hierarchies are not only created by assumptions about knowledge. The rituals, rules and processes that govern the conduct of ceremony, debate and discussion can exclude or include different people. The ceremonies that mark the opening and closing of parliament, or introduce new members, reveal who the central players are in the theatre of democracy and how they are hierarchically organised. To take one example in the State Opening of Westminster, the procession from Buckingham Palace down Pall Mall and into parliament, to finally get to the House of Lords chamber, reveals the status of all those involved. The order of people in the procession, the seating and the uniforms all indicate the status of participants, from the pinnacle of the social pyramid with the monarch down to the Lords, MPs and finally those they rule over. The pomp and traditional clothes, especially those worn by the people more prominent in the procession, reek of alienating privilege for some, while they confer dignity and stability on the proceedings for others. The complex series of rituals evokes different meanings according to the perspective of the observer (Crewe and Evans, 2018).

Those ceremonial rituals that punctuate daily business are in contrast to the everyday rituals you find in parliament that are needed to make laws, scrutinise government or conduct inquiries and, more informally, engage with stakeholders. Conversations in Westminster take place across the Palace and outbuildings in many forms ranging from the most strictly ritualised events (discussion of bills on the floor of the chamber of the House of Lords or House of Commons, questioning ministers at Question Time, votes in their respective division lobbies, public bill committees considering bills) to the least regulatory (meetings in a café) and the many lightly ritualised encounters in between the two extremes (meetings in offices, outreach or private discussion by select committees). The more that is at stake – because the decision will have impact and there are seriously different views about what to do to improve society and the administration of the state – the more the encounter tends to be ritualised. The problems with these rituals are once again in the eye of the beholder. It is only small irritations with procedure that irk some MPs. Some think more expansively and see in parliament mechanisms of exclusion, whether it is the government dominating the rituals and restricting the potential for democratic scrutiny by parliament or citizens being unable to voice their opinions on proposals. Others perceive the more gladiatorial performances of hostility during Question Time as counter to deliberative process and off-putting for citizens, adding to the disillusionment that many feel with 'tribalism' in politics.

 The unwellness of the world shows up in Westminster within relationships between people in various ways, whether as conflict, hostility or abuse. A 24/7 digital revolution, and new culture of leaking, means that government takes place in the public realm to a far greater extent than ever before. Scrutiny and accountability become more intense, but so do the possibilities of undermining your opponents with malicious attacks and allegations. New forms of communications are creating intolerable pressures within parliament. There is an explosion of judgement, especially of those in positions of power with certain groups being attacked more ferociously than others. If you are not White, male and of a certain age, and therefore not seen as a 'natural' leader, then you tend to receive more violent communication, as a politician especially. For example, ethnic minority and government MPs receive more hate on Twitter than others (Agarwal et al, 2021). Another study found that more general and political abuse was directed at men, while women received more sexist abuse (Gorrell et al, 2020). Women are the targets of more toxic attacks, with the risk that this mix of inequality and conflict is leading to a decline in interest in standing as political candidates (Harmer and Southern, 2021) and the possibility that it makes it harder to win a seat (Collignon and Rüdig, 2021). Hate speech arises in part out of, and contributes to, confusion about knowledge. We are not in a post-truth world, I would argue, but living with chronic levels of contestation that work at cross-purposes, leaving people not knowing who to believe or even where to turn to for guidance. Experts are portrayed as unreliable if ideologically unsound. Within parliament we see conflicts of interests and a multitude of different perspectives represented and we need politicians to listen and deliberate on this messy cacophony when deciding what is for the best. When they don't achieve the results they promise, or that we want, we citizens attack them all as an undifferentiated group – sometimes in ways that are abusive, whether or not they were personally responsible for the action.

Arguably this partly explains why many MPs retreat to their constituencies and hold surgeries with individuals who have severe challenges and go to their MP for help. Just as unwellness shows up in Westminster, neglected problems become evident through these encounters between citizens and their MPs (or MPs' staff) and so within relationships but also for individuals and families. While better off people buy the services of lawyers, doctors or accountants to solve problems, for those who are multiply failed by the state, the last resort is your MP. They often see constituents with multiple, complex and interrelated challenges – related to housing, benefits, stress, debt – and MPs and their staff develop both an encyclopaedic knowledge of services provided in their area and plenty of contacts across local government who might assist. The MPs and staff who seem more comfortable doing this mix of social work and citizens advice tend to be women, taking time and energy away from their other responsibilities and arguably promotion opportunities (Crewe, 2015). While this aspect of MPs' work grounds them in the everyday realities of their constituents, so that they deepen their understanding of the problems caused by bad government policy and law, they are not always that well equipped to address the more complex problems – especially when mental illness is involved.

Westminster has a few more of its own forms of more institutional unwellness in the realm of ethics. In the last few years, we have witnessed a more casual attitude to laws, rules and norms within Westminster, culminating in former Prime Minister Boris Johnson resigning his premiership in 2022 because his own MPs no longer trusted him. Where have the ethics deficits emerged from, to take one example? Before postmodern attacks on truth, the digital revolution with its 24/7 news cycle, and the acceleration of change that globalisation has brought with it, the political world was relatively well-ordered. In the House of Lords parliamentarians used to tell me that all new peers 'go native' within six months, or stay away, which usually meant that they complied with the rules and courtly codes of behaviour (Crewe, 2005). In the House of Commons, MPs were once surprisingly obedient to leaders. A decline in deference to party leadership since the 1950s, with MPs increasingly voting against the instructions of their leaders, might be seen as somewhat refreshing. But more recently, it has been Ministers who have broken the rules, challenging the conventions of the House in profound and even destructive ways. Prime Minister Johnson was especially inclined to ignore laws and rules, as detailed by White (2022) and Thévoz (2022). To reverse this decline in standards, we have to understand how it has come about, distinguishing between political attacks and impartial accusations. However, the rhythms of parliamentary work are too frenetic and competitive to allow for the level of reflection and debate that is needed to improve understanding of the relationships and ethics that underlie standards.

When people find problems in organisations, including parliament, they often resolve that the *culture* needs to be changed. However, there is a lack of clarity about what this means or entails. Culture tends to be treated as if it was a residual category by scholars and practitioners alike – viewed as either a set of traditions with valuable functions or a pattern of dysfunctional behaviour that needs to be transformed, depending upon their political ideology. Brian Street (1993) has pointed out that culture can be more usefully conceived of as something people do rather than have – a verb not a noun – and yet many still conceive of it as something outside the everyday interaction between people, akin to the way we think of and idealise 'systems'. If you think of culture as separate from everyday practice, then you are looking in the wrong place and might formulate the wrong recipes. If you see it as a process that arises between people when they negotiate over meaning, symbolism and ritual, rather than as dysfunctional behaviour that can be changed with a new code of practice, then you will turn your attention to the way people communicate, ritualise interaction and organise themselves. However, culture is less malleable than people assume, with ritual being just one example of this: 'We can't do without rituals in politics, any more than we can dispense with language, but you can't make them do what you want either. They can, but do not necessarily, resolve contradictions, create consensus, mobilise consent, shore up existing hierarchies or include/ exclude groups' (Crewe, 2021: 171). We should not get rid of rituals and symbols, because we cannot do politics without them, but we can review and reimagine them with certain principles to guide us.

Principles and opportunities for reimagining interaction in Westminster

If thinking about a reimagination of three important social processes in interaction – rhythms, rituals and symbolism – then it is important to consider what principles might guide this transformation. Taking the key problematic areas and reimagining them into aspirations, I will focus on these principles when considering how to change rhythms, rituals and symbols:

1. *A more inclusive approach to knowledge*: a commitment should be made to judging the value and utility of knowledge with open-mindedness. This assumes that more attention, and sometimes research, would be needed

to evaluate the rigour of knowledge rather than assuming that particular sources, methods or types of experts are intrinsically more reliable.
2. *Promoting diversity, equity and the right to participate in democracy for all*: others are thinking about how to improve the representation of all groups in parliament. The focus here is on changing processes so that they offer greater equality of opportunity for all politicians, citizens and others in society to engage meaningfully in democratic processes, whereby their voices are heard, and their interests considered. This would mean that encounters were more inclusive, less alienating for minorities and able to negotiate through difference with fairness.
3. *Enhancing wellness*: promoting better mental and physical health, as well as relationships between people, within any parliament is not only important for making it work more effectively. It matters because people will stay away if they perceive political work to be disturbing, discriminatory or harmful. Both face-to-face encounters, and interaction on social media, would enable respectful discussion, debate and difficult negotiations between politicians and others they engage with.
4. *Restoring standards and ethics*: a sense of integrity, trustworthiness and honesty needs to be restored in Westminster so that they become social norms (as they often have been) rather than the exceptions. While the abuse of power appears to be a perpetual feature of all political systems, Westminster can only function properly if this becomes a relatively rare event once again.

How do we promote these principles within a broad agenda of change? According to the sociologist Hartmut Rosa (2020), the contemporary pervasive frustration with politics arises in part out of our conviction that we can predict and control the world around us when, clearly, we can't. Once we recognise that reimagining Westminster is not about redesigning its structure, but about creating different potentials and possibilities and learning to think, be and act differently, then we can cope better with feeling, and often being, somewhat out of control. However, there are significant interests marshalled against thinking, being and acting differently within interaction, which I explore in relation to three areas of potential: rhythms, rituals and symbols.

Rhythms

When understanding but also reimagining parliament you need to look at politicians' work. Parliamentary scholars tend to classify their work into roles and measure their activities, votes and outputs, thereby missing some of the contradictory and ambivalent processes in politics. Influenced by Goffman's (1959) theatrical analogy in *The Presentation of Self in Everyday Life*, elsewhere

I have tried to shift attention towards performance and relationships in MPs' political work. These are so changeable and complex we need a systematic way to study this, and I propose two good sources of inspiration. First, Lefebvre's (2013) rhythmanalysis offers a systematic way to research the diversity of MPs' work by looking at the rhythms of performance through time and space. Second, turning to philosopher Stephen Lukes' (1975) analysis of power allows us to think about the impact of rhythms in terms of inclusion and exclusion, highly significant for fathoming who has access to decision-making agendas, places and moments in time.

The rhythms created by people moving their bodies through time and space can be sequential, where people follow each other in concert; have a beginning, a peak and a decline; and be in or out of sync (Lefebvre, 2013: 25). These patterns reveal who is meeting who, how often and for what time period and how it changes over time through different seasons, allowing for comparison across sites (including parliaments). You can see who gets included and excluded in their encounters and whose voice gets prioritised in both the performance and the impact. An abrupt change to rhythms, such as a special sitting, might tell us that parliament is facing a critical event. In a new place of work part of what you have to learn is how to move around different spaces at what time and with whom. In Westminster you have to watch hundreds of rooms, corridors, bars and speaking chambers, and the routes between them, as well as study the rules about where and when people are expected to gather, sit, stand, speak or walk. You have to work out which rhythms are shared with others (for example, in the same party, on the same committee, if voting in the same lobby, all MPs use Portcullis House Atrium to meet certain visitors) and which are idiosyncratic (for example, every MP has their own constituency, every peer has their own network of contacts), so that you know which bodies join at what point, whether in person or virtually.

If you compare MPs' and peers' rhythms of work, and who they share space with for different tasks, much is revealed about their different networks. MPs are elected so travel weekly, or at least fortnightly, to their constituencies; peers are appointed and conceive of themselves as 'experts' to revise law, so meet up with specialists to discuss the latest developments in their area of interest. We could then develop this potentially more systematic way of studying interaction with a view to compiling a picture of who is included and excluded more accurately. In all cases politicians tend to be more responsive than proactive in choosing who to interact with. In constituencies they tend to meet individuals and families who come to them with grievances or problems, or activists whether on their own or as part of organisations, and in both cases, MPs are not usually seeking them out. On the other hand, select committees in both Houses invite witnesses to give evidence – government Ministers, civil servants but also 'friendly witnesses'. But we don't yet know the patterns of structural exclusion based on gender, race, income or disability in either constituencies or parliament, even if we do know that select committees hear from far more male than female witnesses. The House of Commons reported that in the 2021–2022 session select committees heard from 600 men and 346 women (HC 1, 2022: 93). But it is a very positive step that they monitor participation by gender. We could address some of the inequalities in political participation if we had more data on these rhythms of interaction.

Let's shift our attention from quantity to quality of participation. In a general sense it is clear that we are facing an acceleration of rhythms in political workplaces. Rosa (2013) writes about huge sweeping change in contemporary societies, about how change is accelerating as the social bonds and resonant connections that hold us together are loosening, with the result that rigid relationships and alienation are becoming endemic. The representative relationship between politician and citizens is too rigid and hardened; we need a more fluid way of being in the world where 'resonant relationships are an expression of the successful adaptive transformation of the world, not of its appropriation in the sense of expanding one's resources' (Rosa, 2019: 185). When citizens resort to merely laughing with cynicism or shouting with fury and outrage at politicians as a whole, both non-democratic forms of expression he points out, then the potential for resonance is reduced. To understand this political alienation, Rosa invites us to consider how the liberal individualistic way of experiencing politics creates a rhythm that is inherently dissatisfying. 'Modern democracy is rather fundamentally based on the idea that its form of politics gives every individual a voice and allows that voice to be heard, such that the politically shaped world thus becomes an expression of this productive polyphony' (Rosa, 2019: 217). Even voting is the expression of an individual preference. When we debate, we do so in a way that removes the emotion, aesthetics and embodiment of politics. What we need is to change democracy, or to be specific in the way we think about it, so that it is no longer the 'negotiation and settlement of legal claims and conflicts of interests, but rather refers to an ongoing process of becoming more sensitive to a variety of voices in the sense of perspectives, modes of existence, and relationships to the world' (Rosa, 2019: 218). We need to rethink political participation.

The more diverse we are, the more time we need to give to political participation to prevent the exclusion of sectors of the population or even the alienation of the public as a whole. When politicians don't keep up with the pace and substance of change, then politics lags behind social developments and people feel unheard (Rosa, 2019: 223). So, we need to think carefully about how to improve the rhythms of political work, that is how politicians and citizens navigate time and space when encountering each other. The main public space for political encounters is the Palace of

Westminster with its debating chambers, committee rooms and meeting spaces: some love it for its surreal fairy-tale Gothic splendour while others hate its pomposity, inaccessibility and state of disrepair (or a mixture of the two sensibilities). But there are other spaces too. MPs also meet people online, occasionally during trips arranged by committees, and in a range of places in their constituencies: businesses, hospitals, schools, supermarkets, council buildings, and so on (Crewe, 2021: 109). But we don't really know who they meet and what they talk about when they get there. This matters because these rhythms effectively constitute the substance of their representation of a locality.

If we think of this representation work in terms of rhythms, we can more fully understand the nature of representative politics and make informed suggestions for change. As the French anthropologist Bruno Latour (2003: 147) encourages, it is worth rethinking this claim of representation in terms of truth because we shouldn't judge political discourses as we would judge scientific truth: 'political discourse appears to be untruthful only in contrast with other forms of truth'. An elected politician can't reproduce the views or promote the interests of all their constituents because they are diverse and changeable so unknowable in all their richness. She/he can only inquire into a partial selection and convert multiple interests and views into a few, or sometimes one, and put it through the filter of their own understanding and the party manifesto. In that conversion process the representative inevitably mediates between individual differences and shared interests within a community. This means that who they speak to, in which spaces, for how long, and what they speak about reveals much about the content of representation of a locality. Conversely it would be as revealing to know who is ignored and invisible. If MPs revealed information about these interactive encounters, or lack of them, for example in the annual reports that some produce or on their website, then this would make them more accountable to those they claim to represent.

The risk of demanding more information about who MPs interact with could be an unintended perverse incentive for elected representatives to schedule still more encounters just to reassure constituents that they are working hard, and everyone is being represented. One of the major challenges of democracies is that both MPs, and the governments they form in parliamentary systems, over-promise and under-deliver. They make impossible promises, especially when campaigning before an election, that can't be fulfilled, leading to the inevitability of disappointment. Campaigning stretches further and further back into people's terms of office as seats become more marginal. Over-promising is a habit in other organisations too that depend on public support, such as charities and trade unions or even churches, but it has more serious consequences when it happens in the political world. So, a reimagined Westminster (and Whitehall for that matter) would have parliament (and government) doing less but doing it better. What should politicians stop doing to enable them to represent their constituents more inclusively and govern the country more effectively? That is a question that politicians should ask themselves, in consultation with constituents, their party and those they work with, with an awareness that prioritising time and the direction of their attention requires making difficult political decisions. It is at the core of the work of representation. MPs might consider fewer automatic meetings: prioritising advocacy groups that relate to upcoming policies or bills; more irregular visits to institutions in their constituency and choosing those with the greatest challenges; and attending fewer surgery meetings on the basis of urgency or complexity, as examples. They might spend more or less time in the constituency versus media studios versus parliament at certain times of year. They could ration the amount of time they spend on social media. A more effective parliament is only possible if processes of prioritisation, and switching towards quality rather than quantity, become seen as mandatory.

Rituals and symbols

No parliament can function without rituals. They are events of significance that are always reliant on rules, making or remaking meaning, and creating opportunities for demonstrating or contesting hierarchy. Democratic politics in particular needs to ensure that the performance of political debate is free enough for the expression of different opinions and constrained enough for government to get its laws, policies and motions approved eventually, to enable the implementation of the promises made at elections as well as a smooth administration. Five distinct kinds of ritual tend to be required to make politics work and legitimise power in the Westminster parliament: elections, conferences, formal meetings, decision-making and ceremonies of state. They contrast with the very informal meetings, conversations and gossip in the spaces between ritualised encounters that tend to be unregulated, spontaneous, away from public view and less clear in terms of performing hierarchy.

Ritualised processes are continually evolving or sometimes quite abruptly transformed. They are embedded within wider cultural practices found within Westminster, which are created, reproduced and evaluated by different groups, resulting in a huge range of reactions to the way they are at present and how they should evolve. These reactions are partly shaped by ambition. Peers realise that their House of Lords is the secondary revising chamber, while the Commons is primary with more power to dominate the executive, and for some this limit to their power is compensated for by social status. It is as if the symbolic capital of a peerage, a gilded chamber and deferential treatment compensate peers for the restrictions to their political clout and this suits those who are at the end of an illustrious career with far fewer ambitions than MPs. In the House of Commons, where ambition to govern is far more widespread, status is founded on a completely different premise. The symbolism of being referred in the chamber by your constituency (the Honourable Member for Hammersmith, for example) is a continual reminder of an MP's job of representing a locality while depersonalising conflict during debates within the chamber. The endless confusing rules of procedure and conventions that govern the way politics is ritualised both regulate the hierarchies between politicians but also make sure decisions can be made and stuck to in an orderly way. My point here is that rituals and symbols are vitally important in politics but deserve a rethink in any redesign of parliament.

Before redesigning them, once again they have to be understood. Rituals convey clear, even if multiple, messages but also ambiguity, as mentioned earlier. The State Opening of Parliament looks like a completely different ritual depending on whether you are watching from the street, participating in a procession, sitting in the House of Commons listening to Black Rod summoning you to the House of Lords, or a peer dressed in ermine in close proximity to the monarch when they read out the government's programme:

> Parliamentary rituals remind us where protagonists are supposed to be in formal hierarchies, even if the practice of politics entails endless power struggles over these hierarchies. They are also the processes by which moral values, ideas, and relations between people can be performed and contested in ways that avoid violence. But rituals designed to demonstrate solidarity, unity, or common values inevitably carry with them a risk of excluding rather than including – indeed that must be an inevitable part of their purpose. Rituals designed to cement authority carry the risk of appearing to deny dissent. (Crewe and Evans, 2018: 46)

We may need rituals and symbols but that doesn't mean we should attempt to preserve them in aspic, as if such an aim was possible. They can be a way of galvanising people that distracts from repulsive forms of politics, but they can also exclude people by both subtle and unsubtle means. So, a key question is how to change the rituals and symbolism in parliament for deeper inclusion.

We might take more seriously those symbols that alienate on grounds of privilege. In the current House of Lords, the symbols of class status – a name based on a ranked peerage (baron, earl, marquis, duke), ermine robes for ceremonies and habits of deference towards titles – set these parliamentarians above the rest of the population. The UK class system works to make certain groups – notable White men educated in public schools who would have once dominated parliament exclusively – feel that it is natural to inherit or gain these titles of nobility. For others, the experience ranges from acute imposter syndrome, feeling almost like space invaders (Puwar, 2004), to an appreciation at the meritocratic ways that any Britisher can become a peer at least in theory irrespective of gender, class and race. For all it means getting accustomed to being treated as superior to commoners. The abolition of titles and robes would signal a rejection of this hierarchy, while using a designation like 'Senator' or the equivalent might convey a sense of being more like other countries – gaining inclusion but losing distinctiveness. The peers themselves worry that if they lost this form of symbolic reward for political work then they might attract less talented politicians to join the House of Lords. But that view seems outmoded, and it might work the other way: if the House of Lords became a Senate and peers were treated as experts rather than social superiors, then it might be easier to attract those with specialist knowledge. It would also mean that the other House – the House of Commons – needs to change its name too, depending on what other reforms are brought in. On balance, abolishing the symbols of social superiority (rather than political authority) to promote our aspiration of inclusion outweighs the disadvantages, such as loss of formal sense of dignity. Peers should become Senators, and MPs could be Representatives or the equivalent, to emphasise their political rather than social status.

Improving other aspects of equality in the two Houses could also be partly achieved through symbolic means. Sarah Childs' (2016) recommendations for making the House of Commons more equitable in terms of gender are comprehensive, persuasive and practical, suggesting an impressive range of ways to improve representation, infrastructure, communication and accessibility. Influenced by these ideas, Verge (2022) focused in on the symbolic changes needed to make progress on gender equality: challenging masculine social scripts, women's socially assigned roles as caregivers, and harassment by men, while promoting women's spaces and groups while recognising their caring responsibilities. If we summarise Childs' and Verge's recommendations, then a gender-sensitive parliament would need at least the following symbolic shifts:

- redesigning parliamentary space so that women feel more welcome along with their dependents, whether spaces used by all (for example, allowing breastfeeding in the chamber) or by designating women-only rooms;
- parliament recognises the achievements of women as much as men in symbolic ways (for example, rooms named, paintings hung, sculptures and busts put up and exhibitions or events held);
- gender-neutral language is used (not 'lords' or 'chairmen');
- prioritising gender equality and anti-harassment strategies and messages in communications;

- discouraging or even banning all-male panels; and
- women MPs, but also potential candidates, are offered mentoring, space for peer-to-peer solidarity, and other forms of tailored support.

Parallel arguments could be made about equality and inclusion in relation to other disadvantaged groups. Symbolic recognition of the achievements of minority groups who face inequality in British society, and our parliament, would have value for all. Paintings, room names, busts or exhibitions about politicians of colour, or who are young, disabled and/or LGBTQIA+, could act as a challenge to prevailing hierarchies of value. This is important as an act of recognition but also to make those who belong to disadvantaged groups feel that they too can enter the corridors of power and do well when they get there. Exhibitions about how the UK parliament has been historically involved in creating a modern world fraught with global inequalities could be symbolically significant. What was parliament's role in slavery and colonialism, whether active or through negligence? A permanent exhibition about the UK's impact on the world could emphasise our capacity for self-critical learning, an antidote to the populist nationalism that seems to be having a resurgence.

Knowledge could be handled differently within the ritualised encounters in parliament. The negotiation of narratives between politicians but also between them and others in society deserves far more attention as a process. If politicians debated the narratives, knowledge and evidence that emanate from different sources, settings and disciplines, the difference between them and how they should be handled, then they'd be better equipped to make decisions. There is clearly interest within parliament to think more about how knowledge is produced, and progress has already been made, notably in the handling of 'evidence' by committees. The barrier here is that parliamentarians know that knowledge is contested, and that it can be used to win against their opponents, so the politics of the use of evidence in policy making can create incentives to close down such discussions. Similarly, the debates about freedom of speech can sometimes lead to a constraint on academic integrity that would impoverish debate. There is an important role for academics here to keep opening up spaces for discussion about narratives, knowledge and evidence that enable freedom, integrity but also protection from harm.

Finally, in the arena of standards and ethics, once again the rituals deserve our attention. Proposals for the reform of parliament tend to focus on either individuals or wholes (cultures, structures, institutions) while neglecting relationships, including those created within rituals. While I admit that enhancing the capacity of individuals to be ethical, wise and competent is a worthy goal and developing better cultures or structures can be useful, I still hold that the dual obsession with individualism versus institutionalism has its problems, including unintended consequences and missed opportunities. For example, providing support to individual MPs to deal with the increasingly confusing, difficult, hate-filled world to the exclusion of other processes can leave them feeling they are on their own. Measures to hold individuals more accountable for their actions and to higher standards of ethics, as the Committees on Standards and Privileges are tasked to do, are extremely worthwhile. It might be worth strengthening the ritualised processes of accountability on finding wrongdoing, whether it is being reprimanded by the Speaker, or even giving an apology at the bar of either House, or circulating committee findings on breaches far more widely.

However, ethics is often reduced to policy and legal compliance; we need to consider cultural norms as well. We used to take it for granted that politicians generally like to look as if they are obeying the law. But a new attitude prizing disruption has encouraged a casual attitude towards customs, rules and even laws. Disruption as a valued process for its own sake is evident, for example, in the corporate philosophy of many technology companies. The narrative is to make companies, and by analogy governments, so innovative and fast-moving with new disruptive rhythms that they leap ahead of competitors. Disruption is symbolically conveyed through violent language, casting off older symbols and displaying new ones, preferably relying on what we see as the closest thing to magic in the modern world: technology. However, encouraging politicians to be in competition with each other is counterproductive. Rather than pitting politicians against each other – by leaders making promises or threats about their future prospects in return for support or citizens rewarding them for intensifying blame-filled attacks – political parties and citizens should exert pressure on their members and representatives to aspire to a higher standard of ethics through education.

A renewal of ethics implies a process of education for all of us. Dewey's thinking about how democracy and education rely on each other remains pertinent today. To make democracy work properly you need an educated citizenry: 'a government resting upon popular suffrage cannot be successful unless those who elect and who obey their governors are educated. Since a democratic society repudiates the principle of external authority, it must find a substitute in voluntary disposition and interest; these can be created only by education' (Dewey, 1916 [2008]). He does not mean this in the technical sense of knowing how to participate; it is not just about an accumulation of information about politics. Rather, education enables processes of communication between groups to ensure we can get beyond individual and stratified interests. This means thinking and reimagining for ourselves as individuals but also in different configurations of social networks, encountering each other through rituals. It is in that process of inquiry, deliberation and debate, informed by what Dewey calls practical judgement, that the substance of a reimagined Westminster can be found. Most seem to find political speechifying dull, especially since politicians have been controlled and trained to be on message by spin doctors who have taken charge of communications. Often former journalists, these political communications strategists teach politicians how to handle the media and the result is repetitive and cautious; the flattening out of political talk has made it boring.

Gaffes, jokes, idiosyncratic utterances and vicious personal insults by politicians can inject emotional drama back into political speech, and those politicians who have recently indulged in it – Boris Johnson, Donald Trump and Jair Bolsonaro as examples – are seen by their supporters as authentic, entertaining and relatable. However, it is their lack of interest in striving for truth that is in part having a corrupting influence on narratives within our political rituals. Their supporters do not think this is unusual – they believe that all politicians lie so they may as well support one who creates resonance and does not patronise them. However, we need to recover our expectations of integrity. Tolerating some spin – or a 'mask of virtue' as Runciman (2008) puts it – is necessary in any democracy because it is a competitive form of politics within which political parties, smaller groups and individuals are all trying to win support and promote their causes. Those who pretend it is possible to do politics without creating rosy narratives are lying and it is this form of political hypocrisy, lying about lying, that can have a corrosive effect on democracy itself. What we need is more honest narratives about what politics involves as well as fuller accountability for the actions of government in our political rituals.

Conclusion

In this chapter I have set out some of the problems within the Westminster parliament that lead to inequality, exclusion, unwellness and a shallow ethics. I have proposed four principles to guide us when thinking about how to reimagine parliament:

- a more inclusive approach to knowledge;
- promoting diversity, equity and the right to participate in democracy for all;
- enhancing wellness; and finally
- restoring standards and ethics.

All these aspirations get away from the pervasive fixation on disciplining individuals – with codes of conduct, training or leadership ideas – or restructuring the system – whether changing rules, membership or powers – and focus on relationships that emerge in sociopolitical processes. Individuals and systems may need improvement too, but without addressing the connections between them, it will amount to nothing. This is because the centrality of relationships in political work is universal.

It is within the rhythms, rituals and symbolism of encounters between parliamentarians, and between MPs/peers and others in society, that I have recommended proposals for reimagining. First, I propose that the House of Commons and parliamentary scholars expand the collection of data on the rhythms of who parliaments and parliamentarians interact with and analyse the quality of the interaction, asking who is included and excluded and how might these processes of exclusion be challenged. Second, I recommend a deacceleration of the rhythms of political work to allow parliaments to prioritise. If parliaments and parliamentarians slowed down their rhythms, tackling fewer more urgent global and national challenges rather than rushing around, giving the appearance of busyness, while focusing on the relatively less vital challenges, then both Westminster and society would benefit significantly. Third, I suggest that the symbols of social status in the House of Lords are counterproductive. If social titles were abolished and replaced with political ones, the advantages would outweigh the disadvantages. Senators wearing formal modern dress, but not the uniforms associated with historical privilege, would be taken more seriously as political actors. Fourth, the cultural changes proposed to make Westminster a more gender friendly workplace could be complemented by measures to make other groups feel welcome, for example, by recognising their political contributions. Fifth, a review of how knowledge is valued by parliament and parliamentarians could helpfully lead to a reconsideration of the unequal treatment of 'evidence'. Those people not usually seen as experts, and disciplines with methods of rigour less well understood, might be taken more seriously as a consequence.

Finally, and most importantly, I have argued that ethics and standards need urgent renewal. This is the most complex and delicate area and although it is only the parliamentarians themselves who can demand higher standards of integrity of each other, so that scandals return to their rare occurrence, citizens and commentators can make it plain if they agree that it matters to more effective functioning of democracy. Such changes would complement the others outlined in this book but also enhance their impact and make it more likely that a reimagined Westminster was sustained in the longer term.

Acknowledgements

Emma Crewe's chapter is part of a project that has received funding from the European Research Council (ERC) under the European Union's Horizon 2020 research and innovation programme (Grant agreement No. 834986).

4

Reimagining Parliamentary Representation

David Judge

Introduction

There is a simple, but profound, premise that underpins this chapter: a reimagining of 'parliamentary representation' requires a 'systemic view of representation'. In the words of one of the foremost theorists of representation, Hanna Pitkin (1967: 221–2), 'what makes representation is the overall-structure and functioning of the system, and the patterns emerging from the multiple activities of many people'. Of necessity, therefore, reimagining parliamentary representation involves some notion of an interlocking of electoral modes with non-electoral modes of representation within a system of democratic parliamentarism. Such a reimagining also requires that the resultant paradoxes and contradictions attendant upon this conjunction need to be factored into the analysis. Without this interweaving, on the one hand, a reimagining of the electoral dimensions of representation alone might well be constricted to the narrow boundaries of a 'standard model of representation', while, on the other, a reimagining exclusively of the non-electoral dimensions runs the risk of theorising the institution of parliament out of existence. Before proceeding, therefore, some exposition of the 'standard model' is required, first, to outline its 'imagining' of representation; second, to identify the core principles that underpin that imagining; and third, to use those principles as a guide for a reimagining of parliamentary representation in the United Kingdom. Also, before proceeding further, it needs to be made clear from the outset that the focus here is upon a reimagining of parliament as a *collectivity*. This is both a distinct and specific focus in treating parliament as a collective representative institution, rather than as a set of dyadic representative relationships between individual MPs and individual constituencies, or as a bifurcated institution with one of its parts – the political executive (the government) – enmeshed in broader representational relationships of 'governance' (for the significance of this focus see Judge and Leston-Bandeira, 2018, 2021).

Orthodox imaginings: the standard account of democratic representation

The concepts of representation and legitimation are umbilically connected in democratic parliamentary systems. The basic premise of such systems is that the decisional outputs of government – public policies – are treated as legitimate because the representatives responsible for those decisions are themselves deemed to be legitimate. A comprehensive account of democratic legitimacy has, therefore, to explain why some individuals, in the absence of all other individuals, are believed to have the right to act on behalf of those who are not present at the point of decision.

'The standard account' of representative democracy sketches a basic analytical frame within which to explain this conundrum. In effect, however, there is no single comprehensive 'account' but rather iterations 'of a consolidated view of a model of political representation institutionalised in the course of the twentieth century across a number of constitutional democracies' (Castiglione and Warren, 2019: 45). The advantage of such a consolidated view, for present purposes, is that it provides a basic frame within which to ground the analysis of political representation and from which to launch a consideration of alternative accounts and models.

Under a 'standard account', the legitimacy of political representation is contingent upon, variously, a set of procedural standards, or long-term and systematic institutionalised arrangements, which regulate the authorisation, responsiveness and accountability of representatives. These procedures and arrangements are rooted in an 'electoral representative form' (Castiglione and Warren, 2019: 21) characterised by: first, principal-agent relationships between represented and representatives encompassing processes of authorisation and accountability; second, formalised political decision-making structures including 'some sort of collegiate representative body in a more than advisory capacity', with the legislature most commonly identified with this role at state level (Pitkin, 1967: 227, 235); third, dynamic and dialectic election processes, which institutionalise the principles of inclusion and equality in voting rights, and enable electors to make prospective estimations of the potential performance of their representatives as well as retrospective assessments of actual performance; and, fourth, territorial constituencies with a residence-based franchise, serving to inhere historical claims of relative universality and equality into modern systems of political representation. These four defining elements of the 'standard account' come with concomitant normative assumptions.

First, principal-agent relationships assume two parallel processes of authorisation and accountability: one is a chain of authorisation from voter to representative, the other is a distinct, but complementary, chain of accountability from representative to voter. Underpinning such notions of representative chains is the normative claim that representatives should pursue the preferences of their voters. If they do so, then the interests of principal and agent should align. Representation comes to be seen, therefore, not only as the reflection and transmission of interests and demands held by a principal, but also as a means by which democratic legitimacy can be ascertained and assessed in terms of the degree of responsiveness of the representative towards their constituency and the congruence of 'interests' (broadly conceived in terms of policy positions, issue priorities or ideological preferences) between the represented and representatives. Second, if democratic parliamentarism has 'systematic responsiveness' embedded at its core, then a basic prerequisite is regular elections, which are deemed to be 'genuine', 'free' and 'regular'; and which serve, through equal voting rights, both as 'a simple means and measure of political equality' (Castiglione and Warren, 2006: 1) as well as 'the main institutional mechanisms through which political representation guarantees inclusion' (Castiglione, 2020: 31). Third, and inextricably bound to these electoral dimensions, is the identification of territorially defined constituencies as the basis of elections. Historically, in the development of democratic representation, 'the tendential equalization of constituencies' provided 'a basis for political equality' (Castiglione, 2015: 12). Fourth, and finally, the 'problem of unity' – of how to reconcile the interests of diverse citizens and constituencies with the collective interests of the wider polity – is addressed by invoking the deliberative 'centrality of parliament' as 'the key institutional way in which representation could be made to work democratically' (Castiglione, 2015: 15, see also Pitkin, 1967: 217, 227).

In providing empirical and normative 'imaginings' of how absent citizens are made present in political decision-making, and how the decision-makers and their outputs are legitimated, the 'standard account' serves, as outlined in the preceding paragraph, to reveal how principles of inclusion, equality, responsiveness/congruence and unity/collectivity – or what Urbinati (2010: 83) terms a 'presumption of generality' – are institutionalised in democratic parliamentarism. Equally, however, the 'standard account' also serves to 'problematise' those practical experiences and conventional conceptions (Castiglione and Warren, 2019: 22). Inhered within the standard account are complexities, incongruities and paradoxes which have prompted other 'imaginings' or 'recalibrations' of the principles and institutional modes of representation.

Problematising the standard account: challenges and developments

Before outlining suggestions for a '*re*-imagining' of parliamentary representation in the UK, some understanding of the problematisations associated with the standard account – and in turn identification of existing ideational and institutional responses to incongruity and paradox within that account – will help to identify potential analytical trajectories for further '*re*-imagining'. How these trajectories are determined by the intersection of the principles and problematisations of the standard account will be examined in the following section.

Inclusion/exclusion

One 'problematised' issue of the standard account is the relationship between the constitutional design of democratic parliamentarism (particularly its prioritisation of electoral representation) and patterns of political inclusion and exclusion. While elections have traditionally been identified as 'the starting point' of political representation, there is now more explicit recognition of an inclusion–exclusion paradox wherein citizens are simultaneously linked and separated from decision-makers (Urbinati, 2006: 4, 2011: 24). The punctuated participation of citizens in the electoral process is both decisive in legitimising the decision-making process and its policy outputs, and equally decisive in their *self-exclusion* from the formal representative process thereafter.

A second 'problematised' issue, linked to the first, arises from the premise that political representation constitutes, in essence, a principal-agent relationship. In treating this as a primarily dyadic relationship – where an individual constituent is represented by an individual representative – the standard account and simple agency theories fail to capture the mediated nature of the relationship between constituent, constituency and representative. A systemic perspective on the other hand leads to an awareness that citizens are represented by their elected representatives in the legislature, but this is only part of a larger representative system wherein 'each citizen is represented throughout the system by nonelected, non-legislative representatives in parties, interest groups, nongovernmental organizations, the media, [and citizens informally representing other citizens]' (Mansbridge, 2011: 628, 2020: 18). In which case, attention needs to be paid not only to the process of election but also to 'between-election' modes of representation. An understanding of political representation thus spills out beyond electoral processes to incorporate non-electoral processes and institutions of representation.

Equality

A third 'problematised' issue is the assumption, noted earlier, that electoral representation provides a simple egalitarianism, an equal standing of citizens in the decision-making process. What the practice of representation in democratic parliamentarism reveals however is that 'the notion of formal political equality might not suffice to guarantee the equal consideration of different interests in parliament' (Elässer and Schäfer, 2022: 1363). The extent of this insufficiency has been particularly exposed in numerous theoretical and empirical analyses of the relationship between political equality and descriptive representation. Descriptive representation provides for a more dynamic understanding of legitimation than that provided by standard electoral accounts. It does so through invocation of the notion of 'social proximity' between representatives and represented to explain and examine how the rightfulness and efficacy of the former to 'act for' the latter is justified and measured by the degree to which the former also 'stands for' the latter (in terms of correspondence of social characteristics and shared experiences). In this sense, descriptive representation is seen to be of vital importance in fostering democratic legitimacy: both normatively and substantively.

Indeed, descriptive representation has become one of the key conceptual tools for contesting structural inequalities (see Brown, 2020; Celis and Erzeel, 2020). Yet, a foregrounding of the descriptive dimension in recent imaginings of political representation has brought in its wake 'problematisations' of how exactly does the conceptualisation and operationalisation of descriptive representation address political inequality; and what criteria are to be used in determining which groups have a legitimate case for descriptive representation? Even if the basic criterion – the existence of identified patterns of structured inequality associated with group membership – is invoked in answer to these questions; contingency has been built into its deployment. This conditionality can be observed in the prioritisation of the claims of some groups above the claims of other groups for the redress of the inequalities confronting them. Stated at its starkest, the group claims of women and minority ethnic people have attracted far more attention than the claims of specific socioeconomic groups – the poor or the working class – or groups related to ability/disability.

Beyond questions about the criteria to be used for determining which groups merit descriptive representation, the question of 'what' is being represented substantively is also problematic. One problem is that an answer might spring the trap of 'essentialism' – the assumption that members of a marginalised group by virtue of their membership have unified interests, perspectives or 'issues' that can be represented. Certainly, this assumption has long been critiqued, contested, even repudiated, but, significantly, it has not been resolved (see Phillips, 2020: 180–1). Such critiques have prompted, however, a move beyond single-axis conceptions of group identities, experiences and interests – where heterogeneity of interest is conceived and analysed within the confines of a specific marginalised group – to conceptions and analyses of multiple axes of inequalities which recognise the 'intersectionality' of cross-cutting identities, experiences and interests (see, for example, Gershon et al, 2019; Montoya et al, 2022; Reingold, 2022). As a result, simple questions posed in the initial conceptualisation of descriptive representation become problematised and lead to more difficult, 'messy' and 'more nuanced' questions about 'complex intersections of multiple axes of identity and power as they relate to political representation and our ability to understand it' (Reingold, 2022: 296).

Responsiveness/reflexivity

One of the key characteristics of the standard account is that representation, conceived as a principal-agent relationship, is intrinsically a process of responsiveness. In this account, a legitimate decision-making process is one in which policies made and authorised by elected representatives closely track the interests and preferences of those they represent. Responsiveness is taken, therefore, as an indicator of legitimate representation. Equally, the standard principal-agent account also assumes that political representation provides for elected representatives to be held ultimately responsible and accountable for their actions to the represented. This simple formulation is, however, problematic.

When treated as a simple, dyadic, one-to-one relationship between individual citizen and an individual elected representative, then determining the flow of causality of responsiveness – from the latter to the former – is relatively unproblematic. However, when responsiveness is conceived as a many-to-one relationship (multiple citizens to one representative), or a many-to-many relationship (multiple citizens to multiple representatives), then determining causality becomes more opaque and more problematic. Equally, further problematisation arises from the assumption that responsiveness is a unidirectional process. In the context of contemporary governance, however, responsiveness is effectively a process of multidirectional interactions between elected representatives and citizens. It is a systemic, complex, multidirectional and cyclic process, and extends well beyond ideas of a simple chain of electoral responsibility/accountability to include more expansive notions of 'reflexive' responsiveness.

A detailed consideration of 'reflexivity' extends beyond the immediate focus of the present chapter. Instead, a more immediate concern is to discover the potentiality of 'reflexivity' to address some of the problematisation identified earlier. The key to discovery is to recognise that 'reflexivity' not only allows for mediated representation – through the interactions of political parties, organised groups and social movements with and alongside electoral modes and institutions – but also complements mediation through rooting responsiveness in open and ongoing contestation. In this sense, reflexivity is of importance to a procedural understanding of representation by identifying a dynamic relationship between representatives and represented which 'entails the possibility of sustained deliberation, negotiation and contestation that … demand[s] responsiveness of those governing, not only through elections but also in-between election dates' (König and Siewert, 2021: 693).

Unity and the 'presumption of generality'

Within the institutional frame of democratic parliamentarism there is, as noted earlier, 'the presumption of generality'. Indeed, Urbinati (2010: 83), the author of that phrase, is certain that such a presumption 'is essential to the moral legitimacy of political decisions' in representative democracies. There is no presumption, however, that there is an absence of political divisions, or that parties, groups and movements will not seek to promote their partisan and partial interests; rather there is an expectation that these divisions can be reconciled within an articulation of a collective interest. Indeed, what 'grounds' the representative process in democratic parliamentarism is an assumption of unity. In embodying the idea 'that an elected body of responsible citizens is there to legislate in the name of all' (Eriksen and Fossum, 2012: 328) elected assemblies have come to enjoy a special status. A status derived from the capacity 'of giving [a] community a single voice and acting on its behalf as though it were a single agent' (Brito Vieira and Runciman, 2008: 134). A central tenet of conventional understandings of parliamentary representation, therefore, is this fusion of diversity and unity in the legislature.

If parliamentary representation is thus identified as a process of unification, it also, simultaneously, problematises how such unity is to be achieved. As a process of fusion, the common interest – collective unity – has to be constructed and is not pre-given. Elected representatives through 'sustained deliberation, negotiation and contestation' in the legislature have both to identify and articulate a collective will and, importantly, subject that articulation to 'trial by discussion' in the legislature (Manin, 1997: 191). In a context where discursive competition is framed exclusively in terms of 'autonomous deliberation', where parliamentary representatives act independently from extra-parliamentary mandates and from extra-parliamentary control, then the creation of unity out of diversity is relatively unproblematic. However, in the contemporary context of organised political parties – especially where parties see themselves beholden to their own hard-core electoral 'base' – such a view might be considered somewhat naïve. In its starkest formulation, the allegation may be made that party representation is inimical to the articulation of a cohesive national interest. If this is a problematic issue for contemporary imagining of parliamentary representation, then any future reimagining will also have to address this 'problematisation'.

Reimagining parliamentary representation

The preceding sections serve as a prologue to reimagining: first, in identifying the principles to guide the process of reimagining; second, in explaining and justifying their selection; and third, and importantly, in raising issues of problematisation associated with these principles. The word 'problematise' is used advisably here: 'to view, interpret, or analyse (an issue ...) as a problem or system of problems to be solved' (*Oxford English Dictionary*, 2022). If reimagining is a response to problems of current conceptions and practices of parliamentary representation, then it also needs to offer solutions to those problems.

If solutions are to be found in the following discussion, then they will stem from a recognition that answers will necessarily be complex. There are no simple answers: no simple reimaginings. Instead, there will be a search for answers which acknowledge that: parliamentary representation is nested elementally within a wider representational system; the principles underpinning 'the electoral representative form' are necessarily interlinked; and an expansive process of reimagining will situate the institution of parliament and its elected members as nodal points within intricate and mutating networks of electoral and non-electoral modes of representation. Let the search commence!

'Electoral representative form': principles of equality and inclusion

Political equality, as a condition of legitimacy in democratic parliamentary systems, is institutionalised in electoral institutions and processes and captured in the dictum 'one person, one vote, one value'. The universal franchise provides, in principle, for basic formal political equality through free and fair elections. But as Dahl (2005: 195) makes clear: 'If equality in voting is to be implemented, then clearly ... [t]o be free means that citizens can go to the polls without fear of reprisal; and if they are to be fair, then all votes must be counted as equal.' Moreover, as noted above, the equality of voting power also has as its corollary the more expansive notion of institutionalised inclusion of electors in the representative process.

If the principles of equality and inclusion are to serve as markers for a reimagining of electoral representation, then the UK's current electoral system provides little inspiration for such re-envisaging. By most metrics the UK's current electoral system is deficient in securing voter equality or citizen inclusion in the parliamentary representative process. To take the example of the UK's 2019 general election, the simple plurality (first-past-the-post) electoral system, in the context of the UK's multi-party system, displayed both unequal and exclusionary outcomes. There were manifest inequalities in the share of Westminster seats and a party's national vote share: with the average number of votes needed to elect one MP ranging from 38,264 for the Conservative Party; 50,837 for Labour; 336,038 for Liberal Democrats; through to 866,435 for the Green Party (McInnes, 2020). The Conservative Party, with 44 per cent of the vote, secured 56 per cent of seats at Westminster and a majority of 81 seats over opposition parties. Yet, a majority of voters in the UK secured neither a party candidate of their choice in their own constituency, nor a party in government at the national level. In effect, some estimated 14.5 million voters (45 per cent of all voters) ended up casting their vote for candidates who were not elected (Garland et al, 2020: 6).

Discriminatory, exclusionary outcomes were also evident in the degree to which representatives were 'socially proximate' to the people they represented. While record numbers of women and minority ethnic MPs were elected in the 2019 general election these groups remained proportionately under-represented in the Commons. At that election 220 women became MPs (and by the end of 2022 a further five women had been elected at by-elections). Yet, set against this record, women still accounted for only 35 per cent of MPs although constituting 51 per cent of the UK's population; only 559 women had been elected since 1918, and it has been estimated that it will take a further 45 years for gender parity to be reached in the Commons (Garland et al, 2020: 16). Similarly, a record number of minority ethnic MPs were elected in 2019 (10 per cent of all MPs, n.65), but still short of the 85 MPs that would have been needed to reflect the 13 per cent of the UK's adult population from a minority ethnic background. LGBT+ people fared rather better, with the return of 46 LGBT+ MPs (7 per cent of all MPs in 2019) serving as a positive inclusionary symbol for the 3.4 per cent of the UK population who do not consider themselves to be straight or heterosexual.

The starkest exclusionary electoral outcomes, however, were to be found for people with a disability. After the 2019 election only five MPs (1 per cent) were self-declared disabled (though some disabled people in the Commons may have chosen not to declare their disability for fear of political discrimination [see Hensman and Schendel-Wilson, 2022: 44]); yet some 14.6 million people, 22 per cent of the UK's population, have a reported disability. For this 'representation gap' to be closed would have needed 143 self-declared disabled MPs to be returned to Westminster in 2019. Similarly, there is a significant representation gap when it comes to social class, or more particularly the working class. An estimated 34 per cent of the UK workforce are classified as working class, yet only 13 per cent of Labour MPs and 1 per cent of Conservative MPs had identifiable prior working-class occupational status before entering parliament in 2019. More especially, very few MPs had directly experienced long-term unemployment, and even fewer had endured sustained poverty. Such under-representation, as comparative research demonstrates, matters to the extent that 'differential representation [in legislatures] is always in disfavor of the poor' (Giger et al, 2012: 57; see Elsässer and Schäfer, 2022: 1377).

If the current first-past-the-post electoral system is merciless in its disproportionality and its distortions of voters' choices and diversity, then it would be appropriate to consider other 'electoral representative forms' when reimagining parliamentary representation in the UK. In particular, a new look at parliamentary representation might well be advised to start from Kedar et al's (2016: 677) analysis of numerous empirical studies and their conclusion that 'democracies with proportional representation are characterized by better representation compared with majoritarian democracies'. The established benefits of proportional representation, listed by Kedar et al (2016: 677), are that it: 'allows diverse voices and interests to be heard and considered in parliament, government, and the policymaking process'; 'enables better representation of minority groups as well as women'; provides 'better ideological congruence between the government and voters in comparison to majoritarian systems'; and allocates parliamentary seats '(more or less) proportionately to the votes obtained by the different parties'.

There are of course many systems of proportional representation: some of which are currently used in the parliaments and assemblies of the devolved nations of the UK (Single Transferable Vote for the Northern Ireland Assembly, and the Additional Member System for the Scottish and Welsh Parliaments); and many of which are used in Westminster-derived parliaments in Commonwealth countries. Exactly which system should be adopted in a reimagined 'electoral representative form' is not for recommendation here. Nor for that matter should the choice of a new electoral system be left to elected representatives alone (even if that choice is then subject to confirmation by MPs and ultimately referendum). Crucially, and in preface to the consideration of responsiveness in a reimagined representative system (see the section on responsiveness below), campaigning groups have already argued that the choice of a new system should ideally be determined by a citizen-led, open and inclusive deliberative process. It would be incumbent upon elected representatives in the UK parliament to be both engaged with this process and responsive to its outcomes.

A reimagining of formal electoral rules alone, however, would be insufficient to secure greater equality and inclusiveness in the representative process. The conceptualisation of equality needs to be broadened beyond 'equal opportunity' or 'competitive equality' to encompass 'equality of result' (see IDEA, 2022). The latter would require positive actions, including compensatory measures, to challenge those structural barriers which perpetuate representational inequalities. The neutralisation of inequalities which restrict the political presence of marginalised groups thus provides a powerful justification for positive, affirmative action, and has provided the underpinning logic for the rapid introduction of group-based electoral quotas throughout the world. However, the practical effectiveness of quotas differs markedly across countries; but, as a general proposition, quotas are often seen to have the greatest impact in proportional representation systems, especially those combining closed party lists and high district magnitudes. Moreover, effectiveness is often linked to the specific type of quota and the political context in which they were introduced.

In essence, quotas are designed to 'jump-start' group representation. There are three main types of electoral quotas: reserved seats, candidate/legislative quotas and political party quotas (see IDEA, 2022). Given the problems and critiques of reserved seats and legislative quotas, perhaps the most appropriate 'jumping off' point when making the argument for the future deployment of quotas in the UK is to analyse the merits of party quotas. The unalloyed merit of party quotas is that they serve to increase the numbers of women candidates and elected representatives. The Labour Party's use of all-women shortlists since 1997, culminated at the 2019 general election, with the party having both the highest number of female candidates (n.335, 53 per cent of all Labour candidates) and the highest number of female MPs (n.204, 51 per cent of all Labour MPs) of any party in any general election. In short, the 'equality guarantee', offered in the Labour Party's use of all-women shortlists, worked.

While gender electoral quotas have been at the centre of most advocacy for, and analyses of, descriptive representation the claims of other under-represented groups – ethnic and racial minorities, disabled, LGBT+, and working class – for 'equality guarantees' through quotas have been amplified in recent years. And, simultaneously, the case for the introduction of youth quotas has gained increased traction. But the creation of separate, single-axis, quotas for under-represented groups generates complex, and possibly insurmountable, problems of co-ordination and implementation. In which case, a reimagining would have to work within an intersectional frame, to address the multiform intersections of gender, ethnicity, race, sexuality, class and age, and to investigate the potentialities of 'nested quotas' (see Phillips, 2020: 184). A reimagining of the 'electoral representative form' thus extends beyond formal electoral institutions and rules; to incorporate a re-envisaging of the 'supply-side' provision of candidates and representatives via political parties.

A further extension of reimagining is also needed to address the broader issue, flagged above by Dahl, that equality in voting can be achieved only in the absence of 'fear of reprisal'. While Dahl's focus was upon voters, his caution also applies forcefully to candidates and elected representatives. Indeed, there is compelling evidence in the UK that the daily abuse, harassment and intimidation suffered by women inhibits them from seeking and reaching elected office. At the 2019 general election, women candidates were significantly more likely to suffer abuse both online and offline than men, and to be 'very concerned' and 'very fearful' when campaigning (Collignon et al, 2022: 35–7). Indeed, as Collignon and Rüdig (2021: 443) conclude, the abuse suffered by women candidates 'impacts the representation of women because it makes it more difficult for them to get elected by forcing them to modify their campaign behaviour in meaningful ways'. Ultimately, therefore, harassment, abuse and intimidation serve to constrain gender equality in representation, both through women's self-limitation of behaviour and self-exclusion from participation. These constraints especially impact Black, Asian and minority ethnic women. Any future reimagining of representation would need both to address these constraints, and to treat them as systemic problems.

Responsiveness: non-electoral representation

Parliamentary representation entails a dynamic relationship between represented and representatives; but, as noted above, this dynamic representational relationship is not confined exclusively to elections. From a systemic perspective, political representation extends beyond electoral processes and institutions to encompass non-electoral processes, and 'informal' or 'self-authorised' modes of representation capable of representing citizens and effecting responsiveness from their representatives.

Adopting a systemic perspective and incorporating non-electoral modes and associated claims-making approaches into a reimagining of parliamentary representation, while necessary, is also problematic and runs the risks of generating something tantamount to a conceptual black hole into which all existing ideas about political representation might be sucked. To avoid this fate, therefore, the following discussion will focus exclusively on the responsiveness dynamic between electoral modes and non-electoral modes of representation.

Claims to represent 'the *interests* of a *specified group*' (Saward, 2010: 95, original emphasis) are a key characteristic of non-electoral representation. These claims are advanced by a wide range of non-statal groups, such as interest groups, social movements, civil society organisations or nongovernmental organisations (both national and international) as well as by critical actors. And the view that 'representative democracy is all about elections' has long been challenged in the UK in the extent to which other non-electoral models, modes and experiments – pluralist, neo-corporatist and network governance, to name but a few – have featured in the post-war period. But these modes and models have pivoted primarily around the mediated relationship between groups and the *executive* rather than between groups and *parliament*. What needs to be reimagined, therefore, is how these groups may be incorporated, or, more accurately, be 'institutionalised', into an encompassing system of *parliamentary* responsiveness.

Indeed, in many respects, this call for an institutionalised interconnection of parliamentary and non-electoral modes of representation is the obverse of mounting calls for democratic innovation, particularly for the institutionalisation of democratic mini-publics or sortitioned citizen panels into existing systems of representative democracy (see Chapter 5). The key question to be addressed here, however, is the extent to which such innovations, as modes of representation, are compatible with, or fundamentally challenge, parliamentary representation. If it is the latter, then a reimagining would undermine the electoral foundations of parliamentary representation and so detach legitimation from electoral processes and the institutional form of a representative parliament. What would be created would be a new 'non-electoral institutional form' and one based upon alternative principles of legitimation.

At its furthest extreme, a reimagining of representation in accordance with theories of deliberation and sortition – in its 'open democracy' variant – is meant to be 'not just an improved, more participatory, or differently representative version of representative democracy but a different paradigm altogether', and to constitute 'a radical break from electoral representation' (Landemore, 2021: 71, 76). The central institutional feature of this new democracy would not be parliament but 'an open mini-public' as 'an all-purpose, randomly selected body open to the input of the larger public via citizen initiatives and rights of referral as well as a permanent online crowdsourcing and deliberative platform, and ultimately connected to a demos-wide referendum on central issues' (Landemore, 2020: 218). In contrast with electoral representation, the representative base would be 'lottocratic' or 'self-selected' in nature. Clearly, 'open democracy' is distinctly, and intentionally, different, therefore, from electoral parliamentary modes of representation. Less radically, but still radically, advocates of 'liquid democracy' – premised on vote delegation, proxy voting and voters having the capacity to choose different representatives for different issues – do not rule out the possibility that such a system might be 'a potential complement' to existing forms of democratic representation, and capable of being integrated into existing democratic systems (Valsangiacomo, 2021: 2). But the word 'potential' does some 'heavy lifting' in such a presumption.

More pragmatically, one way to institutionalise sortition into democratic parliamentarism would be through 'hybrid bicameralism'. This institutional form would combine elections and sortition by having one elected and one randomly selected chamber. Proponents argue that such a scheme would enhance legitimacy in the parliamentary system as a whole, as a sortition second chamber would 'instantiate political equality' and be 'presumptively responsive to people's interests' (Abizadeh, 2020: 800), and have proffered elaborate schemes of 'intelligent institutional design' for the implementation of hybrid bicameralism and the institutionalisation of sortition in a parliamentary system (see Gastil and Olin Wright, 2018; Abizadeh, 2020; Sortition Foundation, 2022).

Another way of connecting sortition with parliamentary representation – in a quasi-institutional form – is through the establishment of permanent deliberative mini-publics 'very tightly coupled with the representative system' (Curato et al, 2021: 125). The 'Ostbelgien model', examined in Chapter 5, provides a particularly striking example of this linkage. This model is of particular importance for the proponents of sortition as it is seen as a critical test of how such a quasi-institutional form would work 'in the wild'. Yet the model comes with its own problematisations. Obviously, this is not the place to examine these issues in detail other than to note that these issues are endemic in the use of mini-publics generally, and to highlight two specific problems.

The first concerns the extent to which mini-publics are conceived as decision-makers, as being 'consequential when it comes to affecting the content of collective decisions' (Dryzek, 2010: 23); or are seen simply as a means of 'enhancing the responsiveness of the [extant] political system to the interests, views and policy objectives of the citizenry' (Lafont, 2017: 97). Hence a central, perpetual, problem has been whether, and how, mini-publics should be connected to the 'main game' of 'central decision-making processes' in the polity (Goodin, 2012: 806). In turn, the second problem is linked directly to this first problem. In essence, this is a problem of legitimation. Generally, if mini-publics are part of an institutional design for a legitimate political order based upon deliberative praxis, then rooting that order in the macro-deliberative system of parliamentary democracy, which privileges electoral representative institutions, generates fundamental conceptual and practical incongruities (see Judge, 2014: 136–47). In essence there is a 'legitimacy tension'. A tension which is apparent in institutional designs seeking to integrate mini-publics into statal policy making and confer upon them decisional power, and so to transition away from advisory or consultative status.

A related problem is that, if one of the legitimacy claims of mini-publics rests in their descriptive representativeness of society, then the processes by which members are selected are key to sustaining this claim. Hence, selection algorithms designed to optimise fairness in these processes are essential to bolster these legitimation claims (see Flanigan et al, 2021). Beyond their use in sortition processes, however, algorithms are of significance to a wider reimagining of representational responsiveness. If a key dimension of political responsiveness is congruence – of aligning the activities of representatives to the preferences of the represented – then the accurate discovery of what these preferences are and how they are articulated in a dynamic, complex, multi-directional and cyclic relationship should be factored into a reimagining of parliamentary representation. 'Algorithmisation' – exemplified in artificial intelligence, data-mining and big-data analytics – provides opportunities for representatives to anticipate and align the preferences of the represented. Already notions of 'government by algorithm' and 'e-policy' initiatives – where big data and artificial intelligence enable governments 'to undertake better assessments of the preferences of citizens' and make them 'more accountable to citizens and even transform the traditional governance model' (Pencheva et al, 2020) – are driving reimagining of public policy making. There is scope, therefore, for a cross-over from these initiatives into a reimagined sphere of parliamentary representation. Obviously, any 'algorithmisation' of the representative process would have to confront the many problematisations – not the least of which is regulation – associated with this idea; but, given the pace of technological advance, the merits and demerits of such digital innovation warrant urgent attention (see Cavaliere and Romeo, 2022: 440–1).

Unity and the 'presumption of generality'

There is, as noted earlier, a rudimentary consensus that the 'presumption of generality' provides one of the guiding principles of democratic parliamentarism. One of the 'most important features' of this representative system is 'its capacity for resolving the conflicting claims of the parts [of the nation], on the basis of their common interest in the welfare of the whole' (Pitkin, 1967: 217). This capacity is 'peculiar' in that it stems from the combination of the legitimation principles of election and from the legitimation principles of deliberation. It is also 'peculiar' when contrasted with the representative claims made by non-electoral representatives to speak for the collective interest (see Judge, 2014: 10–12, 136–9).

If the 'presumption of generality' is to be realised within a reimagined institutional frame of democratic parliamentarism, then the 'peculiar' conjunction of the legitimation principles of election and deliberation needs not only to be recognised but also instantiated. Equally the problematisations of this conjunction need to be both acknowledged and addressed. A starting point would be to accept that 'to fulfil the promise to create unity out of diversity without eradicating the latter' requires an institutionalised process of 'sustained deliberation, negotiation and contestation' (König and Siewert, 2021: 693). In other words, it requires reflexivity. And, as Knight and Johnson (2007: 56) emphasise, parliaments, as democratic institutions, 'enable a level of reflexivity unavailable in other institutional forms' in allowing for the collective reconsideration and revisiting of the 'terms of ongoing interactions' and inducing 'common or shared understandings of what is at issue in particular circumstances'. An increase in institutional inclusiveness and equality, prospected above in a reimagined 'electoral representative form', would be expected to boost such dynamic reflexivity.

Moreover, the principles of equality and inclusion could be further embedded in dynamic reflexivity at Westminster if, for instance, the plurinational nature of the UK state, and the conflicting claims of its territorial 'parts', were reflected in a second chamber based upon the principle of election but structured around territorial difference of the nations and regions of the UK. Such a chamber would institutionalise reflexivity in the search for unity out of territorial diversity.

Beyond reform of the 'electoral representative form', further enhancement of dynamic reflexivity is promised in designs for the institutionalisation of non-electoral representation (see the section on responsiveness above). Other institutional designs, many of which pre-date current 'democratic innovation', are on offer for the incorporation of non-electoral voices into parliamentary deliberations. The creation of second or third parliamentary chambers selected in accordance with functional or associative notions of representation have reappeared throughout the past century: such as proposals for a 'House of Industry' or a 'Social Parliament' in the UK in the 1920s and 1930s, or further afield in the establishment of the European Union's Economic and Social Committee in 1957. The inclusion of more, and more diverse, voices in the deliberation of public policies, certainly fits with ideas of enhanced reflexivity, and also fits with established ideas that democratic parliamentarism is a system wherein 'everything has to be justified in debate' and subject to 'the trial of discussion' (Manin, 1997: 191). Less certain, however, is the compatibility of institutionalising 'the interests of a specified group' (Saward's definition of non-electoral representation) with ensuring that 'citizens have to see and understand that they have something in common that unifies them' (Urbinati, 2006: 134). As Runciman (2007: 113) notes, 'a scheme that prioritises variety over uniformity in political representation is not without its costs'. The way to minimise these costs is to recognise that democratic parliamentarism does so by allowing elected representatives to claim to represent the people 'as a whole', yet also provides institutionalised capacity for contestation of such a claim. Such a process of justification, and hence of legitimation, serves to differentiate collectively accountable (and collectively authorised) elected representatives and electoral representative institutions from 'self-authorised' non-electoral representatives and institutions.

Conclusion

In many ways what has been offered in this chapter has been 'bounded reimagining'. Bounded in multiple ways. First, in focusing upon parliament as a collectivity, rather than addressing narrow dyadic individual representative relationships or the broad representative relationships of governance focused upon the political executive. Second, in not prospecting the extremities of democratic innovation which offer alternative paradigms to, and radical breaks from, parliamentary representation. Third, in leaving uncoupled the interconnectedness of the specific dimensions of reimagining. Fourth, in not investigating how a systemic view of representation is nested ultimately for its success in far wider, and existential, systemic perspectives on the UK's polity, society and economy. Fifth, and finally, in tempering the positivity and dynamism of reimagining with the caution and pessimism entailed in 'problematising' the processes of renewal. But each of these boundaries, although in need of transgression in the future, have helped to map out the widest and elemental boundary – of a 'systemic view of representation' – within which reimagining of parliamentary representation needs to be conducted.

The starting point of this chapter was the claim that a reimagining of parliamentary representation requires a systemic view of representation. A reimagined UK parliament should serve, therefore, as a key nodal point in intricate networks of electoral and non-electoral representation. To reach this point requires aggregation of the constituent elements of reimagining outlined in this chapter: parliamentary representation needs to be more equal, inclusive, reflexive and responsive; more digitally agile in its embrace of algorithms and artificial intelligence; and more accommodative to non-electoral modes of representation. Such a process of aggregation, however, would not be a matter of simple addition – of mechanistically combining diverse elements together – but of prioritising distinct preferences (a choice would have to made, for example, between the various principles ascribed to a reimagined second chamber – territorial, functional, electoral or sortition). Nonetheless, reimagination of parliamentary representation would be systemic in scope, cumulative in approach and expansive in its ambition.

5

Reimagining Engagement between Citizens and Parliament

Cristina Leston-Bandeira, Didier Caluwaerts and Daan Vermassen

Introduction

This chapter's reimagining challenge seems more straightforward than in the other chapters in this book, as it deals with a far more recent reality. While the other chapters focus on areas of activity with centuries' old practice, here we focus on a relatively new development: parliamentary public engagement. As such, there may be less to unpick and reimagine, as parliaments simply have not yet fully 'imagined' it in their own current practice. Parliamentary public engagement draws from, and extends, notions of representation, but it is a product of modern societies, having only become a distinguishable activity since the turn of the 21st century. However, the principles of engagement often run contrary to core parliamentary principles, making this chapter's reimagining task nonetheless as challenging. We start the chapter by establishing the significance of public engagement to today's parliament, to then outline the core principles and tensions between public engagement and parliament. We then proceed to outline a reimagined engagement between citizens and the UK parliament, to finally reflect on how close or distant this is from current practice.

Why focus on engagement

The UK parliament is first and foremost an institution that legitimises political decision-making through its law-making, scrutiny and representation roles. However, to ignore its public engagement role is to misunderstand the type of societies we live in: a digitally connected society of 24/7 communication, with an ever-expanding civil society, high expectations of governance and critical citizens. Political institutions locked away from the citizenry are unthinkable today. Likewise, to think of the relationship between citizens and parliament confined to the opportunity to participate in elections every few years is to misunderstand today's expectations of having a say.

Parliament's core institutional framework, practices and role may have been shaped over centuries, but its relationship with the public has changed dramatically since the turn of the 21st century. In a context of pulverised interests, a ubiquitous civil society, hyper voter volatility, unpredictable politics and decline in party membership, the modern parliament acts as the Mediator Parliament (Leston-Bandeira, 2016): an institution that assumes a key role in mediating inputs and outputs between society and governance, but not necessarily just through the representative accountability chain. It is a parliament that needs to combine representation with other mechanisms to connect with the public; a parliament that needs to reach out, to be open and accessible, and integrate participatory mechanisms which facilitate the involvement of people's voices and lived experiences within decision-making processes. Either as a response to the alleged crisis of democracy or as a recognition of today's expectation of more openness, parliamentary public engagement has become a key area of development for parliaments across the world (Leston-Bandeira and Siefken, 2023). This is illustrated by the Inter-Parliamentary Union (IPU), the international organisation of parliaments, selecting the theme of public engagement as the focus of its latest global report (IPU and UNDP 2022).

It is in this context that the UK parliament's role of public engagement has expanded and strengthened over the past couple of decades. The 2009 expenses scandal only reinforced a development that had already been set in motion since the turn of the century, namely through the publication of the *Connecting with the Public* 2004 report. This report gave a mandate to parliament's services to invest in and expand on public engagement (Leston-Bandeira, 2016). The aftermath of the expenses scandal that brought parliament's reputation to tatters would strengthen this path, as officials attempted to redress declining levels of trust. Since then, public engagement services have expanded across all types of engagement activities, from education to participation, as this chapter's last section shows. This development is clearly patent across parliament, but it is also patchy and its impact is often unclear.

Engagement both strengthens and supplements parliament's traditional roles of law-making, scrutiny and representation. It is not just an expectation from citizens, it is also becoming part of the fabric of parliamentary business.

Principles and tensions between public engagement and parliament

Before we outline what a reimagined engagement between parliament and citizens would look like, we establish the core principles of public engagement and its inherent tensions with the nature of the institution of parliament, after briefly establishing what we understand by public engagement.

The meaning of public engagement

Public engagement is often reduced to meaning participation. The two are often assumed to be interchangeable, but they are not. Participation can be one element of engagement, a type of activity seeking to involve the public in a process and/or event, but engagement is far broader than participation. Indeed, public engagement in the specific context of parliament can be embodied in the following five types of activities: information, education, communication, consultation and participation (IPU and UNDP, 2022). Ultimately, public engagement is about empowering people in relation to their surroundings, be it because they feel better informed, confident enough to get involved, or indeed decide to participate in a political event.

Initially conceptualised as public understanding within the realms of the arts and the sciences (Sanders and Moles, 2013), the concept of public engagement has since developed to include a much broader and nuanced spectrum of connections between citizen and realm (in the present case, politics), which assume non-unidirectional relationships and an enduring effect on the citizen beyond the actual public engagement event. That is, public engagement should involve a dialogical relationship rather than a one-way flow of information and be outcome-led rather than activity focused: public engagement is not simply about going through an activity or event, it should linger beyond the occurrence of these and have an effect on the citizen. This effect could be of feeling more confident, welcomed, listened or valued, in short empowered, or indeed, when done badly, less confident, unwelcomed, not listened to or unvalued, in short disempowered. But engagement is not just about the citizen. It is also about making better science, arts or politics. It is, in the context of parliament, about enhancing parliamentary decisions and decision-making processes by making these more meaningful to the citizen – both in how the citizen perceives them and in the quality of the decisions taken.

The core principles of engagement

As established in the previous section, public engagement entails different types of activities, from providing information (for example, parliamentary websites) to enabling citizen participation in parliamentary proceedings (for example, petitions). We are thus referring to potentially very different types of activities. But across these, we establish five core principles of public engagement with parliament: (1) inclusivity, (2) relevance, (3) relatability, (4) continuity and (5) sustainability.

1. Inclusive engagement reaches out to a wide range of audiences, going beyond those often referred to as the 'usual suspects'. Those who get involved in politics tend to be older, White and from well-off socioeconomic backgrounds. Engagement needs thus to be particularly focused on those groups who would not normally get involved. This is about reaching diverse people and community groups, but also about facilitating spaces and processes that feel inclusive.
2. For engagement to chime and lead to consequences, it needs to be relevant; relevant to the people it focuses on, to the issues it addresses, and to the parliamentary processes in place. This requires engagement with specific issues, groups and processes. Engagement methods may be generalised, but their sense of relevance needs to be kept to each instance of engagement activity.
3. Engagement is based on connections; subjective connections that make you feel you belong, that it is worth it and that someone is listening. For those connections to take place, the citizen needs to feel they can relate to the organisation leading on the engagement initiative, be it parliament overall, a select committee, an official or indeed an MP. Meaningful engagement does not take place when it feels distant and abstract.
4. Engagement should not be a one-off. It should be built upon structures and processes that enable a continuity of contact, which assist parliament and parliamentarians in being aware of the issues, interests and needs affecting citizens.
5. Finally, public engagement practices, processes and outcomes need to be sustainable. This is for two reasons. First, they need to be sustainable to be run in the medium and long-term to preserve connections between parliament and citizens. There is little point in creating initiatives that cannot be replicated or sustainably run within the parameters of parliamentary practices. Second, and more importantly, engagement needs to consider the consequences of today's decisions for tomorrow's generations. It should facilitate discussions which consider the impact on future generations of specific decisions and policy, both those who are already born and those yet to be born.

In our reimagined parliament, these core principles of engagement would therefore be at the forefront of its relationship with citizens. However, these core principles are not necessarily in line with core parliamentary principles, as we explore next.

The tensions between public engagement and parliament

Parliaments were created to represent people and take decisions on their behalf. They were not created to engage with people.[1] To represent and to engage are clearly linked, but they are not the same. As institutions of democratic political governance, parliaments embody characteristics and principles that are in tension with the principles of public engagement outlined earlier. We explore five of these next.

First, the collective nature of parliaments. As explored elsewhere (Leston-Bandeira, 2014), parliaments represent everyone and no one specifically. They lack a single identity (Kelso, 2007). They bring together different political groups which, collectively, represent a nation. However, these groups have different agendas, being often opposed to each other. Despite being constituted of 650 MPs and 800 odd peers, due to its collective nature the UK parliament is an abstract and anonymous entity as it cannot represent one single identity, representing vastly different realities across the country.

When considering the importance of establishing connections at the core of engagement, it becomes clear that the UK parliament does not have the characteristics to make it relatable. As a large, abstract organisation, it lacks the flexibility and persona needed to embed engagement initiatives that are relatable to the citizen. This can of course be counteracted by focusing engagement on MPs and peers individually, issues or indeed committees and their chairs. But as a core principle, the collective and abstract nature of the UK parliament makes it intuitively a poor vessel for relatable engagement practices.

Linked to this, the UK parliament is also a highly hierarchical institution, where rituals and symbols set the pace and mood of the institution by reproducing distant pasts and associated senses of privilege (Puwar, 2004). Again, in many ways, this is due to its nature: all parliaments are hierarchical. This derives essentially from the processes associated with attributing legitimacy to MPs, as elected representatives and servers of the public; but also in establishing the legitimacy of the institution of parliament. Stripped of the symbols, rituals, practices and denominations which embed representatives with their status, MPs and peers would simply be people; likewise, parliamentary spaces would simply be just another building. Still, the UK parliament goes well beyond other parliaments in being particularly hierarchical, in great part due to its reliance on practice, precedence and history as part of its legitimacy mantle. Much has been done in recent years to redress this, but again this is part of parliament's nature, and contrary to engagement's core principle of inclusivity; particularly as there are wider factors that make politics exclusionary and the realm of narrow groups of people. This means that our reimagined parliament needs to actively nurture ways to make it more inclusive to foster proper engagement.

Our third parliamentary feature in conflict with the core principles of engagement is parliament's main House's dependency on electoral cycles. Elections are of course a key vehicle in ascribing legitimacy to parliaments.

However, by their very nature they also introduce priorities and narrow MPs' attention foci. Electoral cycles can be counter to the continuous nature that should characterise engagement processes. More importantly, electoral cycles and their inherent accountability to today's voters mean that MPs rarely consider consequences beyond the immediate election and voters; this encourages short-term thinking. It hinders sustainable approaches to policy making and engagement. Within the context of an electoral cycle, engagement can become about how to win an election, rather than about the lived experiences of specific policies or their consequences for generations to come.

Fourth, the model of representative parliamentary democracy is based on the principle of aggregation of interests following the will of the majority. This is a practical way of transforming people's needs and preferences into a governing system. However, engagement is anything but aggregation and majorities. It is about shaping processes to reach out to specific groups of people, to identify ways of making the issues of minorities come to the fore and to go beyond the majority and find solutions that are commonly accepted and based on lived experiences.

Finally, we turn to the pace of politics. Parliamentary representative democracy frameworks are in place to establish processes that facilitate governance in a timely manner – a small group of representatives making the decisions on behalf of millions. It is a system that ensures decisions are taken in a timely manner. Asking, checking and conferring with the public on all policy decisions would not be practical or even possible. Governance includes hundreds of small weekly policy decisions, many of which are of no relevance or importance to most people. Added to this, a politics highly visible under the spotlight of 24/7 communications introduces an even quicker pace to politics. This pace is often in contradiction to engagement, which requires time to be undertaken properly.

There are therefore many practical problems in harmonising the work of parliament and public engagement. Understanding how citizens feel about issues all the time is not practical and would make policy making an impossible task. Likewise, keeping connections and making parliament seem relevant is a difficult task. Making representatives think about future generations that are not yet born and relevant for their voting basis is the stuff of science fiction. However, none of this means that our reimagined parliament would not be able to bring in practices and processes reasserting the principles of public engagement at the core of parliamentary practice. We may simply need to think about it in a more creative way and to see engagement as a core priority. The reimagined engagement between citizens and parliament would adopt a more continuous and integrated approach between engagement and parliament's core roles of representation, law-making and scrutiny.

A reimagined parliamentary public engagement

A reimagined parliamentary public engagement would abide by the principles outlined here. It would feel welcoming and inclusive, be continuous throughout the parliamentary year and term, feel relevant to audiences and parliamentary processes, be relatable through Members, peers and staff, but also through stories and issues, and importantly it would be sustainable and future generations aware.

Welcoming and inclusive

The first stop for this reimagined journey is the parliamentary space. Parliaments in their current form are often perceived as rather unapproachable spaces for engagement. They are physically and symbolically distant places for citizens. Their status, their location at the centre of political life, often in the capital, and even their formal architecture can be a barrier for meaningful and purposive public engagement.

In our reimagined parliament, the physical and symbolic space would feel inclusive and welcoming. It would reflect the fabric of the country and its people. Rather than a space for them, it would feel as a space for us all. It would obviously be accessible for people of all abilities and disabilities (see Chapter 2). But part of reimagining the parliamentary space is also about forging this space, with its actors and practices, outside of its building. A reimagined parliament would take parliamentary business to local communities across the country regularly, rather than expect others to come to the building. This outreach could be through a range of practices such as committee sessions in constituencies, or through key officers such as the Speaker having dedicated days in constituencies outside the Palace of Westminster. In a reimagined parliament, MPs would also have welcoming, and inclusive, spaces within their constituency offices to engage with their constituents.

The next stop would be parliamentary language and the way parliament communicates to external audiences, particularly the general public. Parliamentary language can seem opaque to the public. It is complex and has its own jargon, as many other professions do. But the difference between parliamentary and other sectors' activities is that this is about the public. New Zealand has passed a law that commits decision-makers to use plain language (New Zealand Parliament, 2022). Our reimagined parliament would update its antiquated language to a more modern familiar vocabulary; a simple example could be the term 'divisions' becoming 'votes'. However, recognising that parliamentary language is always going to be complex by the nature of what it addresses, our reimagined parliament would mainly invest in effective translation processes. This can be in the form of the development of guides explaining parliamentary practice tailored to a range of audiences, to the availability of translation of parliamentary business such as into British Sign Language.

A reimagined parliament would be welcoming and inclusive across its parliamentary business. Citizens invited to give oral evidence to committees, for instance, would feel at ease to talk to MPs and peers, by, for example, having all the information needed to prepare themselves and to understand what a committee evidence session entails. Processes supporting any activities oriented to the public would be communicated in a clear and accessible manner, taking into account respective target audiences. Often parliaments introduce public engagement initiatives which end up by having poor take-up because they are simply poorly communicated and feel exclusive in the way they are set up (Leston-Bandeira and Thompson, 2017). Just because an initiative exists, it does not mean it is a good initiative or that the public will feel encouraged to get involved. For diverse publics to get involved, citizens need to understand the purpose of the initiative and feel that it is worth them engaging with it. In short, the initiative needs to be appropriately communicated and set out.

Continuous

As explained, parliaments across the globe are increasingly employing a wide range of engagement strategies to reconnect with citizens in-between elections. However, one of the main shortcomings of these strategies is that they are often ad-hoc and short-term initiatives. They are organised, for example, whenever a political or policy problem presents itself or whenever a public call for more engagement is aired. Engagement is therefore often instrumental in defusing political conflicts and crises, and as a logical corollary, the commitment to facilitating engagement is usually short-lived.

In our reimagined parliament, in contrast, public engagement would be a structurally embedded practice, as a sustained and structural interaction between political decision-making, parliamentary administrations and the citizens. Permanency and continuity would therefore be a core element of our reimagined parliamentary engagement. Our reimagined parliament would institutionalise citizen engagement: engagement strategies would allow citizens and policy makers to engage in meaningful and transformative interactions on a continuous basis and as part of a long-term strategy, rather than in sequences of ad-hoc engagement or participatory iterations.

The continuous character of engagement in a reimagined parliament would also imply the formalisation of engagement strategies and practices. Engagement plans reaching well beyond the next election would be adopted transversally within parliament, and engagement officers would ideally be appointed to develop, implement and follow-up on the progress made and results achieved, across parliamentary business.

The continuous nature of engagement is therefore about regular practice that happens throughout a parliamentary term because processes are in place to activate engagement initiatives, rather than being dependent on ad-hoc decisions. But it is also about having systems in place that enable parliament to have an ongoing understanding of the core issues concerning people. One such mechanism is the 'post bag' of MPs. When the implementation of policies goes badly wrong, MPs soon start hearing about it through their post bags – see, for instance, the massive increase of casework as a result of the pandemic COVID-19 (Salisbury, 2021). However, this does not necessarily lead to a collective action or go beyond MPs and their offices individually taken.

One way of ensuring this continuity of contact and presence would be having a very good network of parliamentary officers across the country. As we see in our assessment of the UK parliament later in this chapter, outreach officers already exist. But these are relatively few and spread across the country. The Parliament of South Africa, by contrast, has parliamentary offices in every single constituency (Begg, 2022). These offices serve parliament, not the MP, and play an important role in establishing links between citizens across the country and the institution. Our reimagined parliament would have a network of parliamentary offices across the country's constituencies, which would not only disseminate the work of parliament and seek to understand and listen to the public's views on specific issues, but also provide a bottom-up way of citizens raising issues. This continuity of access can also take place through, for instance, phone and digital post boxes, such as Brazil's Congress's free phone number (*Disque Câmara*), which is used by millions (Barros et al, 2012). Of course, for these to be meaningful, they would need to be serviced with staff who would acknowledge inputs from citizens and direct them to a relevant service, such as a committee.

Another way of ensuring some continuity of awareness of the core concerns affecting people is through building communities of practice around specific policy areas. An obvious locus for this work would be departmental (Lords' investigative) select committees. Communities of practice would be open networks of organisations from the third and public sectors relevant for a specific policy area. For example, the Commons' Education Committee could maintain a community of practice with organisations representing key stakeholders, such as teachers, parents, schools, and so on; this could be maintained across both Houses, supporting, in this case, also the Lords' Public Services Committee. Each community of practice would maintain a list of contacts which would enable committees and MPs and peers to reach out to relevant and diverse groups according to the issues they were addressing at the time, but also meet on a regular basis. In a 21st-century society, parliament needs far more embedded and effective mechanisms to connect with outside organisations.

Relevant

As mentioned before, parliaments tend to be hierarchical spaces of symbolism, historical custom and ritual. As such, they are often more engaging for those who are familiar and comfortable with the usually highly formalised procedures and language of parliament. In our reimagined parliament, engagement strategies would cater to a wide diversity of audiences and groups. Moreover, it would do so in languages and practices that are not only inclusive, but also demonstrate the relevance of parliamentary practices and political decisions to all. In order to do so, our reimagined parliament would rely on a wide range of engagement practices from online surveys, through permanent exhibitions and mobile roadshows, taking parliament to the people nation-wide, to practices of participatory and deliberative democracy.

To ensure relevance to a diversity of groups and people, engagement strategies would be co-created with citizens. Instead of determining engagement policies top-down, citizens' views on effective engagement should also be taken into account bottom-up while developing policies. This generates the legitimacy, effectiveness and smooth implementation of such engagement strategies.

One noteworthy evolution in recent years is the use of mini-publics by parliaments. In several countries, parliaments have begun fundamentally reimagining their relationship with citizens by relying on democratic innovations within parliament (Setälä, 2017), complementing traditional representative procedures with more participatory innovations. For instance, the parliament of the German-speaking community of Belgium has adopted a model of democracy in which a council of 24 randomly selected citizens can decide to organise a citizen assembly to prepare recommendations on specific policies (Niessen and Reuchamps, 2022). These recommendations are subsequently presented to parliament. Another way of introducing citizens at the heart of parliamentary decision-making has been adopted by the Brussels regional parliament in Belgium, through its so-called mixed parliamentary committees. In these parliamentary committees, elected politicians and randomly selected citizens deliberate and formulate recommendations on themes or bills under consideration in parliament. Afterwards, the Brussels parliament is expected to vote on these recommendations, and if rejected, it needs to explain within three months why it has not adopted the committee's ideas. There are many other examples, demonstrating that parliaments are increasingly seeking connections with citizens in a co-creative process of making political decisions and integrating those connections in their day-to-day procedures. Our reimagined parliament would integrate a permanent structure that would facilitate co-creation with citizens through deliberative democracy processes.

While the UK parliament already has a rich portfolio of different types of engagement practices, as we see in what follows, our reimagined parliament would make sure that staff, MPs and peers were aware of which types of initiatives may be most suitable for each circumstance, according to the type of issue, context and target audience(s). Different methods of engagement would be deployed according to relevance of the method to the issue, context and audience(s) at stake. This would be simple to apply because our reimagined parliament would offer resources and specialised staff able to offer this advice. Crucially also, our reimagined parliament would have processes in place which would integrate a public engagement stage in each instance of law-making and scrutiny consideration.

Relatable

Our reimagined parliament would also feel to citizens as something they can relate to. As we explained, engagement is about connections, subjective feelings through which people can relate to others. Our reimagined parliament would focus on stories, issues and people, rather than processes and structures.

Engagement initiatives and points of access would be created around specific people and/or issues, so that citizens can more easily relate to these. Rather than inviting citizens, for instance, to submit their views to parliament, our reimagined parliament would showcase the issues it is covering and reach out to those who may be affected by those issues. Likewise, citizens need to feel that parliament addresses issues that matter to them. So, for instance, an education programme that simply tells pupils about the different stages of the legislative process but fails to connect to the specific context of the pupils it is targeting, by for instance outlining issues of relevance that committees may be addressing or specific critical bills passed, will be doing little in engaging and being seen as relatable. Instead, it is reproducing the idea that parliament is this abstract thing that other people deal with; it does not relate to our everyday life. Our reimagined parliament would engage through issues instead of processes.

Another way of making engagement more relatable is through people. This is often an issue for parliamentary public engagement, as staff are not meant to be seen, named, individualised, but it is often staff who implement public engagement initiatives. Our reimagined parliament would not shy away from building contacts between staff and external stakeholders. More importantly though, it would channel engagement initiatives through Members and peers. They are the ones who give a face to parliament, who can act and take decisions, who need to profile engagement initiatives. A simple way of doing this could be through a recording of an MP introducing an online survey meant to inform their debate in the chamber; or by including peers in a workshop with citizens on a specific issue for a committee inquiry.

Besides focusing engagement on issues and people, our reimagined parliament would close the feedback loop effectively. One of the main problems with parliamentary public participation initiatives is the lack of feedback to those who get involved, to relate in what way the citizens' contributions have informed parliamentary business. This is often due to lack of time and resources, but it does not need to be done at an individual level for each citizen or issue, it can be done collectively, simply giving a sense that someone did listen. Our reimagined parliament would include reports for each committee inquiry, for instance, giving an indication of the sort of issues raised by citizens and how these informed parliamentary business. In our reimagined parliament, committees' reports would refer to citizens inputs just as any other 'expert' type of evidence. What is more, short accessible reports would be created for each committee report aiming at the general public to explain the inputs suggested by citizens. These would be communicated back to citizens who had contributed.

Consequential

In our reimagined parliament, democratic engagement would matter, it would have an impact. Engagement strategies envisage rekindling the democratic linkage between parliaments and citizens, implying that engagement should affect both Members of Parliament and members of the public.

The literatures on participatory and deliberative democracy often speak of formal political uptake as a necessary condition for success. If engagement practices want to contribute to the institutional legitimacy of parliaments, they need to be linked in some way to political decision-making (Edwards, 2007), otherwise they are merely democratic experimentation with little practical use (Chambers, 2009). Even though engagement generally does not lead to substantive shifts in policies, a reimagined parliament would at the very least give meaningful consideration to citizens' opinions on substantive or procedural issues; crucially, it would be integrated with parliamentary business processes. Moreover, our reimagined parliament would offer citizens the opportunity to exchange views and ideas. If, for example, Members decided not to enact citizens' opinions, they would need to explain and justify their choice to gain public acceptance of that decision.

Consequentiality can also be situated at the level of individual citizens. The success of engagement strategies is contingent upon the level of enlightened understanding citizens gain during the process (O'Flynn and Sood, 2014). All participants should be able to develop an informed opinion, have the opportunity to process information in a non-coercive setting, that is, a setting in which strategic and power considerations are bracketed. Through this process of information gathering and processing, parliamentary engagement would act as a learning school for democracy: citizens are enabled to critically assess their own views on political issues, and in doing so, citizens learn about the challenges and difficulties inherent in political decision-making (Caluwaerts and Reuchamps, 2018). Citizens would also feel listened to, a key element of engagement often wanting in parliamentary practices (Leston-Bandeira and Thompson, 2017). Democratic engagement is therefore legitimate to the extent that it fosters interaction between parliament and citizens, and among citizens.

Future generations aware

The decisions taken by parliament today affect not only the current electorate, but many generations to come. Because future generations will bear the consequences of our current decisions, they should be engaged in the process leading up to those decisions (Goodin, 2007). A lack of consideration for future generations infringes the principles (outlined earlier) of inclusiveness and sustainability, leading to intergenerational injustices. Our reimagined engagement between parliament and citizens would therefore consider the interests of future generations.

While the dangers to the principles of inclusiveness and sustainability apply to both the young and the unborn, the two groups differ in their relation with engagement. The young are only excluded from formal modes of representation, that is, elections, but they can get involved in diverse engagement activities. The unborn, on the other hand, cannot be part of any direct form of public engagement. Indeed, engagement with those who are not yet alive is practically impossible. Not only are they not able to voice their interests, but their interests have not even been materialised and will depend on current and future decisions. Reimagining public engagement with these two groups requires a different approach each. We discuss these in turn.

In democracies, the politically underaged suffer from a double absence, both as electors and as elected representatives. Consequently, their interests and their lived experiences receive less attention in the political process. This double absence poses risks for the principles of relevance and relatability. That is, the under-representation of youth in parliamentary politics makes it hard for them to make their voices heard and hampers the salience of issues that are relevant to them. This can give minors the feeling that they do not belong, or that they are overlooked in the political process.

To empower the young, all possible activities of public engagement would be employed to make sure young people are communicated with and listened to. Engagement with the underaged would therefore go beyond the classic perception of minors as passive citizens who must only be educated to fulfil their political role when they reach adulthood. Instead, our reimagined parliament would establish interaction channels to specifically inform young people and set up consultation and participation initiatives to give the underaged a voice in the political process. This inclusion would eventually lead to young people feeling more relevant and being able to relate more to parliamentary work.

The unborn also suffer from a double absence, but they cannot be engaged with directly. The only means to engage with future publics is the unidirectional way of information-giving on the reasons why we make certain policy decisions. While this form of engagement may seem blatantly insufficient compared to the drastic ways in which we impact the futures of the unborn, it is nevertheless crucial for two reasons. First, providing future generations with information on the 'why' of our decisions entails taking the possible impact of our decisions on those generations into account. By engaging with future generations by means of reason-giving, parliaments must justify their actions towards the unborn. This justification and consideration of future generations' perspectives are beneficial for the principles of inclusiveness and sustainability. Second, providing information to future publics by justifying our decisions further increases sustainability since it allows for policy coordination across generations (MacKenzie, 2021). Every generation has the potential to cause policy reversal, which can be detrimental for long-term policies that need to be sustained to provide future benefits. The reason-giving by current parliaments provides a much-needed transparency for coordinating actions across time.

Making parliaments future generations aware does not limit itself to engagement with those future generations. The future is not an inevitable series of events waiting to unfold. Instead, the decisions we make today shape the future in many ways and even determine who will live. What this future should look like cannot be decided by abstract philosophical principles or by supposedly neutral technocratic decisions but should be the product of inclusive and deliberative processes (MacKenzie, 2021). This means that our reimagined parliament would employ a wide range of engagement mechanisms, as explored earlier, to engage with citizens to collectively explore possible futures and decide on the desired future. Again, this would strengthen the principles of sustainability and inclusiveness.

How far off is the UK parliament from this reimagined reality?

Despite all criticism of the UK parliament and the patent low levels of trust over the past few decades, this is actually a very active institution in enhancing its engagement with citizens. As explained at the start of this chapter, public engagement is a relatively new activity for parliaments across the world and the vast majority are well away from our reimagined parliament (Leston-Bandeira and Siefken, 2023). The UK parliament is not quite there, but recent years have seen considerable development of its capacity to develop public engagement practices.

Indeed, this institution has seen significant developments since around 2005 in all five core public engagement activities – information, education, communication, consultation and participation (Leston-Bandeira and Walker, 2018). This has been possible thanks to a considerable expansion of its staff and services specifically focused on engagement activities, such as the bicameral Participation Team (which covers such wide-ranging areas as visits, education, outreach and chamber digital engagement) or the Select Committees Engagement Team, specifically focused on supporting committees in their public engagement activities. Since 2015, the House of Commons also has an e-petitions system, with an associated new Petitions Committee, which has brought a significant addition to the direct relationship between parliament and citizens, performing a clear public engagement role (Leston-Bandeira, 2019).

These new structures have enabled the following developments, among others, in the areas of information, education and communication: a better awareness of publics beyond those who tend to engage (such as a library briefing identifying those groups who tend to engage less with parliament as a key informant of engagement strategies; easy read guides; use of British Sign language in Prime Minister's Questions); an education programme specifically aimed at special educational needs children; an expansion of the education services and visits to parliament, supported by the innovative multi-purpose Centre for Education and the development of a pioneering Teacher Ambassadors programme; the implementation of a network of outreach officers across the country, who work with local organisations to develop information sessions on parliament; and better tailored services to communicate about parliament's activity, including a range of podcasts such as one specialising on committee work.

There has also been considerable expansion in the areas of consultation and participation, namely within select committees and in both Houses. Committees now regularly consult the public as part of their inquiries, through a range of methods such as online surveys and workshops. These activities aim mainly to collate evidence on the lived experiences of the public for MPs to consider in committee inquiries, including the use of citizens assemblies and deliberative workshops, as well as enabling citizens to define the agenda of committees. This expansion of consultation and participation opportunities goes beyond committees, such as the work of the Chamber Engagement Team with Westminster Hall debates, through which MPs are able to integrate into their speeches the views and lived experiences of the public, or the Youth Select Committee, developed in partnership with the British Youth Council. MPs also often consult their constituents to inform their practice, such as Chris Bryant MP's choice of a topic for his Private Member Bill in 2017, which eventually became law (UK Parliament, 2018). Finally, the new e-petitions system has encapsulated considerable and innovative public engagement practices, many of which enabling citizens to shape government policy (Leston-Bandeira, 2019).

There is no doubt therefore that the UK parliament has considerable and innovative activity in public engagement. However, to become our reimagined parliament, this practice needs to be far more institutionalised and better resourced. Notably, understanding and appreciation of public engagement and of its value towards enhancing core parliamentary business – such as scrutiny and law-making – needs to be more embedded. Often public engagement is still too patchy and an after-thought. While some staff and Members understand the importance and value of public engagement, the majority still views it with suspicion and a possible clash with representative mandates (Matthews, 2021).

Having a more institutionalised approach to public engagement would ensure that it becomes a more continuous practice and better linked to ongoing parliamentary business. It would also contribute towards developing a better understanding of public engagement among both staff and Members. A more institutionalised approach may include, for example, committee inquiries always considering the public engagement angle at the early stages of planning and including a default section on public engagement in committee reports. It may also include the presence of public engagement officers in core business teams. A much wider network of public engagement officers and of parliamentary offices in the constituencies would also help keeping more continuous connections between the institution and citizens.

While some public engagement initiatives lead to change already and are fed back to the public, our reimagined UK parliament would have clear processes linking public engagement activity and output, be it linking it with parliamentary business, or be it with explaining to citizens how their input was used (closing the feedback loop), supported by well-resourced capacity. This may include better systems to convey to Members key messages from citizen evidence, a clearer reference to citizens' inputs in committee reports (acknowledging the value and role of this type of evidence, besides expert evidence), more regular and explicit explanations to the public on how their evidence informed parliamentary business.

To develop a more institutionalised approach to engagement, our reimagined UK parliament would need to expand further its services (and staff) working on engagement and, crucially, skill up in digital capacities and systems. One of the challenges staff currently face is the inability to process high volumes of inputs from citizens in a timely and meaningful fashion. Parliament simply does not have the resources to do this, and yet digitally this is possible with ever more user-friendly solutions. Our reimagined parliament would have flexible processes enabling it to adapt to technological developments.

Finally, our reimagined UK parliament would have systematic processes for evaluation of public engagement practice. Evaluation is still only fledgling, despite important initiatives such as feedback questionnaires in outreach sessions and the start of monitoring of diversity of committee oral witnesses. Our reimagined UK parliament would have far more comprehensive and systematic processes to evaluate ongoing practices and draw lessons for future practice.

Conclusion

This chapter has focused on parliamentary public engagement, a practice that is not necessarily embedded in centuries' old traditions, but that has gained significant traction among politicians and the public in recent years. The alleged crisis of democracy, and the perceived disconnect between citizens and their representatives, have propelled the demand for new engagement strategies, which spans a wide range of activities from informing and educating citizens, to formally including citizens in the process of political decision-making.

Even though many parliaments have tried to imagine public engagement in recent years with varying levels of success, we set out to reimagine what engagement strategies would look like in our reimagined UK parliament. Ever-louder calls for the UK parliament to position itself as a mediator between the inputs of society and the outputs of politics also sparked the need for a critical assessment of existing practices, and creative imagination of future practices. To guide our process of thinking through engagement, we conceptualised that a reimagined engagement would fulfil six key criteria. Engagement would only be able to create legitimacy and bridge the gap to the extent that it is inclusive and welcoming, continuous, relevant, relatable, consequential and future generations aware.

On most of these criteria, the UK parliament has made significant progress in recent years. It has taken multiple initiatives to improve its informational, educational, consultative and participatory functions, and it is currently able to engage a wide range of citizens on relatable political topics. Moreover, parliament's organisation has professionalised to further strengthen and support its engagement initiatives.

However, our exercise of reimagining parliamentary public engagement in the UK has also pointed out its weak spots. Despite an active strategy of reconnecting parliament with the people, most initiatives lack institutionalisation, integration and embeddedness. Even though parliament's engagement repertoire has broadened in recent years, its permanency and its connectedness to the parliament's key roles – scrutiny and law-making – remains limited. A reimagined engagement between the UK parliament and its citizens would be supported by far better resources and be pervasive across parliamentary practice. Crucially, it would consider impact on future generations.

Acknowledgements

Cristina Leston-Bandeira's contribution to this chapter is part of a project that has received funding from the European Research Council under the European Union's Horizon 2020 research and innovation programme (Grant agreement No. 834986).

Didier Caluwaerts's and Daan Vermassen's contribution to this chapter was made possible with funding from the Research Foundation – Flanders (FWO Vlaanderen) (Grant agreement No. G027019N).

Note

[1] One could argue that the early parliaments were not really about *representing* groups of people, but about *engaging* with specific groups of people on specific issues, be it the Athenian agoras or the English medieval curia; as parliaments were then ad-hoc gatherings to discuss specific matters. This could almost look like engaging if it was not limited to very restrictive groups of people.

6

Reimagining Working: Who Works and How?

Hannah White

Introduction

This chapter examines how the Westminster parliament functions as a workplace – a reality that is often absent from popular narratives which, understandably, focus instead on its central role in our democracy. If parliament is acknowledged to be a place of work then it is usually only 'Members' – those who are elected or appointed – who are imagined to be working, and their roles are often characterised more as vocation than as employment. Indeed, they are not employees in any normal sense. Meanwhile the role of the 'non-Member' staff employed directly by Members or by the legislature, is often elided. This has consequences for workplace dynamics, for the relative prioritisation of the rights and responsibilities of different groups of workers and for the effectiveness of parliament as an institution, many of which were highlighted by parliament's experience of the COVID-19 pandemic. This chapter reimagines what a future parliamentary workplace could look like, focusing on where the legislature departs from the principles which should underpin any modern workplace, and considering how its deficiencies could be addressed.

Who works and where?

There are three main categories of workers in parliament: 'Members' of the legislature who sit in the Commons and the Lords; 'Members' staff' who work directly for individual MPs and peers; and, 'House staff' who perform a wide range of roles from catering and maintenance to research and procedural advice. There are also some workers who are given permission to undertake their work on the parliamentary estate but not employed directly by or elected to parliament, such as lobby journalists or specialist craftspeople brought in to help maintain the estate. Still others may be working when they exercise their rights as members of the public to enter parliament – for example to lobby MPs on behalf of their industry or business. This chapter focuses on three categories of workers: those who are elected or appointed, those directly employed by MPs or peers and those employed by the parliamentary administration – Members, Members' staff and House staff.

Between these three groups, the major axis of difference which fundamentally shapes parliament as a workplace is between 'Members' (MPs and peers) who are elected or appointed to their roles in parliament, and those who are employed – sometimes referred to collectively in the negative as 'non-Members'. Partly this distinction is practical – in terms of the nature of the employment of the three groups. MPs are office-holders, elected to serve in the Commons at the pleasure of their constituents. They are not formally employed by anyone, have no 'contract' as such and cannot be removed except at a general election (or in certain circumstances via a 'recall' by-election between general elections). Peers have their positions for life having been appointed to the Lords by the monarch on the advice of the government, *ex officio* in the case of the Lords Spiritual or – in the case of 75 hereditary peers – following election by their hereditary peers (with 15 more elected by the whole house as office-holders and two other hereditaries chosen by other means bringing the total to 92). They have no contract of employment or salary but do have the right to claim attendance allowances for each day they attend parliament. Since 2014 it has been possible for a peer to voluntarily relinquish their seat, to be removed for non-attendance or to have their position terminated through expulsion.

By contrast, the other two categories of people who work in parliament have more conventional employment arrangements. Members' staff are hired, employed and fired by individual Members, paid for by a staffing budget allocated to each MP. House staff are employed by the Commons or Lords administration, mostly on permanent employment contracts, on terms similar to those of civil servants. The vast majority of parliamentary workers belong to or are employed within either the Commons or the Lords, although there are some parliamentary staff who work for departments which span both Houses – such as the Parliamentary Digital Service.

The distinction between 'Members' and 'non-Members' extends beyond formal employment arrangements and deep into parliamentary culture. The purpose of parliament as a workplace is to enable Members to play their roles in the democratic institution, so the spaces, processes and work of non-Members in Westminster are all designed to facilitate the performance of those roles. The language of 'membership' is significant – and parliament operates in a way that is analogous to other clubs – those who work in parliament by virtue of election or appointment are afforded rights and opportunities that others are denied. There is a clear hierarchy in the rights and privileges of people working within parliament.

A further distinction between different categories of parliamentary workers is between those who are political and those who are non-partisan. Many Members' staff – but by no means all – share the political convictions of their employer. By contrast, House staff are explicitly non-partisan, serving all current members of the Commons or the Lords. The vast majority of MPs affiliate to a political party – apart from a handful of independents or those who have had the party 'whip' removed for some form of misdemeanour (a sizeable group in the 2019–2024 parliament). The majority of peers belong to a party-political grouping, although the Lords has a large contingent of 'cross-bench' members who are not party affiliated.

The parliamentary estate is the UK parliament's main workplace – the collection of buildings centred around the 19th-century Palace of Westminster and the 20th-century Portcullis House, on the north bank of the Thames due south of the centre of government in Whitehall. Workers employed directly by the House administration are employed almost entirely on the estate while Members and their staff also undertake parliamentary work across the UK – in their constituencies, offices and other locations which they are required to visit to perform their roles – such as schools, hospitals, businesses and council buildings.

What principles should shape a workplace?

In order to assess parliament as a workplace and consider how it might be reimagined, it is instructive to consider how it compares to other workplaces. In order to do this, it is useful to identify the key principles which underpin any effective, modern workplace. The question of what these principles should be is the subject of a broad literature focusing on organisations and approaches to management. It is also a question that many organisations have recently had cause to consider in a very practical way, having been brought strongly into relief by the COVID-19 pandemic.

Parliament was just one of millions of organisations forced to grapple with workforce questions raised by the COVID-19 pandemic. The social distancing necessitated by the pandemic required organisations to consider the importance of the physical workplace for their ability to fulfil their purpose. The responsibility of employers to keep workers physically safe was a key consideration for leaders deciding how to manage their workers. Some were readily able to move aspects of their operations online, allowing workers to avoid physical interaction, while for others this was impossible. The different policies and approaches adopted in order to keep organisations functioning had equality impacts for workers with differing personal characteristics and circumstances. In the aftermath of the pandemic many organisations have retained innovations forced on them by the crisis, working from home has become more common and technological innovations facilitating work online are now far more widely used.

Drawing in part on the experience of COVID-19, which has changed the nature of many jobs and the environment in which they are done, it is possible to identify three sets of key principles that should underpin any mid-21st-century workplace. These are certainly not the only principles that are important but are three of the most salient for a consideration of how parliament might be reimagined as a workplace.

First, a workplace should provide a safe, secure environment for workers. This means meeting appropriate standards of physical health and safety, adapting these to risks as they develop and change. Second, any workplace should encourage equality, diversity and inclusion among its workers, and avoid unlawful discrimination. Again, as circumstances change an organisation may need to flex the characteristics of its workplace to ensure it achieves this goal. For most workplaces in the UK, the minimum standards that should be met in relation to these first two principles are set out in statute and regulations which require appropriate policies and processes to be in place. The third principle is that any workplace should create and maintain a culture and environment that supports its organisational goals so that it operates effectively – training and developing workers, and embracing innovations which facilitate their work. There is no legislative basis for this principle, but its validity is underpinned by swathes of literature on management best practice and organisational effectiveness.

How does parliament match up against these principles?

Physical safety and security
Any workplace needs to mitigate physical risks to its employees. Depending on the nature of the work involved these may range from biological or chemical threats (including pandemic disease) to physical risks and environmental hazards. Broadly, parliament is an office environment – which means it is inherently safer than some workplaces which involve heavy machinery, chemicals, transport or other physical hazards – but it also has some particular features that increase the threat to its employees.

The most obvious threat to parliament is the physical risk to the estate and its workers from terrorism or other violent attack. As a high-profile national institution and as the workplace of individuals with a significant public profile, the parliamentary estate, and other locations where politicians work such as constituency offices, are subject to elevated risk. This was tragically demonstrated by the murders of MPs Jo Cox and David Amess while attending their constituency surgeries, and the terrorist attack on the parliamentary estate in March 2017 which led to the death of PC Keith Palmer. MPs, in particular female Members, frequently report receiving threats of physical and sexual violence, and police investigations and prosecutions for such behaviour are not uncommon. In response to the risk of violence against its workers, the parliamentary authorities, police forces and the Independent Parliamentary Standards Authority (IPSA) have taken steps to increase the physical security of the estate and to fund security measures for MPs in their constituencies.

A second area of elevated risk for parliamentary workers arises from the historic nature of the parliamentary estate – in particular the dilapidated state of the Palace of Westminster. Technically, as it is a royal palace, health and safety law does not apply to the Palace. While the parliamentary authorities have nonetheless committed to implementing its provisions, some MPs are conscious of the unique status of their workplace and inclined to use this as an argument that parliament should be exempt from the rules governing other places of work. Such 'exceptionalist' arguments were made, for example, in the context of debates over physical presence on the estate during the COVID-19 pandemic – for example over whether the advice of the Health and Safety Executive against voting in the confined space of the lobbies should be followed (White, 2022). While facilities for remote working – including remote participation in chamber proceedings – were developed during the pandemic, the physical constraints of the Palace of Westminster – its narrow corridors, small lifts, confined offices and confrontational chamber configurations – increased the difficulty for the parliamentary authorities of keeping workers safe on the estate.

Even during normal times, the Palace of Westminster – as a historic building built in the 19th century, presents various hazards to those who work there (see Chapter 2). These range from the inconvenient (mice and clothes moths), via the unpleasant (sewage leaks), to the seriously life-threatening (fire, flood, Legionnaires' disease, asbestos and falling masonry). Managing these risks while keeping the Palace functioning as the seat of British democracy is a constant challenge for the parliamentary authorities, with the annual cost of running repairs – which must be performed in ways that cause minimal disruption to parliamentary proceedings – in the tens of millions of pounds. A series of reviews conducted over recent decades have repeatedly identified a larger scale 'Restoration and Renewal' (R&R) of the Palace as an urgent priority, but these more ambitious plans have been repeatedly rejected by MPs due to the astronomical cost and because the scale of the works required would entail parliamentarians moving out of the building for years. The implicit or explicit decisions taken by generations of MPs to manage the physical decline of the Palace through running repairs rather than full R&R mean that the risks to those who work on the estate have remained considerable and are only growing.

Equality, inclusion and non-discrimination

The second set of principles that should underpin any workplace is that it should encourage equality, diversity and inclusion, and that workers should not be subject to illegal discrimination. In part, these principles are underpinned by the basic individual rights established under the Equality Act 2010 which extends to the workplace by providing that workers should not be discriminated against in recruitment, employment terms and conditions, training, pay and benefits, promotion and transfer opportunities, dismissal or redundancy. Sexual harassment may be both a matter of employment rights and criminal law – under the Protection from Harassment Act 1997.

In theory at least, this set of principles is embedded in the employment policies and processes which apply to House staff, and in some respects to members and their staff. For example, the *House of Commons Staff Handbook* identifies the principles of 'equality, diversity and inclusion' as being at the heart of the Commons administration's Diversity and Inclusion Strategy, there is a Human Resources Diversity and Inclusion Team and a series of Workplace Equality Networks have been established to bring together House staff to focus on different protected characteristics. In 2018, in the wake of the #MeToo movement, after serious concerns were raised about bullying and harassment through the parliamentary community, a *Behaviour Code* was introduced, designed to identify and encourage positive behaviours. The code applies to everyone present on the parliamentary estate and is referenced in the MPs' and peers' codes of conduct. Breaches of the Behaviour Code by parliamentary workers – including Members – may be independently investigated under the Independent Complaints and Grievance Scheme and can result in serious consequences. The former Speaker, John Bercow, for example, was excluded for life from the parliamentary estate after serious allegations that he had bullied House staff were upheld. The introduction of the Independent Complaints and Grievance Scheme was a step change in the ability of workers to challenge poor behaviours in parliament, but the scheme continues to be subject to criticism – in particular the time taken for complaints to be investigated – and allegations of poor behaviour continue to emerge.

In some legal respects, where Members are concerned, parliament does not adhere to the principles of equality, inclusion and non-discrimination. As office-holders rather than employees, MPs and peers are not subject to the protections of employment law – for example, MPs are not legally protected from sexual harassment nor are they eligible for statutory maternity leave (although this right was extended to ministers via the passage of the

Ministerial and Other Maternity Allowances Act 2021). IPSA provides a financial allowance to allow MPs wishing to take time off after becoming a parent to pay for additional support, but the House authorities have taken the view that – constitutionally – certain parliamentary duties such as speaking in the chamber and voting cannot be undertaken by an alternate to the elected member. This means MPs must choose between spending time with their new children and undertaking key parliamentary duties on behalf of their constituents.

While peers benefit from jobs for life, the employment of MPs is unusually precarious. Although the normal electoral cycle is for a general election to take place once every five years, the fact that there were three between 2015 and 2019 demonstrates the uncertainty of their tenure. As an office-holder, an MP can be relieved of their position by their constituents at a snap election with just a few weeks' notice. In financial terms, Members who lose their seat at a general election after a period of two years' continuous service are entitled to a loss-of-office payment equal to double the statutory redundancy entitlement. But many MPs who leave parliament with little notice find it a traumatic experience and do not necessarily transition smoothly into subsequent employment (HC 209, 2023).

While MPs' roles are potentially impermanent, while they are working in parliament – MPs and peers benefit from elevated status compared to other workers. In this respect, the idea of equality of treatment between different categories of worker is deliberately set aside. This manifests in various ways, including in terms of physical access to the parliamentary estate which is controlled for reasons of security but also to ensure that parliamentarians have priority access to the facilities they need to fulfil their roles. For example, when a 'division bell' has been rung to signal a vote in one of the two houses there are lifts designated for the use of 'Members only' to ensure MPs and peers can reach the voting lobbies within the requisite eight minutes. Admittance to different areas is policed through the access provided by different grades of security pass (which provide electronic access to some and not others) as well as by security staff who control access to specific places such as the chambers, dining facilities and the terrace that runs along the River Thames.

These restrictions have an impact on parliamentary culture – reinforcing spatially the strong cultural distinction between 'Members' and 'others'. This has consequences for House staff and Members' staff – visibly defining them as lower in status than elected and appointed parliamentarians. This disparity in status supports a power dynamic that has repeatedly been shown to facilitate unfair or even discriminatory behaviours towards Members' staff and House staff (Childs, 2016; Cox, 2018; Ellenbogen, 2019).

Spatial restrictions also have an impact on different groups of members. Female, Black and minoritised members report being frequently challenged when trying to access 'Member only' spaces by security staff questioning their legitimacy as members – one female, minority ethnic MP speaking at a Fawcett Society event in 2023 described the 'exhausting' experience of navigating parliamentary spaces. In a survey of Black, Asian and minority ethnic MPs conducted by ITV in 2020, 62 per cent of respondents said they had experienced racism or racial profiling while working in Westminster, with 51 per cent saying they experienced this from other MPs (Tritschler, 2020). Fawcett Society research published in 2022 found that 37 per cent of women MPs compared with 55 per cent of men agreed that 'the culture in Parliament is inclusive for people like me', and women MPs were significantly more likely to report that parliamentary culture had a negative impact on how they felt about being an MP – 62 per cent – than men – 34 per cent (Shepherd et al, 2023).

It is not just the way that parliamentary spaces are policed, but also their physical characteristics which are discriminatory. Much of the parliamentary estate – in particular the Palace of Westminster – is inaccessible to people with disabilities. As Sarah Childs (2016) documented in her study *The Good Parliament*, the chambers are mainly inaccessible to wheelchair users and there are limited accessible bathrooms, handrails, self-opening doors and lifts. There are few office spaces in close proximity to the chamber which would facilitate access for members with mobility restrictions, and the estate is difficult to navigate for workers with sight impairments. Beyond the physical, parliamentary processes are not designed to facilitate the participation of Members with hidden disabilities – for example, the requirement to be physically present in the chamber throughout a debate in order to be given the opportunity to speak limits the participation of Members who need regular access to medication, sustenance or bathroom facilities.

Effective organisational culture

The final principle that should underpin any effective 21st-century workplace is that it should create and maintain a culture and environment that supports its organisational goals – training and developing its workers and embracing innovations which work within an effective organisation. The characteristics of parliament as an institution make this principle less straightforward to fulfil than for other workplaces.

The Westminster parliament apparently has a clear organisational goal – to play its role as the apex institution within the UK's democratic system. But because the UK has an uncodified constitution, and parliament is a collective formed from the sum of its Members, no single definition exists of what that role should be. At any moment in time the organisational goals of parliament are defined by custom, precedent, centuries of accreted decisions by past parliamentarians and a simple majority of the current membership.¹ As parliament is unique, it lacks direct comparators against which to assess the effectiveness of its working culture and environment. Pride in its long history means there is often a lack of appetite to consider the comparators that do exist – in the form of the devolved legislatures and other countries' parliaments.

The lack of a single definition of parliament's role has consequences for its ability to build and maintain an effective working culture. For MPs, it translates into a strong emphasis on the right of each member to perform their role on behalf of their constituents as they see fit.² This has consequences for Members themselves as well as the staff they employ, including a lack of any culture of evaluation, learning and development or any systematic provision of professional development to parliamentarians during their careers as backbenchers or as ministers.

Many MPs arrive in the Commons wholly unprepared for their responsibilities as small business owners, directly employing their own staff, let alone equipped with the specific skills and knowledge required to operate successfully in parliament. Ad-hoc support is offered by some political parties and the Commons administration makes considerable efforts to provide induction following a general election, but in the absence of a general culture that encourages learning and validates professional development, MPs often fail to fit training into their schedules alongside their numerous other responsibilities. For those who make the transition to ministerial office, support is rarer still – despite the significance of the role and the range of unique responsibilities that it brings, ministers are largely expected to learn 'on the job' with some advice from the civil servants in their private office (Bishop and Barr, 2023).³ The lack of provision of systematic professional development for MPs and ministers leads to clear disparities in their ability to fulfil their roles on behalf of their constituents and to support the endeavours of their political parties while they are in parliament.

The lack of a culture of learning, combined with the conventions of exclusive cognisance (parliament's historic responsibility for administering its own affairs) and parliamentary privilege (the special rights afforded to parliamentarians to do their jobs) embolden some MPs and peers to assume they should be an exception to the rules that others follow. It is only with some reluctance that most parliamentarians have accepted that they should be subject to similar standards of human resources (in relation to their staff), accounting (in relation to their expenses) and behaviour (in relation to bullying and harassment) as those they themselves apply to the rest of the population. These standards are applied through a combination of normal laws and distinct processes set up by parliamentarians. IPSA sets and administers MPs' pay, pensions and allowances, the Standards Committees of the two Houses oversee their respective codes of conduct together with House-appointed standards commissioners, and the newly created Independent Expert Panel plays a role in determining complaints of bullying and harassment. But with unfortunate frequency parliamentarians are investigated – by the police or the Parliamentary Commissioners for Standards – for breaches of the rules.

Inappropriate behaviour by Members can have consequences for everyone else working in parliament; in particular the staff parliamentarians employ directly, who working in small teams, are exposed to the vagaries of different Members' managerial strengths and weaknesses. As Gemma White QC observed in her 2019 report into bullying and harassment of MPs' staff:

> MPs' staff are in a uniquely vulnerable position in the Parliamentary community. Although their salaries are funded by the taxpayer, individual MPs have near complete discretion as to who they employ and, importantly, for how long they employ them. Despite being relatively low paid, their jobs are much coveted, and staff are often reminded that the Member will have no difficulty filling their position with someone else. There is no set of uniform employment procedures for MPs and their staff. Nor is there any collective oversight of MPs' employment practices. The combination of this lack of structure and the demands placed on the MPs themselves is fertile ground for bullying and harassment. (HC 2206, 2019: para 9)

As for Members' staff, opportunities for learning and development are inconsistent – dependent on the inclination of their member employer and the limited provision made by parties and House authorities. Possibilities for progression are limited by the size of the pot available to each MP for staffing and how they choose to spend it. Together this means that rates of burnout and turnover among MPs' staff can be relatively high compared to similar workplaces, so parliament persistently bleeds the experienced and knowledgeable staff that MPs need to fulfil their roles effectively.

Parliamentary culture is changing very slowly. While a significant minority of parliamentarians still see the mere suggestion that they might require support or benefit from professional development as an affront, many select committee members have accepted the value of training in skills such as effective questioning and regular reflection on their approach and impact. But such innovations tend to be hard won in an institution which prides itself on its history and tradition and remains dominated by the older, White men who originally shaped its spaces, practices and procedures.

In the Commons, the very high degree of government control over proceedings means that the executive's vested interest in sustaining certain ways of working that operate to its advantage is rarely challenged. Although MPs are elected as 650 individuals, all the political parties exert strong control over the working lives of MPs – how they arrive in parliament, how their routines are structured and the influence of the party whip (which can be withdrawn for non-conformity with party lines). The parties are also the strongest influence over the collective working conditions of MPs and peers, through their control of the House of Commons and House of Lords Commissions – which have overall responsibility for the House Administrations. The Commissions are responsible for shaping the decisions that the Houses can take about matters such as the upkeep of the parliamentary estate, expenditure on parliamentary proceedings and working conditions, and in practice the executive has a controlling influence over the Commissions.

The implications of parliament's reactionary culture for its role as a workplace were starkly illustrated during the COVID-19 pandemic. The immediate priority when the pandemic arrived was for parliament to continue working – to enable Members to be seen to continue to do their jobs. Rapid innovation by the House Administrations created technical solutions which enabled MPs and peers to meet, debate and vote remotely – while social distancing restrictions were in place across the UK, only 50 MPs were able to safely meet in the House of Commons chamber. Online meetings of select committees enabled MPs to participate from anywhere – limiting the need for risky travel and widening the pool of witnesses able to participate in evidence sessions beyond those willing and able to reach Westminster. The innovations designed to allow Members to continue their work also had benefits for House staff – fewer were required to be physically present in parliament to facilitate proceedings, which limited their exposure to the risks of the covid workplace and journeys to and from work. Most Members' staff were able to work from home or the constituency, with additional allowances provided by IPSA to MPs to set themselves up.

Despite their benefits in terms of diversity and inclusion, these innovations also had downsides. Hybrid proceedings in the chamber necessitated the use of 'call lists' so that Members would know when to appear online to ask a question or contribute to a debate which reduced the spontaneity of debate. Some felt it was more difficult to hold ministers to account online, and the government was concerned that adaptations to proceedings would limit its ability to progress its legislative programme. As a consequence, while the Lords – with many vulnerable Members – retained its hybrid facilities, the government ensured that the Commons returned as fast as possible to its 'normal' way of operating – emphasising the importance of physical presence for the work of Members. This decision privileged the need of the executive to get its business through parliament ahead of the rights of individual Members to do their jobs or their staff to avoid the risks associated with physical presence in Westminster. For the second half of 2020, many MPs who were unable to travel to Westminster were excluded from participating in debates, including the scrutiny of legislation, and greater numbers of House staff were forced back into the workplace to service the needs of Members. The way parliament operated during the pandemic thus clearly illustrates the hierarchies and principles which currently shape its operation as a workplace.

Reimagining who works and how

During the COVID-19 pandemic, parliament failed to fulfil all three of the key principles identified as underpinning any mid-21st-century workplace. First, it did not do everything possible to provide a safe and secure environment for its workers. After a brief period of experimentation, the Commons failed to retain innovations which would have kept Members, their staff and House staff safer during the pandemic. Second, it failed to adopt processes and procedures that were fair and non-discriminatory to all workers – large numbers of MPs and some staff were not able to fulfil their roles in the same way as their colleagues due to the government's decision to allow temporary hybrid facilities to lapse and compel MPs to attend in person. And third, although the parliamentary authorities demonstrated a remarkable ability to innovate at speed, the changes that were introduced were rapidly reversed at the behest of one group of workers to the detriment of many others. The COVID-19 pandemic was an exceptional episode in the recent history of our legislature but it amply demonstrates the potential for reimagining parliament as a workplace.

The overarching principle behind this reimagining is that parliament should see itself as an exemplar of, rather than an exception to, the rules it has established for other workplaces. Best workplace practices should be identified in other parliaments and other organisations, then adopted and championed in parliament. Rather than expecting to be an exception to the rules, Members should expect to be subject to rules except where parliament has taken an explicit decision to exempt them. When passing new legislation relating to workplaces, explicit consideration should be given to how it will be applied in parliament. Maintaining an awareness of the laws and rules to which MPs are subject should be seen as an important responsibility of all Members rather than a discretionary and irksome task and the house authorities should be funded and equipped to support Members in meeting this responsibility.

Parliament will not succeed in becoming an exemplar as a workplace unless it transforms its approach to supporting and developing its Members. The political roles of MPs, peers and ministers are both unique and highly consequential – it is unrealistic to expect any individual to be completely prepared to take them on, nor should the public be satisfied with representatives who believe they have nothing to learn. MPs and peers should expect and be expected to undertake professional development throughout their political careers, from preparatory training as a Prospective Parliamentary Candidate, through compulsory collective induction as a new Member, via annual professional development as an established Member, to career mentoring as a minister. MPs who lose their seats in a general election should receive funded outplacement support to assist them in finding employment after leaving the Commons. Similarly, Members' staff should be supported with ongoing professional development to develop their skills and give them a sense of progression, encouraging them to remain in parliament for longer while preparing them for careers within or beyond the Commons.

MPs come into parliament to fulfil their political goals, not to become small business owners, and many lack the skills and experience to run a successful workplace. The running of MPs' offices, including the recruitment and management of staff, acquisition and running of constituency office premises and provision of professional services should be outsourced; either to a new parliamentary agency, which would ensure a level playing field, or to external companies equipped with the skills and expertise to deliver these services to the high standard MPs would expect. This would increase the consistency of management of Members' staff, and improve the working conditions and safety of some currently subject to inappropriate behaviours by their employers. It would help vulnerable Members avoid making mistakes and discourage ill-intentioned Members from behaving in ways that breach rules and expectations – protecting Members from damaging their political careers because of administrative misdemeanours and safeguarding other workers.

If parliament is to succeed in promoting equality, inclusion and non-discrimination within the workplace, the most important change needed is to break down the hierarchies that characterise the working lives of everyone in parliament – particularly those between Members and non-Members. In some contexts these are strictly necessary to enable parliamentarians to do their jobs effectively, but it is essential that hierarchies should operate only to the extent they are absolutely needed to facilitate the business of parliament. This means the rationale for and limits of any hierarchies must be understood and operationalised. For example, parliament should start from the assumption that all workers should have access to all parts of the estate at all times and work back from there to identify the times and locations when and where this is inappropriate. Removing unjustified hierarchies will help ensure that these do not inadvertently limit the effectiveness of people working in parliament by facilitating bullying, discouraging innovation or creating resentment between different groups of workers.

A reimagined parliamentary workplace should have committed to the renovation of the Palace of Westminster, pushing beyond the basic minimum of restoring the 19th-century buildings, and building on public consultation to enhance the way the public experience democracy in Westminster (see Chapter 2). The renewed Palace of Westminster should be fully accessible to wheelchair users, with chambers and division lobbies redesigned to accommodate Members, other workers and members of the public with a wide range of impairments. Just as with the Victorian palace, a physically renewed parliament should model the use of the most recent innovations, including in energy efficiency and sustainability.

Hybrid technologies should enable Members to participate remotely in proceedings whenever they consider necessary – with individual MPs making the decision about the balance of time they spend in Westminster and in their constituencies. Parliamentary procedures should be adapted to make this possible, opening the possibility of becoming an MP to a more diverse range of people, rather than the narrow demographic who currently sustain historically rooted working practices. The reification of physical presence on the estate should be dismantled – House and Members' staff should be allowed to work wherever they can be most effective, with the default being that they should work remotely unless their presence on the estate is necessary to facilitate parliamentary business.

The decant of all parliamentary workers required to undertake the R&R project as quickly and cheaply as possible should have been used to experiment with different ways of working. Parliament should regularly meet at a number of physical locations around the UK, with select committees able to choose from over 20 alternative centres in small towns across the country equipped to host their evidence sessions (and otherwise available for the use of local communities). Together these innovations should make it possible to shrink the footprint of the parliamentary estate in Westminster, with the sale of prime central London property used to invest in the devolved parliamentary premises. With fewer workers present on the parliamentary estate, the parliamentary estate should be easier and cheaper to maintain.

Conclusion

As a workplace, today's parliament is fundamentally shaped by a hierarchy between Members and non-Members – expressed through rules and spatial restrictions but, more importantly, deeply embedded in the culture of the legislature. This hierarchy is supported by the dualistic political culture of the UK, which hands significant power to the party of government and enables the executive to sustain the parliamentary rules and workplace practices from which it benefits. A historically rooted belief in the importance of physical presence for the proceedings of parliament is a further factor which shapes parliament as a workplace and became particularly evident in the course of the COVID-19 pandemic.

A reimagined parliament would conceptualise itself as an exemplar of best workplace practice and culture, rather than an exception to the rules shaping other workplaces. This would entail distinguishing between constitutionally justifiable differences between Members and non-Members and those which have arisen for reasons of tradition, Members' preference or executive convenience, but which now limit the ability of parliament to operate as effectively as it might. Hierarchies which inappropriately discriminate between different groups of workers should be dismantled. A positive learning culture should be developed in which Members are supported to develop the skills to fulfil their roles, while the parts of their jobs that are not integral to their democratic function – such as managing their parliamentary offices – should be outsourced to professional providers. Meanwhile the parliamentary estate should be restored, renewed and reconceptualised to extend beyond Westminster – allowing Members to work wherever they judge they can be most effective in fulfilling their roles on behalf of the public.

Parliament is some way away from this imagined future, and the prospects of achieving it are reduced by the fact that today's Members – who have all the decision-making power within parliament – are accustomed to the status quo. The first step needs to be for today's Members to pay more attention to the needs and rights of non-Members working on the parliamentary estate, and to balance these more effectively against their own preferences. The more challenging step will be for Members to reflect on how to create a parliament which meets the needs of future generations of workers – elected and unelected – and the public on whose behalf they are working.

Notes

[1] In the Commons this almost invariably translates into the will of the current government, but the Lords – lacking a government majority among its members – maintains a strong tradition of independence, albeit one heavily influenced by consciousness of its lack of legitimacy compared to the elected House of Commons.

[2] There is no such thing as a single job description for an MP (see IPSA, 2012: paras 48–50, 70).

[3] The Institute for Government has provided professional development for ministers on request since 2009 but demand has been low. The Institute for Government Academy launched in 2023 aims to establish an expectation of ministerial support and training and provide systematic support.

7

Reimagining Parliamentary Governance

Ben Yong

Introduction

What would a reimagined set of governance arrangements for the Westminster parliament look like? That is, what would be the ideal set of arrangements to deal with and resolve issues of parliamentary administration – finance, staffing, infrastructure and engagement? Parliamentary governance is an important issue, rarely raised (for exceptions, see Yong, 2018; White, 2022). Most people focus on the partisan debates in the chamber and scrutiny of the executive via committees – even parliamentarians themselves. Questions of internal governance seem boring, but how the legislature organises and maintains itself is a fundamental question of our constitution: it goes to legitimacy and effectiveness of the legislature in carrying out its core constitutional functions. A well-supported legislature makes for a more confident and effective legislature. This requires collective choices to be made on how parliament's resources will be allocated. Determining an appropriate decision-making structure for making those choices is the subject of this chapter.

This chapter is organised thusly. It begins by explaining what governance is, and its key requirements – goal identification, goal reconciliation, implementation and accountability. The Westminster parliament is then used as an example to demonstrate the problems of legislative governance. The chapter then discusses a number of principles to resolve problems of collective action – prioritising the institution; clear governance mechanisms; clear lines of accountability; and representation. It then looks at the Westminster parliament to illustrate the importance of governance, and how far we are from any ideal.

What is governance?

Governance has become a fashionable concept: it straddles disciplines – from politics to economics and sociology. It has been used as a means to capture and understand a broader range of actors (both formal and informal) involved in decision-making in a particular field of action. It can signify a shift towards greater (or lesser) control. It can mean a structure, a process, a mechanism and a strategy (Levi-Faur, 2012: 8). The expansiveness of governance is partly because the notion of governance is 'weak on intension and therefore very strong on extension' (Peters, 2012: 19). That is, the concept has little internal content, and therefore its meaning can be easily stretched.

Still, if the idea of governance is attractive, it is because it is capturing something we think is important. For our purposes, governance can be understood to be about public action and collective decision-making. How can individuals resolve to deal with matters that affect them as a group? There are many pressing issues which cannot be resolved by individuals alone, because of their complexity, because of the scope of the issues and sometimes because of the lack of agreement over the issues and the appropriate response to resolving the issues. And so, we need governance: a decision-making mechanism for collective action, together with some means of implementation and ensuring accountability.

Guy Peters (2012: 22) points out that there are a set of functional requirements for successful governance: *goal selection*; *goal reconciliation and coordination*; *implementation*; and *feedback and accountability*. Goal selection is about determining aims and objectives. Goal reconciliation is necessary because there are always multiple actors involved in governance, and they may all have different goals. Once decisions have been made in the first two stages, these must then be implemented. Finally, there should be means by which these decisions and their implementation can be scrutinised and, where necessary, lessons learned: this will (ideally) improve the decision-making process.

Thus framed, governance still remains very broad: it can apply equally to states, organisations and associations. For our purposes, though, it leads neatly into the governance of parliament and its administration. Governance was defined by a 2014 House of Commons committee examining the Commons' governance arrangements as:

> [T]he way in which organisations are directed, controlled and led. It defines relationships and the distribution of rights and responsibilities among those who work with and in the organisation, determines the rules and procedures through which the organisation's objectives are set, and provides the means of attaining those objectives and

monitoring performance. Importantly, it defines where accountability lies throughout the organisation. (HC 692, 2014: 8)

The Committee's definition of governance connects neatly with Guy Peters' functional requirements. Parliament is an association (and in some capacities an organisation) which requires that certain decisions be made on behalf of the many individuals – elected and non-elected – who work on the parliamentary estate. Some of these decisions are simple; some are complex; but they are collective decisions, which require governance.

Parliamentary governance is therefore about how objectives in parliament are set (goal selection; and coordination and reconciliation); the means of attaining those objectives (implementation); coupled with mechanisms of accountability. In short, parliamentary governance is the set of arrangements which determine the administration of parliament as an organisation and its resources. Parliamentary governance so defined is separate from questions such as who is in control of parliament in the House chambers (for instance), although in practice the distinction is blurred. But broadly, parliamentary administration is less about the day-to-day political battles in chambers and committees, and procedure; and more about the medium- to long-term management of the provision of resources and services necessary for parliamentarians to carry out their functions.

Without proper governance arrangements, parliamentary administration will suffer because of a lack of clarity about goals, weak or no implementation, and limited or no accountability. This will have a knock-on effect on the work of parliamentarians. Good governance should also in theory contribute to a well-functioning, effective and efficient parliament: a parliament that can get things done will boost the institution's legitimacy with both parliamentarians and the public. Good governance can also ensure accountability – to the parliamentarians the House administrations serve; and to the wider public. And a well-governed, responsive parliamentary administration will also encourage trust between the administration and parliamentarians.

But in order to see why *reimagining* governance might be necessary, it is helpful to start with a concrete example. For this, we turn to a brief history of the governance arrangements of the Westminster parliament (for a more comprehensive history, see Yong, 2018). This reveals a set of governance arrangements which have traditionally been ineffective, inefficient and non-transparent.

A brief history of Westminster governance

The modern history of parliamentary governance begins with the slow transfer of control of the Palace of Westminster estate from the executive to parliamentary authorities. This took place in the second half of the 20th century, with key stepping-stones being the establishment of the House of Commons Commission in 1978 and the transfer of complete control of the parliamentary estate in 1992. The Commons Commission was established by statute to give greater parliamentary control over House administration. The Commission's primary roles were primarily to prepare the estimates for the House; and the employment of House staff. It was initially composed of six members: the Speaker (Chair of the Commission), the Leader of the House of Commons, a member nominated by the Leader of the Opposition (usually the shadow Leader of the House); and three other MPs, usually representatives of the two main parties and one of the smaller parties. The posts were (and remain) unpaid.

The Commission was structured to be cross-partisan in composition to insulate it from inappropriate influence by the executive. However, this meant that there needed to be cross-party consensus for decisions – which in practice was not easy to achieve. Commission members are chosen less because they have the interests of the House as institution in mind and more to maintain the status quo between the parties. And Commission members, with the exception of the Speaker, rarely stay in post for long (Yong, 2018).

The upshot of all this is that the Commission has been historically slow to act, if at all: there is very little incentive to do anything, particularly in an intensely political arena like the House of Commons, and where re-election is a much more pressing priority. That is, the Commons Commission's goal selection and reconciliation capacity has historically been weak. Thus, even though in theory it would appear that the Commission is responsible for 'leading' House administration, in practice, much of the day-to-day business of administration and maintaining the institution falls to the Speaker and senior parliamentary officials (mostly clerks). This is problematic, not least in terms of accountability.

In the Commons, the Speaker is an unusually powerful figure in House administration, as the Presiding Officer, being elected by the entire House, and usually having a long tenure (in the Lords it is different: the Lord Speaker is in a much weaker position, being a relatively new office). But this also means that the House's administration tends to be at the whim of a single person; and few actors (other than perhaps the Leader and Shadow Leader) have the courage and power to push back where necessary. It does not help that the extent of the Speaker's powers and discretion is far from clear: there still remains no authoritative list or document of the Speaker's powers (HC 692, 2014). The other problem is the House's administrative wing: the officials, who implement the policies of the Commission. While parliamentary officials are able to compensate, to some extent, for the indecisiveness of the political wing, the impartiality of officials means there are limits to what they are able to do. Maintaining the status quo is the default setting.

The Commission is also supported by a number of domestic committees (so named because they deal with 'domestic' or internal matters; select committees deal with 'external' matters), including the Finance Committee and the Administration Committee (in the Lords the Services Committee). These committees are formally tasked with advising the Commission on various aspects of administration (Lee and Yong, 2022). Further, members and chairs are chosen through the usual channels rather than by election. The result is that domestic committees have a limited role in governance. They sit very much in the background: they are not well-known (not least to parliamentarians) or considered prestigious committees.

Parliamentarians have not helped themselves either. The vast majority have shown little interest in the governance of their respective Houses – as one MP said: 'People do not become Members of Parliament because they want to run the House of Commons' (HC 692, 2014: 15). The 2014 Straw Review (HC 692, 2014), for instance, was the first Member-led review of the House of Commons governance arrangements in over 40 years. The Review did lead to a number of changes in these arrangements: an explicit requirement to consider the strategic priorities and objectives of the House services; and the membership of the Commission was expanded. Whether these changes have improved governance remains unclear, but a recent report on the House of Commons' financial management suggests not (Morse, 2022).

Compounding all this is the problem of accountability, the fourth of Guy Peters' governance requirements. Many a parliamentarian has complained about the opaqueness of the Commissions and the decisions they make; many are simply unaware that the relevant governance arrangements even exist (Yong, 2022). This is unsurprising. The deliberations of the Commissions are not public. They publish minutes of their monthly meetings, but these tend to be quite limited (the Lords being better than the Commons) – rarely giving any substantive detail of discussions. The domestic committees are similar, and even though they have more regular, more substantive meetings with officials, very little is published (again, the Lords are better than the Commons in this respect).

We have not specifically discussed the Lords, whose governance arrangements are deserving of a chapter of their own. But for our purposes there are two problems: Lords governance generally; and the 'bicameral issue'. The Lords governance arrangements are very similar to that of the Commons, but without any statutory underpinning. And because of a greater number of parties, no overall government majority in the Lords and a much more explicit insistence upon 'self-regulation', the Lords governance arrangements are what the Commons governance arrangements would have been but for the pressures of party and more severe public scrutiny in the Commons (Yong, 2018). That is to say, the Lords' arrangements are even less transparent and even more prone to gridlock. In spite of reforms (inspired in part by changes in Commons governance), a recent report suggests that problems of decision-making in the Lords persist (House of Lords Commission, 2021).

There is also the 'bicameral issue' – at least, at Westminster, where parliament is made up of two Houses. The two Houses are of unequal size, powers and functions, with the Commons having a superior position because of its elected status. Historically, there has been limited communication and coordination between the two Houses' Commissions. Partly this is due to the different views that each House has of its own importance, and its perceived status relative to the other. The Commons views the Lords as inferior and mostly unimportant; the Lords view the Commons as capricious and fears losing its own privileges. But it is also about the sheer difficulty of getting two already complex entities with limited governance capacity to simply engage with each other on a regular basis. This has made bicameral cooperation limited and highly uneven, with one or the other House lagging behind the other on various initiatives. In Guy Peters' terms, the bicameral issue necessarily complicates the governance requirements of goal identification, reconciliation and coordination.

The weakness of governance arrangements

In short, the governance arrangements at Westminster are weak and ineffective, and are also non-transparent. Put differently, there are problems with all four of the governance requirements that Guy Peters has identified, and in particular goal identification, reconciliation and coordination. This is because of the way that Westminster is organised, and the nature of the institution: mechanisms for figuring out what the goals of parliament are and should be, and reconciling and coordinating multiple visions of those goals, are limited at best. This state of affairs often goes unacknowledged: where there is noted dysfunction in the legislature, it is usually attributed to the 'malign' influence of the executive. But a key problem for parliament is that it is sometimes not clear, even to the key actors themselves, who is in charge (Norton, 2017; Yong, 2018).

An illustration of the weakness of parliamentary governance is the Restoration and Renewal of the Palace of Westminster. This is dealt with in more detail in Chapter 2 (see also Meakin, 2022), but it is an obvious example of how the governance arrangements at Westminster have failed. The Palace of Westminster has been badly in need of repair for many years – indeed, one report noted that '[i]f the Palace were not a listed building of the highest heritage value, its owners would probably be advised to demolish and rebuild [it]' (House of Commons and House of Lords Study Group, 2012: 5). A 2015 independent report set out a number of options to deal with the crumbling estate, including a partial and full decant of the Palace. A Joint Committee of both Houses recommended a full decant of the Palace (HL

41/HC 659, 2016). It was recognised that the complexity of the restoration and renewal of the Palace was beyond the capacity of parliament (in terms of expertise, and in terms of project management); and so legislation was passed; a Delivery Body and Sponsor Body established. However, a new Commons Speaker and Leader of the House of Commons hostile to the idea of a full decant had, by 2022, effectively stymied any further progress. The result is that the restoration and renewal of the Palace remains in limbo, with costs rising and the danger to parliamentarians and staff alike increasing.

The key principles of parliamentary governance

We have set out the broad functional requirements of successful governance but how might these map onto the specifics of a legislature? Using Westminster as an example, we can see that legislatures are weak in terms of goal selection; goal reconciliation and coordination; and feedback and accountability (we leave aside implementation, which would require a separate chapter on its own). Any reimagination of parliament needs to have principles which satisfy these key requirements. Four are suggested here: prioritising the institution; effective governance mechanisms; clear lines of accountability; and representation.

Prioritising the institution means that ideally, parliamentarians in the governance structures should think of the institution first, or at least, more than they currently do. More often than not, party comes first, fear of how the public might react a close second, and the medium- to long-term health of the institution last. The result is that key decisions are put off, or endlessly debated, and parliament, as an institution, suffers. As Tony Wright, a former MP, noted: '[T]here is no Parliament, in that collective sense, to insist on anything. There are simply Members of Parliament who have preoccupations and inhabit a career structure in which sustained strengthening of the institution is not a central priority' (Wright, 2004: 874). This principle focuses on reimagining parliamentarians and their internal dispositions. What we want in a reimagined set of governance arrangements are parliamentarians who consider the strengthening of parliament to be a central priority. This requires rethinking arrangements so that 'thinking institutionally' is encouraged: this means, among other matters, in any given situation, asking less about 'how can I get what I want?', and more about 'what expectations and conduct would be appropriate of me in my position?'; and valuing the long term over the short term (Heclo, 2008).

Effective governance mechanisms is tautologous, but is a principle which focuses less on the internal dispositions of parliamentarians and more on 'external' organisational mechanisms which ensure effective goal selection, reconciliation and coordination in parliament. It should be clear who is in charge, how decisions are made, and who is responsible for implementing decisions. It is not merely a processual principle, but also a substantive one: it requires that key actors actually make decisions which are in the best interests of parliament as an institution.

Clear lines of accountability is simply the other side of effective governance and leadership: this principle also requires greater transparency of governance arrangements and decision-making – this ensures all actors know who is responsible and will make the key decisions, but that they are also accountable for those decisions as well. Clear lines of accountability will ensure that there is the potential for improving decision-making processes.

Representation has no clear parallel with the general governance requirements noted by Guy Peters. Parliament is, of course, *the* institution of electoral representation in any democratic polity: that is what gives parliament its particular legitimacy. This principle requires that the key governance structures of parliament should be representative of all key parties; but there should also be representation of staff and the public too – since parliament is a workplace and a representative institution. This should increase the overall legitimacy of the governance arrangements, but it may also contribute to better decision-making. But as we shall see, the representation principle also means taking political parties seriously.

Reimagined governance

The starting point of reimagining proposed here is a set of perhaps uncharitable assumptions about parliament and parliamentarians, drawn from, but not limited to, the experience of Westminster. Parliament is a large collection of individuals who do not formally owe each other obedience (Loewenberg, 2011). Under such circumstances, the primary incentive of elected parliamentarians is to gain re-election; and, as a result, they are most likely to work under the auspices of a political party. Indeed, political parties are the primary means by which coordination is achieved in legislatures (Cox, 2009). Even in the Lords, where there is no need to seek re-election, most coordination between peers is done through political parties, although it is true that there is a substantial proportion of peers who are independent or cross-benchers, who, in theory at least, do not vote along party lines.

However, because parliamentarians tend to prioritise party matters and re-election opportunities, any duty they have towards parliament as an institution is very much deprioritised. How can we ensure that parliamentarians in governance offices will put parliament, and not party, first? There is no one answer that would shift parliamentarians' priorities; there probably needs to be a suite of interlocking mechanisms. Some of these are more realistic or capable of being implemented than others.

The Commission's issues are two-fold: an inability to act; and the overwhelming power of the Speaker. To remedy this, a number of changes are suggested. The first is to change the composition of the Commission: the Speaker, Leader and Shadow Leader of the House would no longer be on the Commission (and similarly in the Lords). There is no reason why these senior figures need to sit on the Commission. Membership should not be held concurrently with a ministerial or quasi-ministerial post; and the Speaker has too much power anyway. In effect, the Commission would become a backbench body. The number of members would remain fixed at an odd number – say, seven. But parties with sufficient numbers in the House would each be represented by a single Commission member: no longer would there be any imbalance between smaller and larger parties – although this might increase the possibility of gridlock.

The second change requires that members of the Commissions be elected via the Houses, in the same way that select committee chairs are elected. Election would give Commission members additional legitimacy with House members. It would not 'free' members from party; nor is it intended to. But it might provide a greater incentive for Commission members to prioritise their institutional roles over some of their other roles, at least some of the time. Tenure would be for the entire parliamentary term.

Third, parliamentarians who take on an institutional role should be paid, in the same way that Commons select committee chairs are paid an additional salary for their work as chairs. But the salary should be higher, to reflect the importance of the Commission's work and governance to parliament. Again, this will not 'free' members from their other obligations: it merely provides an extra incentive for members to take their institutional roles more seriously.

The fourth proposed change is that Commission members become responsible for particular portfolios, as happens in other legislatures, such as the European Parliament and the Scottish and Welsh Parliaments. This would be beneficial for a number of reasons. Commission membership, then, offers a non-ministerial career route for parliamentarians and allows Commission members to develop expertise in a particular area. Making Commission members responsible for a particular area may both lead to greater effectiveness – in the sense that members will (ideally) provide the energy, drive and perhaps expertise to provide direction in their area; but also greater transparency and responsibility – allocation of responsibilities may also discourage maverick behaviour. Portfolios would be allocated in the first meeting of the Commission by common agreement. Members would need to think carefully about balancing expertise against other factors such as providing political parties with any institutional power. Portfolios might include such matters as finance, administration, committees, security and engagement. There would also need to be a chair, who would be elected by members of the Commission at the first meeting. The chair would be responsible for the overall functioning of the Commission, and would represent the Commission to the House.

One danger with making Commission membership elected, salaried and more specific is that rather than cultivating institutional loyalty, it intensifies the individualism and fragmentation already present in parliament. For instance, election could lead to the 'celebrity chair' phenomenon which emerged after the Wright reforms (Johnson, 2018: 121). Crudely, this is where office holders of elected posts use their office as a means to garner more public attention (and therefore increase the possibility of re-election). It is not hard to imagine that this might happen with elected Commission members: for instance, some members may want to interrogate (and possibly humiliate) parliamentary staff publicly in order to present themselves as defenders of the taxpayer.

Moreover, there is no obvious reason why there should be 'collective commission responsibility'. There is no incentive for Commission members to maintain a united front so as not to undermine collective decisions made by the Commission. The result is that there is an even greater risk that the elected and salaried status of Commission members will simply reinforce or even intensify the already-existing individualism in parliament, and in the case of Commission work, lead to total gridlock with Commission members heading off in their own separate directions.

All the same, these are risks worth taking, for a number of reasons. The alternative is more of the same: stasis, and the underlying assumption of this chapter is that parliamentary governance cannot and should not stay the same as it currently is. The second is that members will be kept in check by their colleagues. Over time, it seems likely that the Commission will form something akin to collective responsibility, probably as a result of initial mistakes where individual members do try to aggrandise themselves at the expense of the institution. Finally, this could be bolstered by setting out a code of conduct for Commission members – which would include collective responsibility – in standing orders, or in a Commission Manual (on which, see [e.g., House of Lords Commission, 2022]).

Then there are the domestic committees. Why have them at all, given the confusion over their functions and a lack of interest on the part of parliamentarians – and portfolios on the Commission? For one thing, it would help satisfy the requirement of accountability: that there is someone with oversight over the Commission and parliament's administration. Domestic committees would also be an opportunity to increase parliamentarians' expertise in understanding and scrutinising administration. The committees may serve as a fount of institutional memory about how parliament works (or ought to). Membership on one of the domestic committees might also serve as a stepping-stone to Commission membership. Generally, members of domestic committees should be elected rather than be selected by the usual channels. This would encourage members to make their case for membership; but it would also publicise the role of the domestic committees in the governance of the Houses.

A fifth change would be that non-executive or lay members should be appointed to the domestic committees as well as to the commissions; and they should have full voting rights on *both* commission and committee. Both the Commons and Lords Commissions already have appointed lay members, but they currently do not have any voting rights – voting rights would give their views greater weight. Appointment would be determined by necessary expertise: currently, Commission laypeople are usually experienced professionals – lawyers, accountants and businesspeople. What matters is that lay members complement the political expertise of parliamentarians by bringing an experienced, expert eye to governance matters. However, parliamentarian members would continue to have a slim majority over lay members, both on the domestic committees and on the Commissions.

A sixth set of changes would help remedy the 'bicameral issue': the problem of coordination and cooperation between the Houses. A 'simple' solution would be regular joint meetings of the Commissions – but also joint decision-making. This would be coupled with another change: the Chair of the Commons Commission should become an *ex officio* member of the Lords Commission; and the Chair of the Lords Commission should become an *ex officio* member of the Commons Commission. They would not have voting rights. Rather, the point would be to allow a better flow of information between the Houses, and to give some voice to the interests of the other House in Commission deliberations. This role could be delegated, but only to a backbench Commission member.

Finally, more broadly, there should be a general culture shift towards greater transparency. Each House should have a publicly available 'Commission Manual' – the legislative equivalent of the Cabinet Manual – which might set out basic matters such as the powers and responsibilities of the presiding officer and the budget process for the Houses (which again, are not set out formally anywhere: Lee and Yong, 2022). Of course, there is *Erskine May*, but that is a compendium of almost everything: any discussion of governance arrangements is lost among discussions of procedure. The House of Lords Commission does have a Commission Operating Manual (House of Lords Commission, 2022), which covers ways of working and subjects such as the allocation of responsibilities between the Commission and domestic committees, but the Commission Manual would cover more than this. Important governance matters could be covered in a Commission Manual: for instance, a code of conduct for Commission members (including collective Commission responsibility), the Houses' respective budgetary processes, the relationship between the political and official levels of administration, staff impartiality, the relationship between the Houses, and so on. This would be produced by the Commissions themselves, with input and scrutiny from the panoply of domestic committees.

More prosaic transparency reforms would include regular publicly open meetings of the Commissions and domestic committees: not all meetings have to be open, to allow free and frank debate, but there ought to be some – not least to make the Commissions and domestic committees known to parliamentarians themselves and the public. Similarly, reports and minutes of the Commissions and domestic committees should be published regularly; and these reports and minutes should be substantial, not limited to merely recording the topic discussed but covering the substance of discussions as well.

How close are we to this reimagined parliament?

It should be obvious from this description of the current arrangements that we are very, very far from what might be – at least in Westminster (see for example the Restoration and Renewal programme). In the second decade of the 21st century, the Restoration and Renewal programme is in stasis, and is unlikely to be resolved authoritatively unless there is a change in political will, or something catastrophic (sadly, deaths) happens. This is in spite of previous votes by the Houses in favour of a full decant, and an Act of Parliament passed to implement the Restoration and Renewal programme.

It is also hard to see how any of the reimagined governance arrangements suggested could be achieved in Westminster. It is not that the suggested changes are difficult: the problem is rather getting key actors and parliamentarians generally to come to a collective decision on such changes. Reform at Westminster is almost always a result of exogenous change – that is to say, events (Russell, 2011). There appears to be limited interest in reforming governance in either House, and it is far from clear who would initiate such reform – in the past, in practice, it has often been Leaders of the House of Commons (such as Michael Foot or Geoffrey Howe) who pushed through governance reform.

Some changes seem more achievable than others. For instance, the election of Commission members, and giving them additional salaries and portfolios might be more realisable than (say) a wholesale reorganisation of House governance arrangements. Some of these proposed changes (for example, election of members; allocating portfolios to Commission members) are already seen in other legislatures such as the Senedd or the Scottish Parliament. Similarly, adding laypeople to domestic committees is not radical: the Audit Committees (another set of domestic committees) in both Houses are chaired by laypeople. A 'Commission Manual' and other transparency reforms seem relatively straightforward, although this would require a shift in administrative mindset.

Solutions to the bicameralism issue are more difficult, not least because they would require cooperation from both Houses. Regular meetings are easy – that is, relative to the problem of joint decision-making. The latter seems unlikely at the best of times, given the Houses' status relative to each other. Transparency reforms similarly seem unlikely: memories of the expenses scandal cut deeply.

There are also a number of principled objections to these suggested changes. First, they aim to strengthen the legislature as a co-equal branch separate from the executive. That is, they presume a particular configuration of the separation of powers, in which the executive and legislature are in conflict with each other – and that that is a better configuration than the currently existing one. Empirically, of course, in the UK the (political) executive emerges from and is part of the legislature: they are fused. Cooperation and coordination have been the markers of the relationship between the two branches. The reforms may have the effect of sharpening a clearer, more separate identity for the legislature, but also creating conflict between executive and legislature. But since the entire point of the chapter and book is to reimagine parliament, this is not an issue.

Second, the proposed changes might turn the legislature into a version of the executive, with a legislative cabinet at the apex of the administration. This may bring with it the problems we see in the executive: a federalised set of baronies loosely tied together by thin political allegiances. Worse still, the proposals may intensify the problems of individualism and fragmentation which lie at the core of parliamentary governance. One reason why parliamentary governance is so problematic is that there are limited or weak incentives for parliamentarians to act in the collective interest. What the suggested reimagining would do is incentivise individual parliamentarians to prioritise their particular institutional responsibilities: to think institutionally. But what the reimagining might do instead is further individualise institutional ideals – that is, the changes might have the effect of further muting the institutional interest at the expense of individual interest. Thus, there has been a need to combat that tendency with additional changes, such as the requirement of collective commission responsibility.

Third, the suggested transparency changes might turn parliamentary governance and administration into a panopticon-like structure, where everyone is watching each other at the expense of 'real' improvement. Transparency is not an unalloyed good. Parliament is already very much in the public eye, and that intense exposure (and the anticipation of potential exposure) may explain some of key actors' past and current behaviour. Increasing transparency may only intensify malign tendencies.

A final objection turns the previous objections on their head: the suggested changes don't go far enough. Why not reimagine arrangements entirely, and disentangle matters like party and the multiple loyalties that various governance actors have so that they are guided *entirely* by the governance principles set out here? That is, we could make all Commissioners *solely* responsible to parliament; once they become Commissioners, they must leave party loyalty behind altogether. That is one possible answer. But reimagining parliament without parties seems to me to rob parliament of a great deal of what makes it a legislature. An entirely non-partisan Commission may find it difficult to act without the cooperation of parties, or struggle to make its decisions be seen as legitimate by parties if there is no serious party input into decision-making. Representation – the last governance principle – matters. The answer is therefore rather to find a balance between party and institution.

Conclusion

The dilemma of governance – of seeking cross-party consensus and cohesion to achieve the institution's core administrative goals of an effective legislature – is one that all legislatures must face. Governance requires clear goal identification; means to reconcile and coordinate different visions of the good; means to implement decisions; and feedback and accountability mechanisms. But such requirements in legislatures are difficult to achieve because they are highly individualised arenas, with parliamentarians having limited incentives to engage in collective action, particularly on matters where there is no obvious party interest, or where matters cannot be resolved by the fiat of a majority vote.

There is no one size fits all answer. But any reimagining of parliamentary governance would need to be underpinned by four key principles: prioritising the institution; effective governance mechanisms; clear lines of accountability; and representation. These principles aim to remedy problems with goal identification, goal reconciliation and coordination, and accountability that legislatures tend to suffer from. Using these principles and applying them to Westminster, a number of potential changes have been suggested in this chapter which aim to give these principles concrete impact: for instance, removing the Speakers and Leaders of the House from the Commissions, elected and salaried Commission posts, more responsibilities given to parliamentarians, and a Commission Manual setting out the duties of Commissioners and basic facts about key governance processes. These may help resolve some of the common problems seen in parliamentary governance – but they may also intensify some of them. However parliamentary governance is reimagined, it is fair to say that governance at Westminster has a long, long way to go.

8

Reimagining Scrutiny

Lucinda Maer

Introduction

Scrutiny is defined by the Cambridge dictionary as 'the careful and detailed examination of something in order to get information about it'. Parliamentary scrutiny is more than this. Parliamentary scrutiny engages the notion of democratic accountability. This idea, that the government is held to account by Members of Parliament, who in the Commons have a democratic mandate and are accountable themselves to their constituents, is what makes parliamentary scrutiny unique. In the Lords, while members are not elected by the public, appointees bring together a range of specialist knowledge and skills with the ability to make the elected chamber 'think again'. It is then these same parliamentarians who pass bills into law and choose and sustain leaders, and for the majority party, the government. The effectiveness and vitality of scrutiny is therefore crucial for the wider health of the UK's constitutional arrangements.

This chapter seeks to reimagine scrutiny by considering what effective scrutiny would look like, and what would need to change to move us further towards it. It focuses on the House of Commons, as the democratically elected chamber and the chamber whose majority sustains the executive, and primarily on the select committee system within it. The departmental select committee system in the Commons is tasked with scrutiny of the spending, policy and administration of the relevant government department, with cross-cutting committees covering themes such as public administration and human rights (through a joint committee). The Public Accounts Committee considers the value for money of government projects and programmes with the support of the National Audit Office. While briefly considering the procedures available to the Commons to gain access to information, otherwise it sets scrutiny in the chamber aside. The scrutiny of primary and secondary legislation is covered to some extent elsewhere in this volume (see Chapter 9).

In this chapter the principles of what makes 'effective' scrutiny are broadly described as follows:

- It should be based on *gathering and interrogating evidence and information*: it must put information into the public domain while also seeking information that explains and exposes the way in which government decisions are made.
- It should connect *parliament to the public* – as the primary democratic institution in the UK, it is a place that should necessarily listen to and communicate with a wide audience.
- It should be *interconnected to other relevant activity inside and outside parliament* – in order to be efficient and make best use of expertise.
- It should be *engaging* for Members of Parliament – parliamentarians need to want to do it, it must also be beneficial to and not penalise those who take part.
- And most importantly, for parliamentary scrutiny, it should have an *impact on the way in which we are governed* – unlike scrutiny by media or civil society organisations, parliamentary scrutiny is unique in its ability to connect with the executive. If it fails to do so, it becomes just one of a number of scrutiny bodies competing for space rather than sitting, as the Hansard Society once proposed, at the 'apex' of public scrutiny (Hansard Society Commission on Parliamentary Scrutiny, 2001).

The history of the development of departmental select committees (Maer, 2019) shows that how parliament does scrutiny is itself capable of development and change within existing structures and procedures. This suggests that not all reimagining needs to be radical – much is easily within reach. But some of it requires difficult decisions and trade-offs to be made. For example, stronger enforceable powers for committees might mean they become increasingly confrontational and political, losing some of the strength that comes through softer powers of influence and cross-party working. Accessing and publishing increasing volumes of information and evidence might mean that the value of what is available is diluted and the real gems become harder to find. The more technical and detailed the scrutiny that takes place becomes, the more difficult it may be for that scrutiny to engage MPs or engage with their imaginations as politicians rather than technocrats. Deciding between these competing priorities goes beyond the confines of the reimagining process, but setting them out throws into sharp relief the delicate balance between effective parliamentary scrutiny, and the business of careful and detailed examination of something in order to get information about it.

Gathering and interrogating information

The House of Commons chamber has what might be considered strong powers to access information and call ministers to account. Urgent Questions and oral parliamentary questions provide key procedural opportunities for this. MPs question government ministers for an hour at the start of every sitting. The rules require that questions ask for information or press for action, and that the matter being asked about falls into the departmental responsibilities of the minister being asked. If a matter arises which an MP believes requires an immediate answer from a government minister, they may apply to the Speaker to ask an urgent question (HC 314, 2019: S.O.21). As the nature of the procedure is that the matter must be urgent, it means that matters of the day are aired in the House. But it also places parliament at the centre of attempts to hold the government accountable. While an invitation to appear on the BBC's *Today* programme can be turned down, the Speaker's summons cannot.

The practical difficulty of these question procedures, however, is ensuring that answers are provided by ministers to the questions that are asked of them. To take the example of oral parliamentary questions, the Chair is unable to police the answers given by ministers to parliament. While misleading the House is a contempt, and there are procedures in place for ministers who have inadvertently misled the House to correct the record (HC 521, 2023: Q57–78), there is no mechanism outside political and public opinion that is available for making sure the response to the question engages with it at all. Furthermore, the chamber procedures are in practice often highly political, confrontational and, at times, loud. This means the process is often less about gaining information and more about other, equally, important functions of parliament – most notably, the place where politics is done on a national stage. The most famous, and most watched, question time is Prime Minister's Questions. While some might praise a system where the head of government is questioned by Members of Parliament every week, this does not appear to be the public view (Hansard Society, 2015).

Both chambers also assert their power to send for 'persons papers and records' (PPR); that is a power to summon witnesses to appear before it and answer questions and a power of ordering all documents to be laid before it which are necessary for its information (May, 2019: para 11.39). The PPR power has been used in recent times by the Commons to call for the production of papers by means of a motion for a return. Before the 2017 Parliament, a version of this mechanism (known as an 'unopposed return') had traditionally been used by governments to provide parliamentary privilege for reports such as those produced by public inquiries. However, in November 2017 an Opposition motion was passed which required the so-called 'Brexit Impact Assessments' to be made available to the relevant select committee. Since then, the device has been used on many occasions. Recent examples include asking for certain papers regarding the appointment of Evgeny Alexandrovich Lebedev as a Member of the House of Lords; and for papers relating to government contracts awarded to Randox Laboratories during the COVID-19 pandemic. However, using this power relies on a majority being found to do so. In these recent examples, the government chose not to vote against the motion. This power that looks strong is, like much else in parliament, dependent on the assent of those whom it is used to scrutinise: the government.

Select committees are less confrontational and partisan than proceedings in the chamber, and through their more conversational and less formal approach, can provide for more careful and detailed questioning. Questions to ministers can be followed up, the detail can be better interrogated. This does, however, depend on ministers subjecting themselves to questioning at all. Though PPR powers are delegated to select committees, the power to command attendance does not apply to members of either House. This means that ministerial appearances before select committees are voluntary. They do not always agree to appear, or to do so in the timeframe that committees ask for. While Boris Johnson was prime minister, he pulled out of a hearing with the Liaison Committee just 24 hours before it was scheduled to take place.[1] In 2023 the Joint Committee on Human Rights invited the Home Secretary to give evidence for their inquiry on the Illegal Immigration Bill during its passage through parliament. The Home Secretary declined the invitation, citing an 'exceptionally full diary' (Joint Committee on Human Rights, 2023). Furthermore, there is an ongoing debate over the extent of the PPR powers and their effectiveness in relation to private citizens who also don't always wish to answer questions from Members of Parliament (HC 401, 2022).

All this means that the information gathering effectiveness of parliamentary scrutiny depends to a large degree on the willingness of those who are being scrutinised to answer the questions asked of them. It is possible to reimagine a parliament where this is a requirement, based on strict rules with enforceable penalties. But to do so would change the relationships between parliament, government and the public. For committees, it would run the risk of increasing the confrontational nature of scrutiny. It would require more formal processes and procedures that would likely be less flexible and capable of adapting to changing circumstances. Instead, the reimagining might focus on creating more levers of influence, more reasons for it to be of benefit to the executive to allow itself to be held to account.

Parliamentary scrutiny puts large amounts of information in the public domain providing information for other scrutineers to use. During the 2021–2022 Session, House of Commons committees published 304 reports, held public evidence sessions 884 times, hearing evidence from a total of 3,347 witnesses (HC 1, 2022). No statistics are available for the number of written submissions published but this will likely total the tens if not hundreds of thousands. All of these reports, submissions, questions and answers, along with the videos and transcripts of hours of debates and oral evidence sessions are online. But the flip side is that the amount of information made available by parliament is almost overwhelming. The results of select committee scrutiny are usually disseminated either by the media, or directly through social media accounts. Parliament itself publicises key events and publications. Select committee media officers are employed to publicise committee events and outputs, and committees themselves pick out their most interesting information for dissemination through the use of Twitter videos, and quotes in reports.

Parliament has grappled for many years with making its information browsable and searchable in ways which will make it appealing for the public and useful for academics and more specialist audiences. Scrutiny reimagined might put even more resource into the presentation of information in a way that can be searched, browsed, curated and combined for more powerful results. On further reimagining might we say: we have reached capacity for information; any more and we risk diluting its impact; that showing restraint would give the outputs more value (Evans, 2019)? But is it possible for committees to reach a saturation point where they are less competing with other non-parliamentary stories and more with each other, crowding out publicity for one another's work? If it is felt that less might be more, who decides what activity is forsaken? Is it better, as is the case now, for parliamentary activities to compete openly with one another in a marketplace for public interest?

Over the last half century, increasingly large amounts of government information has been made available. Open government gave way to a right to request information under the Freedom of Information Act. The internet has enabled the government to publish large quantities of information in regular data and transparency releases. Parliament is no longer the only mechanism available for gaining access to information and passing it on, through the parliamentary record, to the public. Parliament has to rethink its role in this context: it does not have a monopoly on gathering and interrogating information. In rethinking its role, it needs to focus on what is special about the fact that it is parliament doing it, and that takes us to the connections parliament has with the public, and with the executive.

Engaging the public

The House of Commons chamber has no formal mechanism for the public to engage in its procedures directly. Indirectly, the nature of the democratic link between Members and parliamentarians provides a connection with Members keen to use opportunities available to them to raise constituency issues and opinions. Some procedures are more keenly used for this process: in the chamber, adjournment debates provide Members with 30 minutes of debate with a minister there to respond and these often are on local matters. Westminster Hall provides another avenue to raise matters with ministers on behalf of constituents. And the use of Westminster Hall for debates on e-petitions which have reached the threshold of 100,000 signatures again connects parliament to the public.

Select committees have a key role in 'listening': they typically 'call for evidence' as part of their inquiry work. Committees are increasingly casting the net wide and gathering information through new and more inclusive means (Geddes, 2023). The once typical inquiry pattern of call for evidence, oral evidence sessions, and report is now increasingly frequently supplemented with a range of wider activities. Committees have used online surveys publicised through Twitter to take the temperature of the public on issues from immigration to the government's plans for a Bill of Rights. Committees regularly use 'round-table' events to engage with a wider range of people to listen to lived experience and take evidence in private to give vulnerable witnesses the protection or the privacy they need. Citizens' assemblies have been sponsored by parliament, with one considering the funding of long-term social care (Involve, 2018), and another on climate change (Climate Assembly, 2020). Reimagining might see more use of mechanisms for wider engagement such as these including mini-publics, polling and public events (see Chapter 5). More frequent use of these sorts of initiatives would, however, require a bigger budget. Would scrutiny reimagined include a bigger budget and a requirement to ensure the value for money of such spending? Would more use of such mechanisms create any greater impact for parliamentary scrutiny?

The spaces in which scrutiny happens are also capable of adapting to aid parliament's ability to listen. In 2019, when the Liaison Committee published its report into the impact and influence of the select committee system it challenged parliament to provide 'flexible spaces which can be easily adapted so we can take evidence in different formats and there must be ready access to reliable, and preferably permanently situated, video-conferencing facilities' (HC 1860, 2019: para 125). Just six months later, parliament and its committees had to adapt to the global COVID-19 pandemic and its requirement to stay at home. Suddenly, committees met online with only the smallest possible in-person presence in the committee room and with witnesses and Members alike all appearing online. The speedy provision of video-conferencing facilities by the Parliamentary Broadcasting Unit enabled committees to continue to hold the government to account throughout the pandemic, with those leading the response to the pandemic regularly giving evidence to the Health and Social Care and Science and Technology Committees. Yet committee rooms have retained the same physical horseshoe layout. Might spaces in a reimagined parliament sometimes allow those speaking to select committees to sit alongside members, rather than in front of them? There is certainly nothing in the rules that would prevent such a change and where committees hold 'round-table' events this happens naturally to create a different atmosphere.

Some progress has been made to produce information in various formats. For example, Prime Minister's Questions has British Sign Language translations on the parliament website and a same-day transcript is available before the formal overnight Hansard is produced. However, for committees the reporting of documents to the House as the mechanism for publication by committees means that video and images are not afforded the same status as the written word. Committees cannot accept evidence sent via voice file or by video. If such information is to be reported to the House, it first needs to be transcribed, at once losing some of its power and immediacy.

It would not be difficult to reimagine parliament making the receiving and the publishing of information more open and inclusive in such a way. Indeed, the Liaison Committee in 2019 recommended that '[w]hatever its medium or format, information submitted to committees which they then seek to publish by order of the House ought to be recognised as formal evidence. The House must take the necessary steps to bring about this change' (HC 1860, 2019: para 104). House of Commons committees are already producing information in 'Social Shorthand' format as well as long-form reports; podcasts are aiming to reach a younger and more geographically diverse audience. While it would be possible to produce arguments about the ability and desirability of the extension of parliamentary privilege to a wider range of outputs, the fact that they already exist, and nothing has yet broken as a result, perhaps gives confidence to continue with this more experimental and adaptable approach.

There is also the possibility of reimagining the language and choreography of scrutiny. Such incremental change has also taken place in the Commons chamber itself, with 'private notice questions' being renamed 'urgent', to better explain their function to a wider audience. The 2019 Liaison Committee report on the Impact and Effectiveness of the Select Committee System recommended a move away from the language of 'evidence', favouring instead inviting people to give committees their 'views, concerns and experiences' on a topic, and referring to 'guests' or 'participants' instead of witnesses. Commons committees no longer must refer to themselves as 'select' committees – a term which the Liaison Committee noted was often confusing to the public (HC 1860, 2019: para 229).

Interconnectivity and partnership working

Select committees have already gone some way to recognising the strength of making connections with those inside and outside parliament. As the Commons Liaison Committee explained in its 2019 report, '[o]ne way to maximise the impact of our work is to act in partnerships with others inside and outside the House. As well as working more closely with research communities and civil society, we can continue to form effective working relationships across committees through joint working' (HC 1860, 2019: para 37).

The cumbersome existing procedures for joint working between committees were, in 2018, supplemented by the ability for one committee to invite a 'guest' from another committee to take part in the questioning of witnesses. This new procedure, known as 'guesting', has been widely used. While it is a formal procedure available under standing orders, its success is largely in the informality of its operation in practice. For example, a member of the Joint Committee on Human Rights was a 'guest' on the Northern Ireland Affairs Committee for evidence on the Northern Ireland Troubles (Legacy and Reconciliation) Bill as part of its inquiry on addressing the legacy of Northern Ireland's past. Joint working through correspondence is also increasingly frequent; for example, the Chairs of those committees were joined by the Chair of the Justice Select Committee in November 2022 in writing a joint letter to the Home Secretary about the conditions at Manston asylum processing centre and wider issues with Channel crossings. Co-operation on visits also takes place, for example, members of the Home Affairs Committee, the Women and Equalities Committee and the Joint Committee on Human Rights visited the Manston migrant centre in November 2022.

Working within existing structures, committees have found ways in which to connect with others in their relevant policy fields. The long existing ability of committees to employ specialist advisers has been supplemented by a range of academic fellowships that bring outside experts in to work alongside staff. In the 2019 Parliament, some Commons committees published 'areas of research interest', appealing to the academic community to conduct research and provide information on areas where the committee would focus over the next electoral cycle. The Health Select Committee has innovated in a different way, setting up its own expert panel who are asked by the Committee to evaluate government commitments in various policy areas and report their findings to the committee (House of Commons, 2022b).

There is, perhaps, further reimagining to be done here. There are large numbers of monitoring bodies who have expertise and some of which also have a role in holding the government to account – examples include the Committee on Standards in Public Life, the Office of Budget Responsibility and the Information Commissioner. Committees could build different sorts of relationships with these bodies, and with academic institutions, who could work together to interrogate information provided to committees or work together on projects of shared interest. If we look, for example, at the more formal relationships between the Comptroller and Auditor General and the Public Accounts Committee, and the Parliamentary Ombudsman and the Public Administration and Constitutional Affairs Committee, it is possible to see how reports from these independent parliamentary bodies are given further life by committee interest and involvement. Would other relationships and models be possible in other parts of public life? As public service delivery has become ever more complex, should parliament do more to acknowledge that it cannot do the job of scrutinising the government alone? Should, as the Hansard Society Commission on Parliamentary Scrutiny concluded in 2001, parliament be at 'the apex of this system of scrutiny', providing a 'framework for their activity and us[ing] their investigations as the basis on which to hold ministers to account'? (Hansard Society Commission on Parliamentary Scrutiny, 2001).

The success of joint working between Commons committees has not extended to work between chambers. No equivalent procedure currently exists in the House of Lords, or allows for guests from one chamber to take part in the proceedings of another. Joint correspondence between chairs of committees in the Commons and Lords is rare, but possible (for example, in May 2022, the letter to the Deputy Prime Minister from chairs of four committees including the Lords Constitution Committee asking for the Bill of Rights Bill to be subject to pre-legislative scrutiny). There is already a Standing Order which allows the Welsh Affairs Committee to have meetings with members of the Senedd Cymru. A reimagining could seek to allow for such processes to work between the chambers, the Scottish Parliament and the Northern Ireland Assembly.

Politicians sometimes seek to recommend or to use mechanisms outside of parliament to overcome difficult decisions that are required in the short term for benefits that will be felt long outside the current electoral cycle, or to find solutions to what seem to be intractable problems. For example, public inquiries or Royal Commissions have in the past been used to present more limited options to politicians. More recently, commissions made of the great and the good have fallen out of favour. Instead, more citizens' assemblies, which are made up of a more representative group of the public, have been used to frame debates. Parliamentary committees have sponsored citizens' assemblies to look at complex issues where politicians might find it difficult to agree: for example on the funding of adult social care, and on the response to climate change. Reimagining could continue this trend, using a wider variety of deliberative mechanisms including polling and mini-publics (which are smaller and faster than full citizens' assemblies but still allow for the inclusion of a representative public group to look at an issue), increasing the richness and wealth of evidence available.

The need to engage parliamentarians

Parliamentary scrutiny is uniquely important and has its impact on both government and the public, in the House of Commons at least, because it is carried out by people who are directly elected and accountable to the public, and that the executive is both accountable to parliament, drawn from parliament and sustained in power by parliament. The media, regulatory bodies, charities and academics may all play valuable scrutiny roles, but they lack this central democratic function. For parliamentary scrutiny to be effective, it needs to engage parliamentarians. Without them, it does not exist. They have to want to turn up, ask questions and hold the government to account. The fact that committees meet week after week with, more often than not, a quorum of members present goes some way to suggest that scrutiny by committees can, and does, engage Members. But this should not be taken for granted. In her description of the 'good committee', former Liaison Committee Chair Sarah Wollaston explained that '[the good committee would] engage all its members, giving them opportunities to develop areas of interest and expertise, drawing strength from the fact that it is a committee working across party lines and reflecting a wide range of views' (Wollaston, 2019).

Any reimagining must appreciate that while scrutiny is a key function of parliament, scrutiny work competes in parliamentary time and resources with other functions and motivations of political actors. Along with their role as scrutineers, MPs are also there to deliver on manifesto commitments and sustain their political party at Westminster. While some take a less tribal view and seek to find areas of agreement across the House, others will prioritise spending time on constituency casework and others working with party groups, or indeed all-party groups which operate outside the powers and procedures of the House. It is entirely up to each individual Member to decide how to interpret their role. Ultimately, they are all politicians and their choices, opinions and actions come through a political rather than technocratic lens. But how much should scrutiny be the central duty of parliamentarians, and should the culture of the institution be reimagined to place this at its heart?

It is widely held that Members of the House of Commons often also seek the favour of their front benches and aspire to ministerial office. It has traditionally been thought that asking difficult questions of ministers is not necessarily the best way to achieve promotion and favour. In the House of Commons, select committees have over many years sought to modernise and reform their membership to create greater independence from government and what is often referred to as an 'alternative career path' to ministerial office (Maer, 2019). Following the so-called 'Wright reforms' of 2010, committee chairs are largely elected by the House rather than appointed by party whips, building on the introduction of payment to select committee chairs some years earlier. Research has shown that data on select committee chairs since 2005 seems to undermine the idea of select committee work as a career goal in and of itself, with chairships instead increasingly acting as launchpads for, or interludes between, ministerial or shadow ministerial posts (Holden Bates, 2023). While that might be seen by some as a limitation on scrutiny, the reverse might in fact be true: that spending time holding feet to the fire does not discount politicians from ministerial office and ministerial office can also be a training ground for effective scrutiny.

Many areas of government are increasingly technical and complex. For example, the work of the Treasury Select Committee, that of the Joint Committee on Human Rights and of the (former Commons) Science and Technology Committee can cover issues as complex as the crypto-asset industry, the compatibility of national security legislation with the European Convention of Human Rights and the antimicrobial potential of bacteriophages. The more complex and specialised the issues, the more parliamentary scrutiny requires expert staff to support and advise Members; staff who make complex and technical information understandable and set out the policy questions for political decision. As the complexity of public policy increases, and the volume of scrutiny work rises, there has been a corresponding increase in the number of parliamentary staff. At the same time, surprisingly small numbers of people work to hold large and complex government departments to account. The Home Office in 2022 had 36,500 civil servants (Cabinet Office, 2023); the Home Affairs Select Committee had a staff of nine.

Some focus, in a parliament reimagined, might fall on what the right level of staff should be, and how they should be organised to best aid Members who are seeking to hold government to account. Suggestions for sharing of staff between the two Houses, for creating expert hubs and career paths, and for greater numbers of expert advisers have all featured in blueprints for parliamentary reform. Committees sometimes look somewhat jealously at the resources available to the Public Accounts Committee which can draw on reports of the National Audit Office, and to US Congressional inquiries with their large budgets and staff. Certainly, one area of scrutiny where the imagination of Members is rarely engaged is in scrutiny of departmental spending and budgets. This might be better done if it were largely subcontracted out to a large specialist staff. But if more scrutiny is conducted by staff and becomes ever more technical in nature, will it lose some of the power of its attachment to Members of Parliament and the democratic process? A reimagining might seek ways in which both things are possible with structures that help increase the specialism of Members (through, for example, rapporteur systems or connecting department scrutiny to legislative scrutiny committees). There can be a tension between the process of careful and detailed examination and politics. Can scrutiny be reimagined to ensure these processes work together rather than pull in opposite directions?

As well as providing benefits for MPs who engage in scrutiny, MPs could be held to account by the Commons for the way in which they perform the role. Select committees often struggle to have the minimum attendance allowed for quorum under Standing Orders. The current systems mean that there are officially not vacancies on committees – Members are members of committees until they are replaced. There are procedures available to require a minimum attendance of members, but this presupposes other Members would want to step in when others stand down. Would penalties for non-attendance work? Would they be fair if members have indicated they no longer wish to attend but have not yet been replaced? Would members want to be on committees at all if such penalties existed?

Chairs of committees receive an extra payment for what is often a considerable amount of work they do. Most of them are elected by the House of Commons to their posts. While there are mechanisms for select committee statements on the contents on reports, this differs from a mechanism to report back to their electorate on how they have performed, the way in which they have used the resources available to them, and how effective their work has been. A mechanism for select committee questions for a short period in the chamber with a rota that allows all chairs to answer questions twice a term could provide some scrutiny for the scrutineers.

Impact on those being scrutinised

Effective scrutiny in the parliamentary context means having some sort of an impact on the government. Good scrutiny and good government are, as Robin Cook (2003) once said, inextricably linked. The other factors – being engaging, efficient, connected, informed and accessible – can all be seen as part of good scrutiny, but good scrutiny should feed back into good government. Where scrutiny breaks down altogether, in the chamber and in committees, is when the executive does not engage at all. While committees can continue to carry out valuable work on public engagement and play their part in educating and socialising Members, without impact on government can the work they do really be defined as parliamentary scrutiny? As in any relationship, it is difficult for one side unilaterally to make the other side engage. Reimagining has to encourage that engagement, rather than scare it away.

It is, of course, difficult to measure the impact of select committee work. Even when narrowly conceived as select committee recommendations in reports which are accepted in formal government responses, impact can be difficult to measure or track. While the initial response may say one thing, quite another might happen, or it might have happened even without the intervention of the committee (Benton and Russell, 2013). As Hannah White (2022) has argued, a particular strength of committees is when they move a neglected issue onto the government's agenda, as the Environmental Audit Committee did with its work on microplastics in 2016. As committees increasingly look for faster impacts than the traditional inquiry model of publishing reports, their impact becomes even harder to track – letters may not include recommendations that can easily be accepted or rejected. One-off sessions hastily arranged to hold the feet of ministers or public bodies to the fire can have an impact even before they have taken place, by office-holders acting to pre-empt potential criticism.

Some lessons on impact might be taken from the difference between the more confrontational scrutiny that happens in the chamber, and the more conversational and collaborative cross-party approach of select committees. The most partisan, noisy, confrontational exchange in the Commons chamber is undoubtedly Prime Minister's Questions. But it would be surprising if any such exchange has led directly to a change in the policy or administration of government (although the threat of an embarrassing exchange might precipitate change). On this measure, it is not effective, although, of course, it is not the only measure of the importance and effectiveness of the weekly event: the relative strength and weakness of performances might have an impact on whether backbenchers are rallied, or on the evening's headlines.

Select committees tend to work with softer power. Ministers do not have to attend and, despite their powers, private individuals are rarely summoned. They aren't noisy places. The questioning takes time. While some select committee events are 'box office' dramas, a lot of their work goes on out of the limelight. Discussions or deliberation must take place in private, allowing for conversations, compromise and persuasion to take place in order to get to an agreed view. The reports (usually) have cross-party consensus. And a process exists that allows minority views to be recorded quietly in the minutes of reports. The response comes after time for thought rather than in the instant. Committees can follow up their work, tracking their recommendations and campaigning on issues, building expertise and pressure for change over time. This has led some to call for parliament to become a more committee-based institution with the influential Hansard Society Commission on Strengthening Parliament recommending that 'to be more effective in holding the government to account, Westminster must look to its committees' (Hansard Society Commission on Parliamentary Scrutiny, 2001).

Conclusion

Reimagining is difficult and complicated. You reimagine one thing, and everything else changes. While starting with a blank sheet of paper removes constraints, the realities of the UK's parliamentary democracy, its party system, its spaces and cultures, quickly creep back in. Parliament is also in a continual process of reform. Much of what can be reimagined can be done without large scale structural or procedural change. The lessons of the Urgent Question (previously the Private Notice Question and rarely granted, and now the Urgent Question and granted each day as often as not) shows what can be done within existing systems with imagination. Nothing procedural had to change to allow select committees to start crowdsourcing inquiries on Twitter, or to start having British Sign Language translations of Prime Minister's Questions. More recently, select committees have reinterpreted their remit to include scrutiny not just of government but of 'matters of public concern' more widely. The select committee system has arguably captured the imagination of Members and those who engage with it, who find it one of the more vibrant and positive parts of the parliamentary experience.

We can reimagine scrutiny to engage the imagination of parliamentarians, connect with the public, work with others in the public scrutiny sphere and get access to and disseminate information. But equally importantly, scrutiny needs to impact the government. Governments therefore have to be open to challenge. Robin Cook once explained that good scrutiny meant good government. Scrutiny has to be 'good' for government to welcome it, and government must be open to scrutiny in order for it to be good.

Note

[1] The note he sent to the then Chair, Dr Wollaston, was published on her Twitter feed. It read, 'I promised I will come to the Liaison Committee and I will keep that promise but I am afraid I must focus on delivering Brexit in the difficult circumstances in which we find ourselves, and I believe I would be of greater value if I could postpone for a fixed date nearer 5 or 6 months after I became PM, so that my appearance took place after roughly the same period in office as Gordon Brown, David Cameron and Theresa May. I do hope you understand.'

9

Reimagining Parliamentary Procedure

Paul Evans

Introduction

> The principles evolved in creative and revolutionary periods were laboriously reduced to form, and in the process life and growth were often arrested and tendencies were ossified into dogmas. Parliamentary procedure became a mystery, unintelligible except to the initiated.
>
> Ilbert (1908: xviii)

This chapter considers how we might reimagine the rules and forms by which parliament conducts its business. It focuses on the House of Commons because that is the most rule-bound of the two Houses of Parliament. It identifies four key areas in which the current procedures of the House fail the imagination. These are:

- *Complexity*: the rule book of the House (its 'Standing Orders') has reached a level of complexity which has outstripped the capacity of most MPs to grasp and use effectively; and this complexity creates a barrier to engagement and understanding for those outside Westminster.
- *Executive capture*: the procedures of the House, combined with the fusing of executive, party and parliamentary control, have disempowered MPs to an extent which leaves them disengaged in the critical work of making laws, raising and spending public money, and holding the executive to account.
- *Alienation and illegitimacy*: the procedures of parliament do not resonate with the way we conduct our lives. Parliamentary procedure has become divorced from human procedure. They thus fail to command true consent.

- *Inattention*: these three factors which combine to give an increasingly mechanical quality to parliamentary procedure risk driving out deliberation and separating it from the process of arriving at a decision; evacuating parliament of its key purpose of open decision-making and fostering an occult world of lobbying and deal-making which relates only tangentially to what is happening in the public theatre of politics; which in turn can encourage the privileging within parliament of exaggerated posturing and of instrumental and performative partisanship over the hard graft which may lead to the achievement of compromise and collaboration on which parliamentary democracy depends.

After analysing some of the causes of these defects in parliamentary procedure, the chapter proposes how we might reimagine procedure in ways which could help us escape these dead-ends. Principally this involves finding ways to recover space for deliberation through greater attention to the committee dimension of its proceedings and opening up its scrutiny to better collaboration with the world outside Westminster. The aim is to imagine a world in which parliament better engages the imagination of the electorate in performing its central and crucial roles of both enabling good government and discouraging bad government.

Why reimagine?

Anyone who has attended a poorly run meeting (and few among us have not) will know how quickly such events can become inchoate and formless exchanges of more or less irrelevant opinions and prejudices with no clear decisions or prospect of tangible outcomes. Even cogent arguments made during the meeting may appear to have gone unheard and unanswered, and decisions which are eventually announced seem to have been made elsewhere.

Parliament needs to minimise the risks of such negative experiences. Crucially, because it is the centre of our democratic constitution, it needs to command procedural legitimacy not only among its participants (MPs) but also among its observers (the electorate).

Parliamentary procedure is a sophisticated system, developed over centuries (Evans, 2017), but the rules of procedure, particularly in the Commons, are characterised by complexity. They require a knowledge of context to fill the gaps (provided in the 1,000-pages of *Erskine May's Parliamentary Procedure* [May, 2019]), and sufficient understanding of their overall architecture to enable the reader to supply the silent cross-references. They make extensive use of a private language where words do not operate in their plain and natural meaning.[1]

Making laws and raising and distributing public money (the two key functions of the House of Commons) are complicated activities. But if the rules which govern how we set about doing that are largely incomprehensible there will be a deficit of engagement by both representatives and the public which may lead to a crisis of legitimacy (see White, 2022: 91–119). Or to misunderstanding and apathy. Or to parliament being too much at the mercy of those intermediaries who purport to explain and facilitate access to its activities for those outside its high, forbidding, intricate, Gothic walls.

Procedure is a way for a deliberative body to marry debate with decision. But decision has tended to become prioritised at the expense of debate and deliberation. Much of the complexity of the procedures of the Commons arises from the push to enable the executive to deliver its programme with as little resistance as possible from parliament. Many of its rules are designed to ensure that a party with a majority will be certain to prevail. In particular, these rules have steadily handed control over the agenda of the Commons to the executive.

This is most clearly illustrated in the rules relating to the passage of legislation. Starting with the introduction of the 'closure' rule in 1882 (see Redlich, 1908: 165–85; Lee, 2020: 5–54, 2021: 5–55), and progressing through the institutionalisation of the 'guillotine' after the Second World War to the establishment of 'programming' in 2001, the rules of the Commons have handed increasing control of the legislative agenda to the government.

The changes that occurred in the 19th century after the arrival of nationally organised political parties were, perhaps, inevitable and necessary. But if procedure ever passed through a period of intelligibility, as its rules were increasingly codified throughout the 20th century, it has largely doubled back on itself. Only a minority of MPs now understand, care about and try to utilise procedures for the purposes for which they were designed. And for the wider public, they are mostly baffling.

This complexity also reinforces executive/party control of the Commons. The Conservative Party's backbench 1922 Committee was founded in part to help new MPs feeling 'lost in the maze of parliamentary procedure' (see Ball, 2023) and its weekly meetings are still devoted in large part to explaining to Conservative MPs what they will be voting on the following week. A recent commentary on the House of Commons argues that:

> [New MPs] are suddenly presented with an impossibly complex web of rules, conventions, precedents and demands. ... Most [MPs] remain largely ignorant of parliamentary procedure throughout their time in Parliament. ... The complexity of Parliament and the ignorance of its inhabitants are both part of a system of control. It is useful for the party leadership that the system should remain this way, so it does. (Dunt, 2023)

Perhaps the most brutal – and most criticised – element of executive evasion of parliamentary scrutiny is the use of delegated legislation, laws made by ministers under powers given them in Acts of Parliament. Such laws receive scant scrutiny either at their granting stage (when a Bill is being debated) or at the point at which they are exercised (see HL 105, 2021; HL 106, 2021).

The House of Lords is different. There, the executive has much less control over time, and in the last 20 years or so no single party has enjoyed a majority in that House. The opportunities for discursive examination of the details of legislation are greater. But in the end the Lords must concede to the Commons. And where the executive is disinclined to listen to reasoned opposition, the influence of the Lords is much diminished. And the Lords do not have to worry about taxation or public spending. Parliamentary procedure, particularly legislative and financial procedure, fails to capture the imagination of the electorate. That risks depriving its outcomes (whether laws or other decisions) of process legitimacy. Perhaps more worryingly, it fails to capture the imagination (and therefore attention) even of most MPs. That is why it needs reimagining.

What is to be done? Some principles for reimagining procedure

If remedying these deficits is essential to sustaining parliament's place in our democracy, what are the desiderata that might inform such a reimagining?

- Procedure must confer legitimacy – it is the process by which outcomes are reached, not the outcomes themselves, that matter in this context. The way decisions are reached must be seen to be fair (and so far as possible be enduring because they are fair).
- The elements of procedure which reinforce process-legitimacy are evidence of legislators' attention, debate which allows as many voices to be heard as possible, time which allows the job to be done well, transparency about the rules and how they are being applied.
- The elements which tend to erode process-legitimacy are excessive competition for the attention of legislators, unnecessary and counter-intuitive complexity of process, opacity about the rules, legislators' disinvestment in the process, avoidance of challenge.
- Procedure must be recognisably human.
- Procedure must encourage rather than discourage participation. It must bring in expertise, but not only experts.
- Procedure must encourage debate and deliberation while also delivering decisions. These aims must be held in balance.
- Procedure must empower parliament, not just the executive.
- Procedure must focus attention on what is important and use the time and skills of the Members of the two Houses efficiently.

- Procedure must enable the two Houses to each do what they do best and discourage duplication of effort.
- Procedure must be predictable. But not unchanging.

Reimagining
Some building blocks: the select committees
There is an existing aspect of the procedural landscape of parliament where deliberation is nourished and where procedure is more recognisably human. This is the system of departmental select committees in the Commons. These were established in 1979, since when their influence and visibility has grown immensely and their number greatly increased (see Maer, 2019; Norton, 2019). Increasingly the House of Lords has also adopted select committees as a core aspect of its way of doing business.

Select committees are a largely procedure-free zone and might appear to be outside the scope of this chapter. But that is precisely the point. They deliberate rather than debate, in private. They take their time. In public, they converse (more or less politely and constructively) with the unelected in all shapes and sizes – not only the mighty but sometimes the humble and the meek as well. The public seem to like this style of politics, which tends to seem rather human – though with all the flaws that that implies.

Political science speaks of 'talking' and 'working' parliaments (Steffani, 1979). As one European scholar puts it: 'Talking legislatures are characterized by government control over the agenda ... working legislatures are dominated by powerful committees which are permanent and possess rewrite authority; fully empowered committees are congruent with ministerial departments' (Koß, 2018: 39). The House of Commons is undoubtedly a talking legislature by these criteria. Government control of the agenda is strong. Legislation that gets passed is largely (though not absolutely exclusively) what the government has introduced. The opportunities to modify it are extremely narrow (see Evans, 2021a). To the extent they exist, they often do so outside formal procedural structures (see Russell and Gover, 2017). Financial controls are theoretically immense but in practice weak, and dressed up in impenetrable procedures. It does, however, have a system of permanent committees congruent with government departments. What they lack is what Koß calls 'rewrite authority' – either over legislation or the budget. Legislation is dealt with in a separate set of committees which are not permanent, not expert, with only limited ability to collect evidence and which are subject to complex procedures which are designed to reinforce government control. Public money is dealt with largely through legislation which evades even this level of scrutiny.

So Westminster presents two faces to the world: the one of select committees which is recognisable as familiarly human, relatively informal and involves the participation of non-politicians; and the one of the channels (legislative committees and plenary) through which legislation and budgetary matters pass, which are governed by complex and opaque rules and subject to remorseless control by the government (in collaboration with the opposition parties through the 'usual channels').

Another way of describing this divide might be to use a borrowing from neuropsychology. The select committees may be seen to embody the right-brain, emotional and holistic ways of thinking. The procedure-driven plenary and legislative committees embody the analytical, disintegrative, rational, left-brain way of thinking (McGilchrist, 2009: 330). In the high-functioning human being these two elements balance and check each other. In the House of Commons the political neurosurgeons have cunningly separated the two halves of the brain. They communicate with each other sporadically and falteringly, if at all.

Or, if you prefer a different metaphor drawn from broadly the same area of science but suggesting a slightly different allocation of characteristics, the select committees think slow (deliberate, effortful) and the legislative committees and the plenary think fast (intuitive, associative, metaphorical, automatic, impressionistic) (Kahneman, 2011).

Whichever binary metaphor you may prefer to use, what they suggest is that for a good parliamentary system, as for a good person, the two parts need to work in harmony.

Overall, as noted by Koß (2018: 16), '[w]orking legislatures are characterized by powerful committees and decentralized agenda control, whereas talking legislatures combine government control of the agenda with weak legislative committees'. The rest of this chapter attempts to reimagine procedure so as to push the House of Commons further along the path down which it has been slowly travelling for half a century, of becoming more a working than a talking parliament – but also as one that does not hoard all that work to itself, but involves a much wider range of actors in that labour. The select committees, flexible, resistant to fixed formulation, shaped by experience, involving the world outside Westminster, should be brought into a more fruitful relationship with the automatic, rule-bound, inflexible, time-poor procedures of the legislative and financial processes of the House.

Agenda control

A minor reversal of the inexorable trend towards executive control of the agenda in the House of Commons came with the creation of 'backbench business', controlled by the Backbench Business Committee, in 2010. Though in its early days it scored some notable firsts (see Evans, 2021b), what was heralded as a revolution quite quickly became a humdrum part of parliamentary routine.

Two crucial steps that were never taken may have cemented the reforms of 2010 and genuinely shifted the dominance of agenda control away from the executive. First, the House Business Committee, also proposed as part of these reforms, was postponed and then quietly abandoned. Second, the 'votable agenda' recommended by the Wright Committee (more formally the Select Committee on Reform of the House of Commons, see HC 1117, 2009; HC 372, 2010), where the agenda of the House would have ultimately been subject to a vote of the whole House – which would have been a transformative element during the Brexit wars – was never implemented (see Russell and Gover, 2021; Russell and James, 2023). As a consequence, backbench business soon became routinely consigned to the Thursday afternoon graveyard slot in the plenary, where it languished largely un-whipped and unnoticed.

The 2010 reforms did not then inaugurate a permanent backbench revolution, or create a focus for backbenchers to become a third force in the Commons. Party managers and the usual channels were for a while mildly unsettled but certainly not seriously shaken.

This chapter does not address proposals to reform the mechanics of agenda control in the Commons, which has been extensively debated elsewhere. It is a key aspect of the fusing of party hierarchy, government and management of parliament, the disentangling of which is probably the biggest hurdle to be leapt if procedure is to be genuinely reimagined. In what follows it is proposed that the *content* of debate in the Commons should be far more controlled by what happens in its committees.

The most frequently mounted defence of Westminster's dualist committee system is that by keeping the 'scrutiny' committees away from legislation and the design of taxation and spending they are sufficiently defanged that the party managers can afford to let them go their own sweet way – they are no threat to the central functions of government and do not need to be closely managed. There is undoubtedly some strength in this argument. The counterpoise is that this very quality of harmless impotence deprives the backbenchers on those committees of any strong sense of agency. There is limited purpose apparent in investing time and intellectual effort in select committee work if there are no very tangible outcomes beyond the esteem of the already converted when an existing policy is damned or a new one promoted. Can we reimagine committees as powerful parliamentary agents?

Legislative procedure
Primary legislation

The statute book is necessarily detailed and complex; both these qualities are repugnant to most people. Legislative procedure has developed as a technique for focusing on detail; but the practice of legislative scrutiny in the

Commons has become (perhaps irredeemably) separated from detail. MPs are interested in broad principles; so are the public. Legislative procedure and human interest have become separated. MPs are not technocrats, still less the majority of the public.

Moreover, the key decisions about government legislation are made before it is introduced, often made in private in consultation with powerful interests. Parliament is not a partner in this upstream process but is offered the limited choice of wholesale acceptance, carping criticism or pedantic snagging downstream.

The following are suggestions for how we might try to reimagine the procedure without simply abandoning history. To a significant degree, these proposals are an attempt to rationalise and simplify much of what already happens in an unacknowledged way.

Public participation in the pre-legislative stage would be a step towards making the process more engaging and less closed than it currently appears. An experiment in holding 'public reading' stages was tried on four Bills in the period 2010–2013 (see Kelly, 2014). But it needs to be done better and more honestly, with the engagement taking place before rather than after a policy is fully formed so that it brings parliament and the public together in a genuinely joint endeavour, though an academic analysis of a pilot public reading stage in the Commons showed that designing an effective system that works with parliamentary procedure and for the public is far from straightforward, and needs imagination (Leston-Bandeira and Thompson, 2017).

Bills (perhaps to be renamed 'draft laws' in our search for plain language) should not normally be able to start their career in either House until they had passed through a first reading stage where they were examined, select committee style, by a sector-specialist committee, and reported on by it. This would enable the gathering and publication of evidence, bringing some of the upstream lobbying into the light.

Where a committee considers that the full range of pre-introduction consultation (Green Paper, White Paper, publication of submissions) has been conducted by the government, or where a draft law arose from an exercise such as a citizens' assembly or equivalent, the committee would be able to wave the draft law through for consideration in plenary without an elaborate inquiry stage.

After being given permission to proceed by the plenary (what we now call the second reading), Bills should be referred to a timetabling committee on which most parties are represented in proportion to their strength in the House. It could produce a proposed allocation of time for the draft law at committee and report stage. That proposal would need to be agreed by the House after a short, time-limited debate and amendments could be proposed to it.[2]

If we reimagine the current committee stage (clause-by-clause consideration), we might see a sub-committee drawn from members of the committee propose a more detailed timetable which would allocate specific themes to each of its sittings (or a series of sittings). The committee would begin each sitting with the examination of witnesses relevant to the session's theme and the cross-examination of ministers, officials and legal drafters. Where appropriate, ministers from the devolved governments, and legislators from the devolved parliaments, might be heard. No ministers would normally be members of the committee. Perhaps neither would opposition frontbenchers. Expert witnesses, including those from the civil service, and the broader public would be able to engage directly with the content of the draft law rather than being required, as at present, to speak through a rather clumsy ventriloquist's dummy system.

At the end of its consideration of a draft law, the committee would be required to produce a report (agreed in private – or possibly in public) setting out the amendments it was proposing, along with discursive material if it so chose.

The next stage (broadly equivalent to what is currently the 'report stage'), taken in plenary, would again be divided by the cross-party timetabling committee into themed periods of debate.[3] Its proposals would be agreed by the House on a votable and amendable motion after a short, time-limited debate. Any votes would be taken at the conclusion of debate on each theme, including votes on whether to accept the amendments proposed to the draft law in the committee.

If necessary, the draft law might then be referred to a revision committee which would have power only to make minor necessary and consequential amendments. It would then be considered in plenary for a final time on the motion that the draft law be agreed as a whole.

In some ways these proposed changes would do no more than rationalise and simplify what already happens through the opaque process of 'selection' and 'grouping' of amendments that takes place within the current 'clause by clause' procedures. But legislative procedure in the Commons would now be explicitly designed to focus on the themes and principles of a draft law, less on the words on the page. This is human procedure, examining the purpose of a proposed law slowly and intuitively rather than technocratically.

In our reimagined parliament, we may see the less partisan upper House conducting legislative scrutiny more along traditional lines, preserving some of the undoubted virtues of a long-gestated system. That House is habituated to detail, has less need of connection with the electorate, and enjoys a large degree of control over its own allocation of time. But the current system (consideration of Lords Amendments and 'Messages') for reconciling differences between the two Houses is one of the weakest and most opaque elements of current procedures.

Here we might go back to the future for inspiration. Back in the day (up to the beginning of the 19th century), if the Lords and Commons disagreed about the contents of a Bill they would appoint delegations to meet in a 'conference' to try and reach a compromise. The current system of sending almost incomprehensible messages to and fro between the two Houses in an attempt to find agreement leaves little or no space for having a grown-up conversation, and leaves the initiative almost entirely in the hands of ministers. Hugely important topics in government Bills are disposed of by the Commons in very restricted debates where dispassionate information is almost entirely lacking. We can be certain that few, if any, MPs have acquainted themselves with the relevant debates in the Lords.

We could instead try and reimagine a system where some kind of joint committee would be established to debate and recommend what to do about such disagreements. Or, at a minimum, we could try and imagine a rupture with the past so great that Members of the upper House could address the lower House during debates on their proposed amendments (and, indeed, vice versa from time to time). Yet more radically, we could ask whether the conventions surrounding the system of annual parliamentary sessions, which create the temporal cliff-edges at which the two Houses must regularly conduct an increasingly frenetic conversation on a Bill which they are disputing if it is not to be lost, really does more harm to scrutiny than good.

Draft laws proposed by backbenchers

The House of Commons Procedure Committee has described the current system of what are called Private Members' Bills as 'an exercise in futility' (HC 684, 2016: para 9). It has been conducting an heroic campaign over nearly a decade to do something about this (see HC 188-I, 2013; HC 1171, 2014; HC 684, 2016; HC 701, 2016). But nothing has changed – the government has never seen fit to allow any of its proposals to be put to the House for decision.

As we try to reimagine Private Members' Bills, the first thing would be to adopt one of the more obvious recommendations of the Procedure Committee and rename them 'backbench bills' – or perhaps, to be consistent, draft laws proposed by backbenchers.

There should be fewer of them, better supported, and given some kind of guarantee of time for reaching a decision on each of them. That should be a decision of the whole House, not the result of covert and passive obstruction by the government.

More adventurously, one could imagine a system in which (using petitions or some other route) citizens' groups could put forward proposals for legislation, as is found in several other parliaments worldwide. The preparation of the draft law would then be undertaken by a committee of

MPs working with the proponents of the legislation. Before or after this process, MPs would move a motion for permission to introduce the draft law. If they achieved majority consent, its further progress could be timetabled in much the same way as is proposed for government draft laws.

Delegated legislation

Delegated (or secondary) legislation is law made by ministers under powers granted to them in primary legislation (Acts of Parliament). It has been a subject of controversy almost since its invention. But it is both necessary in the modern world and, in some ways in tune with a reimagined parliament in which MPs are freed up to consider matters of real importance and released from the enervating task of combing through endless piles of incomprehensible, often trivial and usually uncontroversial law.

But both the quantity and scope of delegated powers have grown exponentially in the last few decades, and at an accelerating pace under the combined pressures of Brexit (which required a vast quantity of law to be remade) and the COVID-19 pandemic (which required sweeping legal changes to be made in a tearing hurry). The habit of legislating in this lazy way has become ingrained.

There are two mischiefs that need to be addressed. The first is the carelessness of parliament in granting such powers too readily. The second is the inability (and disinclination) of the House of Commons to exercise proper scrutiny of the exercise of those powers in the form of the 3,000 or so statutory instruments made each year.

Here again, there has been no shortage of more or less imaginative ideas for improving things (see HC 310, 1952; HC 152, 1996; HC 48, 2000). Once again, no government has seen fit to bring these ideas to the House for decision.

The key to any solution is two-fold, and consistent with the need to move Westminster further into the world of the 'working' parliament. The first element is to empower committees to set the agenda for scrutiny of delegated legislation, picking out what is important and deserving of further political attention and able to decide (with appropriate veto powers for opposition and backbenchers) what can be passed without further examination. The second element is to play to the strengths of the upper House and trust it to do much of the detailed work necessary to ensure that delegated legislation is not just politically acceptable but is technically and legally effective (see Hansard Society, 2023).

Scrutiny in this area would be made more meaningful by the involvement of a greater range of expert bodies and (occasionally) the wider public in the pre-legislative scrutiny of proposals for delegated legislation.[4] As with primary legislation, it is the upstream, pre-parliamentary, involvement that is at least as crucial as the procedures of the two Houses themselves.

Financial procedure

There can be no more central question in a democracy than how much to tax whom and on what to spend the money raised. The 'control of supply' is the fundamental tool by which the Commons holds the government in thrall. But MPs give scant attention to the procedures by which this control is supposedly exercised. The Lords are excluded by long-standing constitutional convention from interfering in the business of getting and spending public money. (This convention was to a degree put on a statutory basis by the Parliament Act 1911.)

A key factor in disempowering MPs is the operation of the so-called 'rule of Crown initiative' (see Evans, 2020). This holds (it is not statute law but the common law of parliament) that the Commons cannot amend any spending or taxation proposal put forward by ministers upwards – it can only reduce amounts. It also prevents non-ministerial MPs from introducing their own proposals for novel forms of public expenditure (including that which would be necessary to make proposed legislation effective) without the prior permission of 'the Crown' (otherwise the government of the day).

Empowering committees

The ex-post examination by the Commons in many ways exhibits the approach of a working parliament. In 1852 the Public Accounts Committee and the Exchequer and Audit Department were established to examine whether the money allocated to the government had been spent on the purposes for which it had been intended by parliament. In 1983 the National Audit Act transmogrified the Exchequer and Audit Department into the National Audit Office (NAO), independent but answerable to parliament, and made its chief executive, the Comptroller and Auditor General, an officer of the House of Commons. The system embodies the requirements of a powerful committee, access to expertise, sufficient resources and a large degree of agenda control which our reimagined parliament needs to have.

The system for ex-ante scrutiny of public spending by the Commons is nugatory in comparison with the work of the Public Account Committee/NAO. The old Committee of Supply has been gradually transformed into the 20 days allowed each session to the Opposition to choose the subject of debate, plus three Estimates Days; the old Committee of Ways and Means has effectively been transformed into the five or so days of debate on the financial resolutions put forward by the Chancellor after their Budget Statement. In the 19th century and before, the Commons spent vast tracts of its time sitting as these committees (not always, it has to be said, to much purpose) (see Lee, 2017a, 2017b).

The reformers whose campaign eventually led to the establishment of the departmental select committees in 1979 placed considerable emphasis on these becoming the means by which the Commons could recapture some meaningful control over government spending (see Baines, 1989). The standing orders of these committees charge them with examining '*expenditure*, administration and policy'; but in practice the order of priority has been reversed by the committees and, with a few small (but honourable) exceptions, their examination of departmental spending plans has been often formulaic and always far from systematic.

Formal financial procedure which actually effectively authorises taxation and spending exhibits all the marks of a process designed to keep a parliament firmly in the talking rather than the working category. Vast sums of money are allocated at a tumultuous pace, with the executive once again wielding its power over time to evade parliament. This makes virtually impossible any informed and deliberative public debate over the allocation of taxpayers' money, or about alternative trade-offs between areas of greater or lesser priority. The agenda is entirely dictated by the executive, committees (and indeed the plenary) have no 'rewrite power' as a result of the rule of Crown initiative; the Commons system of permanent and specialist committees congruent with the departments of government do not (with the honourable exception of its Treasury Committee) take financial scrutiny seriously.

To help us reimagine financial procedure, worked-up proposals to push it firmly in the direction of the working parliament model are already available. In July 2019 the Commons Procedure Committee published a report containing its outline proposals for the creation of a 'Budget Committee' (HC 1482, 2019). This was designed to enable the House to take control of the whole bundle of spending plans and Estimates, monitoring the quality of information, engaging in dialogue with the Treasury and other departments, drawing the attention of the House and other committees to key issues, following through on proposals for reform and examples of inadequate attention or timeliness by departments, and so forth. It was designed to be a focus for a genuine dialogue between the House and the Treasury about spending plans.

More imaginatively, such a committee might be a focus for some creative thinking about how the Commons could communicate with the wider public and generate better understanding and some degree of involvement in the processes of spending and taxation.

Crucially, the proposal included the setting up of a proper support system for the Budget Committee, creating an office lying somewhere between the Office for Budget Responsibility and the NAO in both its task and its approach to that task. This would be essential to professionalise the way in which the Commons discharged its responsibilities for the oversight of taxation and spending.

Reimagining the rule of Crown initiative

The more radical procedural change would be to look afresh at the rule of Crown initiative. While most people would agree that it is desirable for the executive to be able to deliver a costed programme of government (and the rule is replicated in some form or other throughout many, if not most, parliamentary democracies), most people might also agree that in a parliamentary democracy alternative programmes should be given some genuine hearing in the legislature, and that a government should be required to justify its opposition to those alternatives and defend them against a potential parliamentary majority, not merely snuff them out through the application of procedural devices.

There is probably a better equilibrium between the visions of anarchy and constitutional collapse put forward by those who adhere to the most stringent defence of the rule of Crown initiative and the somewhat unrealistic aspirations of those who think parliament could, given the opportunity, information and tools, ruthlessly settle on priorities in public expenditure. But maybe the people's representatives *should* be able to decide whether they want to exchange an aircraft carrier for a better-resourced National Health Service; and there are a lot of smaller questions of resourcing that they might well be better placed to decide than the executive. By reimagining the rule we could seek to enable opposition parties and backbench MPs to negotiate in the open with ministers about the cost of any proposals they make, to consider whether there are more cost-effective ways of achieving what they seek, and for them to face up seriously to the trade-offs involved in spending money on their preferred project rather than another.

Conclusion

Time is of the essence. It has always been parliament's most disputed territory, and its supposed scarcity drives the adversarial edge of debate. How much there is, to what it is allocated, whether it can be stretched or squeezed, who gets to fit their quart in a pint pot, how debate can be curtailed and decisions guaranteed, have been the dominating issues of procedural design (see Vieira, 2015; Koß, 2018). When we reimagine procedure we need to find ways of giving the work of parliament more breathing space to engage the heart and imagination in a conversation with the electorate.

As our reimagined parliament travels down the path from a talking legislature to a working one, the time-bound bearpit of the plenary will have to be dethroned and the more open-ended world of committees placed at the centre. The agenda of the plenary will be shaped by the deliberations of committees rather than the diktat of the executive and its shadow.

The committees will have more work to do, including legislative work. That legislative work will be supported in the future by the expert resources which currently serve the select committees.

The House of Commons needs to take control of its own agenda. It needs to create new spaces – temporal, physical and imaginative – for different kinds of work. These spaces need to be imagined in ways which invite more people to be included in new ways in its deliberative work.

The composition and powers of the Lords have been debated (and reformed) for over a century, but the argument continues. Our reimagined parliament may have to encompass a redesigned upper House. The virtues of the present House should be retained – a relatively non-partisan approach, relatively open-ended deliberation, attention to detail, freedom from executive dominance. It should focus on these things it does best, and not seek to superimpose its policy scrutiny on that of the lower House through its own committee system. The Lords is able to think slow, as a counterbalance to the Commons thinking fast. Both are needed, but in our reimagined parliament, while each would focus on what they are better at, they would work far more collaboratively and communicate both more discursively and more effectively than they do now.

The complexity of formal procedure needs to be proportionate to its task, not an impediment to participation. When we come to write down the rules of our reimagined parliament we must do so in language which is natural, plain and transparent. Parliamentary procedure, as noted by Ilbert, should not be 'a mystery, unintelligible except to the initiated'. It should be accessible to all who are prepared to take the trouble to be interested in how their nation is governed, how the laws they obey are made and how decisions have been made about where the money they contribute to the common good is spent.

Much of this reimagining depends upon a rebalancing of power between the executive and parliament. Achieving that is a tall order where government (the 'Crown'), party and parliament are so mysteriously fused as they are in the UK's current constitutional and electoral arrangements. We do, after all, have the examples of the three devolved legislatures of the UK to learn from. Perhaps the imagination will only be freed if the winner-takes-all incentives to power-hoarding of the current electoral system for parliament are addressed. But that is for another, and larger, exercise in reimagination.

Notes

[1] Examples include: S.O. No. 76, which exempts certain participants in certain types of proceedings from 'the rule against speaking more than once', but nowhere in the standing orders is the rule against speaking twice to a question set out; the manner in which on 19 January 2019 Mr Speaker Bercow conjured up a particularly novel interpretation of the word 'forthwith' which caused much controversy which had the standing orders just said what they meant – 'without amendment or debate' – may not have arisen; and the

regular use of the word 'tomorrow' in parliamentary proceedings to mean any future day but tomorrow.
2   Currently House of Commons Standing Order No. 83B provides for a similar (though more restrictive) arrangement. It is never used.
3   A version of this arrangement was used for the Committee of the whole House stages of the Bill to approve the Lisbon Treaty in 2008; see the proceedings of the House of Commons for 29 and 30 January 2008, 5, 6, 20, 25, 26 and 27 February 2008 and 3, 4 and 5 March 2008.
4   Two possible models for expert pre-legislative input into the preparation of delegated legislation already exist in the form of the Social Security Advisory Panel (constituted under the Social Security Act 1992) and the Regulatory Policy Committee, but neither of these bodies is directly responsible to parliament.

10

Conclusion: Thinking Seriously about Starting Over

David Judge and Cristina Leston-Bandeira

Introduction

Reimagining comes in many forms: from 'blue skies thinking', 'thinking outside the box', 'moonshot thinking' and discovering 'what can be' unencumbered by present imaginings of 'what is'; through extrapolating present trends into the future, or modelling prospective scenarios of future events; right through to conceiving reimagining as a process of reciprocal interrogation of 'what does and does not yet exist' (for overviews see, for example, Pulver and Vandeveer, 2009; Cooper, 2019; Inayatullah, 2019; Mention et al, 2019). With this amplitude of forms comes the possibility that adherents of one form might well dismiss other modes of reimagining as suboptimal or even spurious (see, for example, Jackson, 1974: 423). Yet, reimagining is a broad church; capable of accommodating creative thinking which is untethered to current reality, as well as rethinking which prospects the hinterlands between the present and the future. As Kru Desai observed in 2016, when she led KPMG's *Reimagine Public Services* programme, reimagining is not only about boldness and thinking without constraint, but it is also about thinking what might appear 'obvious and simple, because those ideas are often the most creative and innovative' (quoted in Civil Service World, 2016). In many respects, the eclecticism of Desai's approach finds reflection in the preceding chapters of this book: some reimagining is bolder than others and others simpler than some. Nonetheless, all contributors were encouraged to explore and challenge current imaginings of what parliament is and does; with the clear stipulation that the parliament in question was the UK parliament at Westminster. In this sense, reimagining was constrained at its outer limits by the expectation that Westminster would neither be imagined out of existence nor imagined in stasis. Contributors sought, therefore, to break from the pragmatics associated with conventional thinking about parliamentary organisation, behaviours, roles and governance, and rethink, imagine again, what the UK parliament might be and might do. The identification of foundational principles – firmly implanted within encompassing frames of parliamentary space, connectivity and interaction – provided the necessary 'headspace' for making this break. The identified principles were used both to guide the process of reimagining and to provide a touchstone as to how far present parliamentary reality diverged from a reimagined parliamentary future.

Foundational principles

As noted in Chapter 1, in asking contributors to identify a set of basic principles with which to drive a reimagining of parliament the intention was to break with current institutional imaginings. From the outset, therefore, each contributor was left free to identify and justify which principles provided the basis for their prospective reimagining. They were, however, expected to explain why the identified principles were deemed to be foundational, and why they mattered. From this process, two broad categories of principles could be discerned. In overview, the principles in the first category are reflective of broad liberal democratic and social liberal norms and practices and include openness; engagement/connectedness; accessibility; inclusion; equality; fairness; and responsiveness/accountability. Principles in the second category are reflective of more focused spatial, cultural and organisational norms and practices and include: wellness; ethical propriety; sustainability; organisational flexibility; institutional prioritisation; and effective governance. This distinction is not intended to connote a hierarchy of importance, nor are the categories mutually exclusive, instead it simply provides a means of structuring the following discussion.

Category one principles
Openness, connectedness and accessibility

Openness and accessibility were identified by Alex Meakin, in Chapter 2, as elemental principles with which to guide rethinking of parliamentary space at Westminster. First, openness in the architectural sense of designing more open-plan spaces within which parliamentarians and staff could meet and work; and of an opening up of the dark recesses of the parliamentary estate to allow in more natural light and ventilation. Second, openness in the sense of parliament being open to the public and infusing the principle of public access into the architectural design and necessary security structures and working regimes at Westminster. A fundamental question asked by

Meakin, and one requiring an answer in a reimagination of Westminster, is what would the building look like if the public's access to democracy was the primary purpose for the design? An answer would have to envisage direct access for people with disabilities (both visible and non-visible); for those seeking to engage with their representatives; or for those simply seeking to tour parliament to learn more about its history and contemporary workings. Equally, prioritisation of the principle of accessibility would require a holistic approach to balancing the rights of physical access and presence with those of virtual access and participation, and so require a rethinking of the spatial requirements needed to secure such a rebalancing.

The reimagining of parliamentary engagement, by Cristina Leston-Bandeira, Didier Caluwaerts and Daan Vermassen in Chapter 5, starts with the observation that openness is key in modern parliamentary democracies both as an expectation and as a principle. Building from the spatial openness noted by Chapter 2, Leston-Bandeira et al argue that the principle of accessibility should be ingrained in the engagement networks, mechanisms and processes of parliament and should inform its information, education, communication, consultation and participation activities. In part this prioritisation of openness reflects growing citizen expectations of more openness within parliamentary democracies across the world; and with these increased expectations comes the stimulus for rethinking parliamentary public engagement. Yet, Leston-Bandeira et al also argue that, while the principles of openness and accessibility provide keystones for such engagement activities, their interconnectedness with other principles – of relatability, relevance, continuity and sustainability – is vital to reimagining public engagement.

The principles of openness, connectedness and accessibility also feature in the chapters focused upon inter- and intra-institutional interactions. In Chapter 8 Lucinda Maer argues that effective parliamentary scrutiny should be underpinned by the principles of access, connection and interconnection, and engagement. Access in the sense of the ability to obtain information from government and citizens and the capacity to receive (and publish) information in a more open way – through reimagining the technologies (digital, audio-visual, and so on), the language and the choreography of scrutiny. Connection in the sense of linking parliament to the public, and the prosecution of the concerns and issues of citizens through parliamentary scrutiny of the executive and its agencies. A reimagining of connectedness would include greater deliberative innovation into the scrutiny process; alongside a rethinking of partnership working both within Westminster and between parliaments and assemblies in the UK; as well as enhanced networking with other monitoring and regulatory bodies. In turn, the principle of engagement for Maer can be used not only to guide a reimagining of the relationship between citizens and parliament but also to rethink the relationship between parliamentarians and scrutiny processes.

She argues forcefully that: '[f]or parliamentary scrutiny to be effective, it needs to engage parliamentarians. Without them, it does not exist. They have to want to turn up, ask questions and hold the government to account'.

In examining the case for a reimagining of parliamentary procedure, Paul Evans (Chapter 9) starts from the observation that procedural evolution through the years has resulted in levels of complexity, unintelligibility and impotence that have both disempowered and disengaged MPs – and so ultimately their constituents – from the core tasks of parliament. If these historical deficits are to be remedied then a reimagining, drawing upon principles of openness, connectedness and accessibility, is required. In slightly transmuted form, these principles would inform a reimagining of parliamentary procedure to make it accessible to parliamentarians and citizens and, to this end, should be transparent both in the sense of being 'open' about the rules governing parliamentary behaviour and how they are applied, as well as being presented in 'language which is natural, plain and transparent'. Moreover, echoes of some of the 'second category' principles identified earlier in Chapter 5 reverberate in Evans's reimagining: 'relatability' inasmuch as procedure 'must be recognisably human'; 'relevance' insofar as procedure 'must focus attention on what is important'; and 'continuity' to the extent that procedure 'must be predictable' without being unchanging.

Inclusion, equality, fairness and responsiveness

Of all the core principles to be inhered in a reimagining of parliament, that of inclusion provides a tensile thread running through most chapters. Closely interlinked with the principles of openness, connectedness and accessibility, the principle of inclusion signifies the necessary representation of diverse bodies, abilities, voices, opinions, backgrounds, races, ethnicities, genders and identities in parliamentary activities. Thus, inclusion/inclusivity is deemed of central importance in how parliamentary space should be re-envisioned (Chapter 2); how parliamentary rhythms, rituals and symbols might be transformed (Chapter 3); how the 'electoral representative form' of parliament could be creatively reconceived to be more inclusive and to encompass non-electoral modes of representation (Chapter 4); how a rethinking of engagement might produce a parliament that was more welcoming, more relatable and more relevant both to current generations and to future generations of parliamentarians and citizens (Chapter 5); and how a reimagining of the patterns of social interactions, working routines and 'people policies' at Westminster should be underpinned by this principle and so encourage diversity (Chapter 6).

Equality is a foundational principle of democracy. As Saward (2003: 162) notes: 'no system can be minimally democratic without institutionalising equality'. In turn, there is a close connection between the principles of equality and inclusion, for, as Saward (2003: 162) goes on to observe, 'it is difficult to see how anything other than an inclusive, involving form of institutionalising political equality can be acceptable democratically'. This connection of the principles of equality and inclusion is evident in Emma Crewe's discussion in Chapter 3. There she points out how a reimagining of parliamentary symbols and rituals can be used to progress greater equality and inclusion in relation to currently under-represented or un-represented groups in parliament. In her words, 'symbolic recognition of the achievements of minority groups … could act as a challenge to prevailing hierarchies of value'. Alongside such symbolic shifts, equality could be further advanced through redesigning parliamentary space, parliamentary communication and messaging strategies, and the adoption of neutral (non-exclusionary) language. Similarly, in Chapter 4, David Judge reveals how the principles of equality and inclusion are institutionalised, and problematised, in democratic parliamentarism. In his reimagining of parliamentary representation, changes to formal electoral rules would be required but would be insufficient in themselves to secure greater equality and inclusiveness in the representative process. Positive, affirmative action, including compensatory measures, would be needed to challenge the structural and attitudinal barriers which perpetuate representational inequalities. The inclusion of more, and more diverse, voices in the deliberation of public policies through such institutional actions and measures, alongside the situating of parliament as a key nodal point in intricate networks of electoral and non-electoral representation, are essential elements of reimagining parliamentary representation.

The principle of fairness also intersects with the discussion of representational equality, not least in the maxim that formal political equality is secured through free and fair elections. Similarly, Emma Crewe identifies equity, which in its literal sense is something that is fair and just, as one of the principles guiding her reimagining of rhythms, rituals and symbols at Westminster. In Chapter 6 Hannah White maintains that fairness, closely aligned with the principle of non-discrimination, should be at the centre of parliament's people policies and practices. Parliament should not be seen, therefore, to be exempt – or to be capable of exempting itself – from the general right of workers in any workplace to be treated fairly and not to be discriminated against. And, as Paul Evans points out in Chapter 9, if procedure is essential to conferring legitimacy upon the processes and outputs of parliament then 'the way decisions are reached must be seen to be fair (and, so far as possible, be enduring because they are fair)'.

The principles of responsiveness and accountability are distinct but proximate (see Bovens et al, 2014: 8). Responsiveness is taken, in Chapter 4, as an indicator of legitimate representation. In this sense a key dimension of political responsiveness is congruence – of aligning the activities of representatives to the preferences of the represented – and a reimagining of parliamentary representation would explore the institutionalisation of an encompassing system of responsiveness. But Chapter 4 also highlights how the principle of reflexivity may be used to enhance a procedural understanding of responsiveness. In identifying a dynamic interactive process of sustained deliberation, negotiation and contestation between representatives and represented, reflexivity extends the conception of parliamentary responsiveness beyond electoral forms to include non-electoral modes of representation.

Accountability, in a broad sense, comes close to responsiveness in that it is a relational concept – with elected representatives held responsible for their actions and having to answer, or account, for their actions to the represented. When it comes to reimagining parliamentary scrutiny, Lucinda Maer is clear that what makes parliamentary scrutiny unique, and distinct therefore from other forms of scrutiny of executive actions, is that it engages the notion of democratic accountability. And this engagement – this distinctiveness – makes reimagining not only difficult and complicated, but also necessary. Ben Yong, when reimagining parliamentary governance in Chapter 7, identifies parliamentary administration which is both responsive and responsible to be a touchstone of good governance. In particular, he argues that internal governance processes could be reimagined by invoking the principle of 'clear lines of accountability'. This principle when operationalised would provide greater transparency of governance arrangements; and ensure that those making key administrative decisions are clearly identifiable and known to be responsible and accountable for those decisions.

Category two principles

If the principles in the first category are deemed foundational in the sense of being derived from, or associated with, basic liberal democratic and social liberal norms and maxims, the principles identified in this second category are largely, but not exclusively, derived from, or associated with, the tenets of diverse theories of organisation, administration, governance and human resource management.

Wellness as identified by Emma Crewe may be considered something of a crossover principle between the two categories. In part this is reflective of a growing acceptance of the discourses and practices of wellness approaches and regimes within wider state and organisational policies, and in personal relationships. In part, it is also reflective of the specific current 'unwellness' of both internal and external relationships at Westminster; and the need to redress this malaise through the pursuit of wellness. A particular obstacle in such a pursuit, identified by Crewe, is the frenetic and competitive rhythms of parliamentary work. In counterpoint, what Crewe proposes, therefore, is a deacceleration of the rhythms of parliament and of parliamentarians.

As part of this slowing of rhythms, time would be afforded to parliament and parliamentarians to reflect upon how 'the unwellness of the world' has intruded into Westminster in various guises – in 'chronic levels of contestation', 'casual attitude[s] to laws, rules and norms' and a 'challenging of the conventions ... in profound and even destructive ways'. In other words, there is an unwellness in the realm of ethics. A broad agenda of reimagining would have at its heart, therefore, a restoration of the social norm of ethical propriety – encompassing integrity, trustworthiness and honesty.

Similarly, the principle of sustainability has crossover characteristics. In Chapter 5, Leston-Bandeira et al make the case that, in a limited sense, there is 'little point in creating initiatives that cannot be replicated or sustainably run within the parameters of parliamentary practices', but, in a much broader sense, 'engagement needs to consider the consequences of today's decisions for tomorrow's generations'. Transformative thinking in most major policy domains – including the environment, economics, energy, health, agriculture, social welfare – has led to growing recognition of the impact that present decisions have upon future generations and hence the need for 'future-aware' policy generation and policy making. A reimagined parliament should, therefore, embrace such transformative thinking and the promotion of the principle of sustainability through a wide range of engagement mechanisms. This would ensure that parliament would be enabled 'to engage with citizens to collectively explore possible futures and decide on the desired future'.

In his consideration of parliamentary governance, Ben Yong invokes key institutional principles to guide reimagining. His first identified principle – 'prioritising the institution' – might at first sight appear somewhat nebulous, but in the context of parliamentary governance is both clear and directly pertinent to reimagining. If reimagining is going to be impactful, realignment of the current priorities of parliamentarians is required so that governance arrangements and the internal dispositions of parliamentarians have as their central priority the strengthening of the institution of parliament. The principle of 'prioritising the institution' is essential, therefore, in face of the UK parliament's struggle 'with its identity as a holistic institution' (Kelso, 2007: 372; see also Judge and Leston-Bandeira, 2018: 162). As Yong argues, the current ranking of parliamentarians' priorities needs to be inverted so that no longer would 'party come first, fear of how the public might react a close second, and the medium to long term health of the institution last'.

Another key principle invoked by Yong (alongside the principles of 'clear accountability' and 'representation' considered earlier) is 'effective governance'. The trace elements of this principle are effective goal selection, reconciliation and coordination in parliament, clarity as to 'who is in charge, how decisions are made, and who is responsible for implementing decisions', and that governance decisions are made in the 'best interests of parliament as an institution'. Yong concedes that this principle might be considered tautologous, but, nonetheless, serves to redirect thinking towards how effective internal governance can promote the broader effectiveness and legitimacy of the institution of parliament itself. Similarly, Hannah White argues that parliament should aim to create and maintain a workplace culture and environment which would sustain best practice and promote the principle of organisational effectiveness. In her reimagining, parliament 'would conceptualise itself as an exemplar of best workplace practice and culture, rather than an exception to the rules shaping other workplaces'.

Principles, reimagining and further reimagining

Contributors to this book have not found it hard to identify principles to guide a reimagining of parliament. Collectively they have produced listings of principles that are either generic (in their association with liberal democratic and social liberal norms and maxims) or more particularised (in their connection with spatial, cultural, and organisational norms and maxims). Nor have contributors found it hard to identify how these principles have impacted current imaginings of parliament. In essence, the UK parliament in the 2020s can now be seen to be more inclusive; more engaged; more accessible; more representative of the UK's citizenry; more aware that its symbols and rituals should reflect the diversity of the UK population; more committed organisationally to address bullying, harassment or sexual misconduct; and more adept, in its creative use of parliamentary processes and procedures, in scrutinising the executive and holding it to account. But, and it is a significant 'but', contributors also have not found it hard to demonstrate how distant the UK parliament still remains from a comprehensive and profound embodiment of the identified elemental principles across all of its activities. From this position, contributors have offered a range of practical proposals of how this distance between principle and practice might be lessened. Taken together these proposals map a reimagined parliamentary future. This is not a definitive map – in the sense of recording all possible pathways and highways to change – it is more of an indicative map outlining possible routes that others might explore, or divert from, according to which guiding principles are accepted and how these are prioritised. Nonetheless, the following indictive listing emphasises just how broad rethinking needs to be:

- *A reimagining of the parliamentary estate* as a democratic space focuses attention upon new spatial designs for mass public access; safer, shared, collaborative and creatively engaging workspaces; more flexible use of physical space; blended on-site and remote working and participation. In summary what is proposed is a parliamentary building that is accessible

and usable for all, and one that reframes the idea of citizenship and the relationship between the public and the institution of parliament.
- *A reimagining of rhythms, rituals and symbols* necessitates a rethinking of the way social interaction is organised in parliament. A cinemascopic perspective scans the complexity and value of different kinds of knowledge; issues of diversity, equity and inclusion; notions of wellness; and norms associated with ethics and standards. A rethinking of parliamentary interactions prompts among other things, first, a review of how knowledge is valued by parliament and parliamentarians and a reconsideration of the nature and deployment of 'evidence' within Westminster. Second, expansion of the collection of data on the rhythms of who parliament and parliamentarians interact with, and analysis of the quality of those interactions. Third, a deacceleration of the rhythms of political work to allow greater prioritisation of effort. Fourth, abolition of social titles in Westminster and replacement with political ones – of 'Representative' and 'Senator' respectively in the Commons and Lords. Fifth, changes of symbols, culture and rituals to secure not only a gender-sensitive parliament but one also welcoming of other disadvantaged and minority groups. Sixth, a sustained renewal of ethics and standards encompassing cultural norms, education, rituals and recovery of expectations of integrity in political life.
- *A reimagining of parliamentary representation* prompts consideration of an interlocking of electoral modes of representation with non-electoral modes; reconsideration of present 'electoral representative forms' to move to a more proportional electoral system; extended use of electoral quotas and investigation of the potentialities of intersectional 'nested quotas'; institutionalisation of other modes of representation (whether functional; associative; geographical; sortition) into the bicameral system; and positive deployment of regulated artificial intelligence, data-mining and big-data analytics in the representative process.
- *A reimagining of parliamentary public engagement* would take parliamentary business to local communities through expanded outreach programmes; co-create engagement strategies with citizens; integrate deliberative democracy processes; and make parliament more relatable by engaging people through issues rather than processes and through building regularised contacts with external stakeholders. In addition, consideration of the interests of future generations would be promoted through initiatives to give the underaged a voice, and to expect 'reason-giving' from parliamentarians to justify their action to the unborn. All of which would require significant investment in engagement services and staffing.
- *A reimagining of parliament as a workplace* would require parliament to be an exemplar in identifying, adopting and championing best workplace practices. It would lead to the removal of unjustified hierarchies in

the parliamentary workplace; the provision of career-long professional development for parliamentarians and staff; and the outsourcing of recruitment and management of staff and the provision of professional services. The use of hybrid technologies would be maximised to enable appropriate remote participation of parliamentarians in proceedings. Overall, there would be an overarching commitment to the rigorous pursuit of policies to ensure a safe, secure and accessible environment for all those working in Westminster.

- *A reimagining of parliamentary governance* generates practical proposals to encourage parliamentarians to 'think institutionally' and to identify the strengthening of parliament as a central priority. A suite of interlocking mechanisms would be required, including changes to the composition of the Commons Commission to ensure its essential backbench nature; the introduction of a system of elections for its members; additional payment of its members as an extra incentive for MPs to take their institutional roles more seriously. Furthermore, there should be development of portfolio expertise among Commission members; regulation through a Commission code of conduct in standing orders and a Commission Manual; extension of voting rights to appointed lay members; greater transparency of Commission proceedings and deliberations; and promotion of greater coordination and cooperation between the Commissions of the Commons and Lords.
- *A reimagining of parliamentary scrutiny* does not necessarily require radical transformation. Extrapolation from current practices points to ways in which parliamentary scrutiny can be enhanced in the future: captured, for instance, in the imaginative use of urgent questioning procedures; the innovative use of powers to send for 'persons papers and records'; the democratic innovations in engaging the public in committee inquiries; the extension of partnership working to connect research communities and civil society groups with parliamentarians, and committee joint working within Westminster to connect their activities and their members; and new ways of gathering and disseminating information. Ultimately, reimagining of parliamentary scrutiny needs not only to engage the imagination of parliamentarians but also requires the engagement of the executive to maximise the impact of that scrutiny.
- *A reimagining of procedure*, while recognising the sophistication and complexity of the systems for making laws and distributing public money, nonetheless, those systems need to be made more comprehensible and engaging for parliamentarians and public alike. To this end, proposed changes to legislative procedure require a more explicit focus on the themes and principles of draft legislation; and recognition that the intent of legislative proposals should be examined intuitively rather than technocratically. Associated changes would also include: more extensive

public participation at the pre-legislative stage; sector-specialist committee examination of draft laws before consideration by plenary; responsibility for the allocation of time to be placed in the hands of a cross-party timetabling committee; clause-by-clause scrutiny to be conducted by committees, populated by backbenchers, which would be empowered to cross-examine ministers, officials and legal drafters, to engage with expert witnesses, and to report on proposed amendments. In turn, pivotal changes to financial procedure would follow from the creation of a 'Budget Committee' designed to enable the Commons to take control of the whole bundle of executive spending plans and estimates, to open up communication channels with the public, as well as generating wider understanding of the processes of spending and taxation. Cumulatively these changes would assist the Commons to take control of its own agenda, to 'speak human' and 'act human', and to prompt consideration of the wider issue of a rebalancing of power between executive and parliament.

Bounded reimagining and beyond

From the outset, as noted in Chapter 1, the specific focus of this book has been the UK parliament, rooted as it is in a system of representative democracy and in a 'fused-powers' (Kreppel, 2014: 84) system of representative government where the political executive is drawn from and formally responsible to parliament. Reimagining has thus been conducted within specific institutional perimeters demarcated by encircling systemic boundaries; and in this sense what has been produced has been 'bounded reimagining'. Not surprisingly, perhaps, contributors have on occasion found their own reimaginings of parliament chafing against these boundaries. Such friction leads to the conclusion, which is simultaneously both platitudinous yet profound, that a principled metamorphosis of Westminster – a 'starting over' for parliament – is ultimately linked to broader political and social reimaginings within the UK.

The conclusion that reimagining parliament is contingent upon broader reimaginings for its ultimate success does not diminish the rethinking that has been achieved in the preceding chapters. In different ways, each chapter reveals how the boundaries of institutional reimagining illuminate the systemic constraints of the UK's polity and society. In essence, as explained in Chapter 1, reimagining has been conceived as a stepwise process (in its literal sense) in this book. Step 1 was to identify foundational principles to guide rethinking of the specific institution of the UK parliament; step 2 was to explain why these principles are fundamental; step 3 was to outline what a reimagined parliament would look like if it was to align with these principles; and step 4 was to gauge the distance between current imaginings and the principled reimagining of parliament. In taking this last step, however, several contributors not only measured this distance but also identified systemic impediments to a lessening of this gap; and in so doing sketched, in almost spectral form, a fifth step.

Paradoxically this fifth step is a 'step too far' for a book focused exclusively upon reimagining the UK parliament, yet it is a step that needs to be taken for that reimagining to have positive practical effects. This book should serve, therefore, as a prompt for further principled reimagining of key aspects of the broader systems – of parliamentary democracy and parliamentary government – within which the institution of parliament operates in the UK. The conclusion of this book is not the place to consider the exact form that such reimagining should take, yet a few directional pointers can be provided here.

Parliamentary democracy

In terms of parliamentary democracy, and its specific 'electoral representative form', wider structural barriers which perpetuate representational inequalities and exclusions would need to be breached. A future reimagined parliament that privileges the principles of equality and inclusion – in the sense of being optimally representative of UK citizens – would arguably need to be centred within broader reimaginings, separately or collectively, of the UK's electoral system; the candidate selection processes of political parties; and wider social attitudes and state policies and programmes in relation to the abuse, harassment and intimidation (whether in physical, psychological or digital form) encountered daily by women, and a host of minority groups. A reimagining of parliamentary engagement designed to institutionalise continuous 'meaningful and transformative interactions' between parliament and citizens might, arguably, prompt more expansive reimagining beyond parliament itself. A broader reimagining of 'public space' or 'civic space' would acknowledge that 'meaningful public engagement requires civic space for public debate' (IPU, 2022: 14). This reimagining encompasses both the sustenance of basic human rights, as well as the promotion of new online spaces for citizens to exercise these freedoms, and to create and support 'dynamic and inclusive public discourse marked by greater activism and engagement' (IPU, 2022: 15). While a reimagining of parliamentary engagement is necessarily delimited by the organisational logic of this book it is, nonetheless, driven by an expansive imperative, in its push to understand the society in which these political interactions take place. Equally, a reimagining of more open and inclusive processes of parliamentary scrutiny and deliberation, through the gathering and disseminating of a wider and more diverse range of information, should prompt a more fundamental reconsideration of the very nature of 'evidence' and 'knowledge' – of sourcing, validation and evaluation – deployed in parliamentary processes (see, for example, Geddes, 2020b, 2023). By extension, therefore, more basic questions are triggered about what constitutes evidence and knowledge in the 2020s, and how narratives among and between politicians and citizens are negotiated. And, by further extension still, questions need to be addressed as to how rapid developments in the use and regulation of new technologies – such as artificial intelligence, data-mining and big-data analytics – will impact core dynamics of parliamentary democracy.

Parliamentary government

In terms of parliamentary government, the institutional balance between parliament and government would need to be reimagined. The requirement for this broader reimagining can be inferred from the cumulative analyses of specific chapters (not that individual authors would necessarily, or explicitly, take this next step). The current imbalance between the legislature and the executive in the UK is apparent in the chapters analysing the inter- and intra-institutional dimensions of reimagining. Where scrutiny is concerned, Lucinda Maer points out that parliament is, in the last instance, dependent upon the executive being willing to have its actions scrutinised. Where workplace and workforce conditions in Westminster are concerned, Hannah White observes that the executive has not only a vested interest in maintaining working conditions that operate to its advantage but also has the controlling capacity to sustain its own interest. Where procedure is concerned, Paul Evans concludes that MPs have been disempowered and disengaged in the performance of their legislative and scrutinising functions by 'executive capture' of the procedures of parliament. Astutely, Evans points out that his reimagining ultimately depends, therefore, upon a 'rebalancing of power between the executive and parliament', and that achieving this would be 'a tall order … in the UK's current constitutional and electoral arrangements'.

A further step of reimagining, therefore, would be to address this 'tall order' head-on. Yet, it is a step that is beyond the specific remit of each contributor to this book, and a step that not all would wish to take. Indeed, to address the source of executive dominance might very well require a fundamental disentangling of the conjoined leadership hierarchies of government, party and parliament. This would entail cascaded reimagining of many of the key elements of the UK's political and constitutional systems: of the electoral system; of the nature of political parties – of inter-party competition, intra-party organisation, leadership, and interaction between parliamentary and constituency parties; of the interface between the political and administrative branches of the UK's executive – of the respective individual and collective responsibilities of ministers, and the convoluted accountabilities of ministers, their political advisers and civil servants; let alone the complications of attempts to rebalance the relations between the executive, the legislature and the judiciary.

Cascaded reimagining

That a cascaded reimagining of parliamentary democracy and parliamentary government is beyond the boundaries of this book should be apparent from the preceding chapters. That such a cascaded reimagining is needed is evident from the preceding paragraphs of this concluding chapter. While the specific focus of this book has been 'to think seriously about starting over' in conceptualising parliamentary space, connectivity and interaction in Westminster, it has, nevertheless, also prompted questions about the necessity of further serious thinking about reimagining the broader institutions and processes of parliamentary democracy and parliamentary government in the UK. A fitting end to this book, therefore, is simply to call for the boundaries of this book to be breached by a cascade of further reimaginings by others!

References

Abizadeh, A. (2020) 'Representation, bicameralism, political equality, and sortition: reconstituting the second chamber as a randomly selected assembly', *Perspectives on Politics*, 19(3): 791–806.

Adonis, A. (2022) 'Relocating parliament to Birmingham or Manchester is an idea whose time has come', *Prospect*. Available at: https://www.prospectmagazine.co.uk/politics/38288/relocating-parliament-to-birmingham-or-manchester-is-an-idea-whose-time-has-come [Accessed 23 April 2023].

Agarwal, P., Hawkins, O., Amaxopoulou, M., Dempsey, N., Sastry, N. and Wood, E. (2021) 'Hate speech in political discourse: a case study of UK MPs on Twitter', in *Proceedings of the 32nd ACM Conference on Hypertext and Social Media*, New York: Association for Computing Machinery, pp 5–16. https://doi.org/10.1145/3465336.3475113

Baines, P. (1989) 'History and rationale of the 1979 reforms', in G. Drewry (ed), *The New Select Committees* (2nd edn), Oxford: Oxford University Press, pp 13–36.

Ball, S. (2023) 'The 1922 Committee: what are its origins?', *Hansard Society Blog*, 14 April, London: Hansard Society.

Barrett, V.M. (2022) *Parliament: A Question of Management*, Canberra: Australian National University.

Barros, A., Bernardes, C. and Rehbein Rodrigues, M. (2012) 'Comunicação publica e participação política: o caso do Disque-Câmara', *Revista de Estudos de Comunicação*, 13(31): 159–69.

Begg, R.K. (2022) *Reaching Out to Remote Communities: The Case of South Africa*, IPEN (International Parliament Engagement Network) seminar, 9 November.

Benton, M. and Russell, M. (2013) 'Assessing the impact of parliamentary oversight committees: the select committees in the British House of Commons', *Parliamentary Affairs*, 66(4): 772–97.

Besly, N. and Goldsmith, T. (2019) *How Parliament Works* (8th edn), London: Routledge.

Bishop, M. and Barr, B. (2023) *Strengthening Private Office: How the Civil Service Should Improve Support for Ministers*. Available at: https://www.instituteforgovernment.org.uk/sites/default/files/2023-05/strengthening-private-office.pdf [Accessed 5 June 2023].

Block, I. (2019) 'Brexit deadlock could be broken with parliament redesign says Axiom Architects', *Dezeen*. Available at: https://www.dezeen.com/2019/04/05/brexit-deadlock-parliament-re-design-axiom-architects/ [Accessed 13 February 2023].

Bovens, M., Schillemans, T. and Goodin, R.E. (2014) 'Public accountability', in M. Bovens, R.E. Goodin and T. Schillemans (eds), *Oxford Handbook of Public Accountability*, Oxford: Oxford University Press, pp 1–10.

Brito Vieira, M. and Runciman, D. (2008) *Representation*, Cambridge: Polity.

Brown, M.B. (2020) 'Democracy and representation', in M. Cotta and F. Russo (eds) *Research Handbook on Political Representation*, Cheltenham: Edward Elgar, pp 36–47.

Bryant, C. (2017) *Private Member's Bill*. Available at: https://www.chrisbryantmp.org.uk/private-members-bill/ [Accessed 12 April 2023].

Cabinet Office (2023) *Civil Service Statistics: 2022*. Available at: https://www.gov.uk/government/statistics/civil-service-statistics-2022#full-publication-update history [Accessed 9 May 2023].

Caluwaerts, D. and Reuchamps, M. (2018) *The Legitimacy of Citizen-led Deliberative Democracy: The G1000 in Belgium*, London: Routledge.

Campbell, S. (2021) 'Lessons from lockdown', *Baroness Campbell of Surbiton DBE*. Available at: https://baronesscampbellofsurbiton.uk/2021/05/04/lessons-from-lockdown/ [Accessed 17 November 2022].

Castiglione, D. (2015) 'Trajectories and transformations of the democratic representative system', *Global Policy*, 6(1): 8–16.

Castiglione, D. (2020) 'The system of democratic representation and its normative principles', in M. Cotta and F. Russo (eds) *Research Handbook on Political Representation*, Cheltenham: Edward Elgar, pp 16–35.

Castiglione, D. and Warren, M.E. (2006) 'Rethinking democratic representation: eight theoretical issues', paper prepared for *Rethinking Democratic Representation*, Centre for the Study of Democratic Institutions, University of British Columbia, 18–19 May.

Castiglione, D. and Warren, M.E. (2019) 'Rethinking democratic representation: eight theoretical issues and a postscript', in L. Disch (ed), *The Constructivist Turn in Political Representation*, Edinburgh: Edinburgh University Press, pp 21–47.

Cavaliere, P. and Romeo, G. (2022) 'From poisons to antidotes: algorithms as democratic boosters', *European Journal of Risk Regulation*, 13(3): 411–42.

Celis, K. and Erzeel, S. (2020) 'Gender equality', in R. Rohrschneider and J. Thomassen (eds), *Oxford Handbook of Political Representation in Liberal Democracies*, Oxford: Oxford University Press, pp 192–210.

Chambers, S. (2009) 'Rhetoric and the public sphere: has deliberative democracy abandoned mass democracy?', *Political Theory*, 37(3): 323–50.

Childs, S. (2016) *The Good Parliament*, Bristol: University of Bristol.

Civil Service World (2016) 'Reimagining government', *Civil Service World*, 12 March. Available at: https://www.civilserviceworld.com/in-depth/article/reimagining-government [Accessed 11 June 2023].

Climate Assembly (2020) *The Path to Net Zero: Climate Assembly UK Full Report*. Available at: https://www.climateassembly.uk/report/read/final-report.pdf [Accessed 9 May 2023].

Coleman, S. and Moss, G. (2022) '"Politicians don't understand people like me": a qualitative analysis of a lament', *Representation*, 59(2): 155–70.

Collignon, S. and Rüdig, W. (2021) 'Increasing the cost of female representation? The gendered effects of harassment, abuse and intimidation towards parliamentary candidates in the UK', *Journal of Elections, Public Opinion and Parties*, 31(4): 429–49

Collignon, S., Campbell, R. and Rüdig, W. (2022) 'The gendered harassment of parliamentary candidates in the UK', *Political Quarterly*, 93(1): 32–8.

Connolly, J., Flinders, M., Judge, D., Torrance, M. and Tudor, P. (2022) 'Institutions ignored: a history of select committee scrutiny in the House of Lords, 1968–2021', *Parliamentary History*, 41(3): 463–90.

Cook, R. (2003) *Point of Departure*, London: Simon & Schuster.

Cooper, D. (2019) 'Introduction', in D. Cooper, N. Dhawan and J. Newman (eds), *Reimagining the State: Theoretical Challenges and Transformative Possibilities*, London: Routledge, pp 1–15.

Cowley, P. (2001) 'The Commons: Mr Blair's lapdog?', *Parliamentary Affairs*, 54(4): 815–28.

Cox, G. (2009) 'The organization of democratic legislatures', in B. Weingast and D. Wittman (eds), *The Oxford Handbook of Political Economy*, Oxford: Oxford University Press, pp 141–61.

Cox, L. (2018) *The Bullying and Harassment of House of Commons Staff*, Independent Inquiry Report by Dame Laura Cox DBE, London: House of Commons.

Crewe, E. (2005) *Lords of Parliament: Manners, Rituals and Power*, Manchester: Manchester University Press.

Crewe, E. (2015) *House of Commons: An Anthropology of the Work of MPs*, London: Bloomsbury.

Crewe, E. (2021) *The Anthropology of Parliaments: Entanglements in Democratic Politics*, London: Routledge.

Crewe, E. and Evans, P. (2018) 'The significance of rituals in parliament', in C. Leston-Bandeira and L. Thompson (eds), *Exploring Parliament*, Oxford: Oxford University Press, pp 43–52.

Curato, N., Farrell, D., Geißel, B., Grönlund, K., Mockler, P., Pilet, J.-B., Renwick, A., Rose, J., Setälä, M. and Suiter, J. (2021) *Deliberative Mini-Publics: Core Design Features*, Bristol: Bristol University Press.

Dahl, R.A. (2005) 'What political institutions does large-scale democracy require?', *Political Science Quarterly*, 120(2): 187–97.

Dávid-Barrett, E. (2022) 'Shirking self-regulation? Parliamentary standards in the UK', *Public Integrity*. https://doi.org/10.1080/10999922.2022.2075632

Dewey, J. (1916 [2008]) *Democracy and Education: An Introduction to the Philosophy of Education*. The Project Gutenberg eBook of Democracy and Education. Available at: https://www.gutenberg.org/files/852/852-h/852-h.htm. [Accessed 23 November 2022].

Dryzek, J.S. (2010) *Foundations and Frontiers of Deliberative Governance*, Oxford: Oxford University Press.

Dunt, I. (2023) *How Parliament Works ... and Why it Doesn't*, London: Weidenfeld & Nicholson.

Edwards, A. (2007) 'Embedding deliberative democracy: local environmental forums in the Netherlands and the United States', in V. Bekkers, G. Dijkstra and M. Fenger (eds), *Governance and the Democratic Deficit: Assessing the Legitimacy of Governance Practices*, Aldershot: Ashgate, pp 165–82.

Elässer, L. and Schäfer, A. (2022) '(N)one of us? The case for descriptive representation of the contemporary working class', *West European Politics*, 45(6): 1361–84.

Ellenbogen, N. (2019) *An Independent Inquiry into Bullying and Harassment in the House of Lords*. Available at: https://www.parliament.uk/globalassets/documents/lords-committees/house-of-lords-commission/2017-19/ellenbogen-report.pdf [Accessed 19 September 2019].

Ellison, J., Rowley-Conwy, E. and Sims, A. (2022) 'Saving the seat of democracy: the restoration of the Palace of Westminster', *Journal of Legislative Studies*, 67(S1): 69–76.

Eriksen, E.O. and Fossum, J.E. (2012) 'Representation through deliberation: the European case', *Constellations*, 19(2): 325–39.

Evans, P. (2017) 'The growth of many centuries', in P. Evans (ed), *Essays on the History of Parliamentary Procedure: In Honour of Thomas Erskine May*, London: Bloomsbury, pp 1–18.

Evans, P. (2019) 'Select committees 40 years on: wider still and wider may their bounds be set?', *Hansard Society Blog*, 19 November, London: Hansard Society. Available at: https://www.hansardsociety.org.uk/blog/select-committees-40-years-on-wider-still-and-wider-may-their-bounds-be-set [Accessed 9 May 2023].

Evans, P. (2020) *Braking the Law*, London: The Constitution Unit.

Evans, P. (2021a) 'Ping pong and packaging', *Hansard Society Blog*, 13 February, London: Hansard Society.

Evans, P. (2021b) 'The backbench business committee: an unfinished revolution?', *The Constitution Unit Blog*, 22 January, London: University College London Constitution Unit.

Flanigan, B., Gölz, P., Gupta, A., Brett Hennig, B. and Procaccia, A.D. (2021) 'Fair algorithms for selecting citizens' assemblies', *Nature*, 596: 548–52.

Fleming, T.G. (2021) 'Parliamentary procedure under Theresa May: nothing has changed?', *Parliamentary Affairs*, 74(4): 943–63.

Flinders, M., Meakin, A. and Anderson, A. (2019) 'The restoration and renewal of the Palace of Westminster: avoiding the trap and realising the promise', *Political Quarterly*, 90(3): 488–95.

Flinders, M., Judge, D., Rhodes, R.A.W. and Vatter, A. (2022) '"Stretched but not snapped": a response to Russell and Serban on retiring the "Westminster Model"', *Government & Opposition*, 57(2): 353–69.

Garland, J., Palese, M. and Simpson, I. (2020) *Voters Left Voiceless: The 2019 General Election*, London: Electoral Reform Society.

Gastil, J. and Olin Wright, E. (2018) 'Legislature by lot: envisioning sortition within a bicameral system', *Politics & Society*, 46(3): 303–30.

Geddes, M. (2020a) *Dramas at Westminster: Select Committees and the Quest for Accountability*, Manchester: Manchester University Press.

Geddes, M. (2020b) 'The webs of belief around "evidence" in legislatures: the case of select committees in the UK House of Commons', *Public Administration*, 99(1): 40–54.

Geddes, M. (2023) *Good Evidence: How do Select Committees Use Evidence to Support Their Work?*, Edinburgh: University of Edinburgh.

Gershon, S.A., Montoya, C., Bejarano, C. and Brown, N. (2019) 'Intersectional linked fate and political representation', *Politics, Groups, and Identities*, 7(3): 642–53.

Giger, N., Rosset, J. and Bernauer, J. (2012) 'The poor political representation of the poor in comparative perspective', *Representation*, 48(1): 47–61.

Goffman, E. (1959) *The Presentation of Self in Everyday Life*, New York: Doubleday.

Goodin, R.E. (2007) 'Enfranchising all affected interests, and its alternatives', *Philosophy & Public Affairs*, 35(1): 40–68.

Goodin, R.E. (2012) 'How can deliberative democracy get a grip', *Political Quarterly*, 83(4): 806–11.

Gorrell, G., Bakir, M.E., Roberts, I., Greenwood, M.A. and Bontcheva, K. (2020) 'Which politicians receive abuse? Four factors illuminated in the UK general election 2019', *EPJ Data Science*, 9(18): 1–20.

Hansard Society (2011) *A Place for People: Proposals for Enhancing Visitor Engagement with Parliament's Environs*, London: Hansard Society.

Hansard Society (2015) 'Prime Minister's Questions: public attitudes to "People's PMQs"', *Hansard Society Blog*, 11 October, London: Hansard Society. Available at: https://www.hansardsociety.org.uk/blog/public-attitudes-to-peoples-pmqs-infographic [Accessed 9 May 2023].

REFERENCES

Hansard Society (2019) *Audit of Political Engagement 16: The 2019 Report*, London: Hansard Society.

Hansard Society (2023) *Proposals for a New System for Delegated Legislation: A Working Paper of the Hansard Society Delegated Legislation Review*, London: Hansard Society.

Hansard Society Commission on Parliamentary Scrutiny (2001) *The Challenge for Parliament: Making Government Accountable*, London: Vacher Dod.

Harmer, E.R. and Southern, R. (2021) 'Digital microaggressions and everyday othering: an analysis of tweets sent to women members of Parliament in the UK', *Information, Communication & Society*, 24(14): 1998–2015.

HC 1 (2022) *Sessional Returns. House of Commons 2021–22*, London: House of Commons.

HC 48 (2000) *Delegated Legislation*, Procedure Committee, First Report of Session 1999–2000, London: House of Commons.

HC 152 (1996) *Delegated Legislation,* Procedure Committee: First Report of Session 1995–96, London: House of Commons.

HC 188–1 (2013) *Private Members' Bills*, Procedure Committee, Second Report of Session 2013–14, London: House of Commons.

HC 209 (2023) *Smoothing the Cliff Edge: Supporting MPs at Their Point of Departure from Elected Office*, Administration Committee, First Report of Session 2022–23, London: House of Commons.

HC 310 (1952) *Report from the Select Committee on Delegated Legislation*, Session 1952–53, London: House of Commons.

HC 314 (2019) *Standing Orders: Public Business 2019*, London: House of Commons.

HC 372 (2010) *Rebuilding the House: Implementation*, Select Committee on Reform of the House of Commons, First Report of Session 2009–10, London: House of Commons.

HC 401 (2022) *First Report – Select Committees and Contempts: Review of Consultation on Committee Proposals*, Committee of Privileges, First Report of Session 2022–23, London: House of Commons.

HC 521 (2023) *Oral Evidence: Correcting the Record*, Procedure Committee, 30 January 2023. Available at: https://committees.parliament.uk/oralevidence/12606/pdf/ [Accessed 9 May 2023].

HC 684 (2016) *Private Members' Bills*, Procedure Committee, Third Report of Session 2015–16, London: House of Commons.

HC 692 (2014) *House of Commons Governance*, Report of the House of Commons Governance Committee, Session 2014–15, London: House of Commons.

HC 701 (2016) *Private Members' Bills: Observations on the Government Response to the Committee's Third Report of Session 2015–16 HC 684*, Procedure Committee, Second Report of Session 2016–17, London: House of Commons.

HC 1100 (2022) *Oral Evidence: Restoration and Renewal of Parliament*, Public Accounts Committee, 14 March 2022. Available at: https://committees.parliament.uk/oralevidence/10030/default [Accessed 12 May 2022].

HC 1117 (2009) *Rebuilding the House*, Select Committee on Reform of the House of Commons, First Report of Session 2008–09, London: House of Commons.

HC 1171 (2014) *Private Members' Bills: Government Response and Revised Proposals*, Procedure Committee, Fifth Report of Session 2013–14, London: House of Commons.

HC 1482 (2019) *Should There be a Commons Budget Committee*, Procedure Committee, Tenth Report of Session 2017–19, London: House of Commons.

HC 1860 (2019) *The Effectiveness and Influence of the Select Committee System*, Liaison Committee, Fourth Report Session 2017–19, London: House of Commons.

HC 2206 (2019) *Bullying and Harassment of MPs' Parliamentary Staff*, Independent Inquiry Report by Gemma White QC, London: House of Commons.

Heclo, H. (2008) 'Thinking institutionally', in R.A.W. Rhodes, S. Binder and B. Rockman (eds), *The Oxford Handbook of Political Institutions*, Oxford: Oxford University Press, pp 731–42.

Hensman, C. and Schendel-Wilson, C. (2022) *Breaking Down Barriers: Improving Disabled Political Representation and Participation across the United Kingdom*, London: Disability Policy Centre. Available at: https://static1.squarespace.com/static/619e1d7a522f9748f55d6a17/t/6217a1260df6fb6a8f05dcfa/1645715752837/Disabled+Representation+Paper+PDF.pdf [Accessed 24 August 2023].

HL 41/HC 659 (2016) *Restoration and Renewal of the Palace of Westminster*, House of Lords, House of Commons Joint Committee on the Palace of Westminster, First Report of Session 2016–17, London: House of Parliament.

HL 105 (2021) *Government by Diktat: A Call to Return Power to Parliament*, Secondary Legislation Scrutiny Committee, Twentieth Report of Session 2021–22, London: House of Lords.

HL 106 (2021) *Democracy Denied? The Urgent Need to Rebalance Power between Parliament and the Executive*, Delegated Powers and Regulatory Reform Committee, Twelfth Report of Session 2021–22, London: House of Lords.

Holden Bates, S. (2023) 'Is chairing select committees in the House of Commons really an "alternative career"?', *Hansard Society Blog*, 5 January, London: Hansard Society. Available at: https://www.hansardsociety.org.uk/blog/is-chairing-select-committees-in-the-house-of-commons-really-an-alternative [Accessed 9 May 2023].

House of Commons (2022a) *Annual Report to the Finance Committee*, Speaker's Advisory Committee on Works of Art, London: House of Commons.

House of Commons (2022b) *The Health and Social Care Committee's Expert Panel*. Available at: https://ukparliament.shorthandstories.com/health-and-social-care-committee-expert-panel/index.html [Accessed 9 May 2023].

House of Commons and House of Lords Study Group (2012) *Restoration and Renewal of the Palace of Westminster: Pre-Feasibility Study and Preliminary Strategic Business Case*, London: Houses of Parliament.

House of Commons Library (2023) *Number of Urgent Questions in the House of Commons Since 1997*. Available at: https://commonslibrary.parliament.uk/research-briefings/cbp-8344/ [Accessed 30 April 2023].

House of Lords (2022) *Statistics on Business and Membership Session 2021–2022*, London: House of Lords.

House of Lords Commission (2021) *House of Lords External Management Review*, London: House of Lords.

House of Lords Commission (2022) *Commission Operating Manual*. Available at: https://www.parliament.uk/globalassets/documents/lords-committees/house-of-lords-commission/2022-23/commission-working-practices-and-operating-manual-final.pdf [Accessed 1 May 2022].

IDEA (2022) *Gender Quotas Database*, Stockholm: International Institute for Democracy and Electoral Assistance. Available at: https://www.idea.int/data-tools/data/gender-quotas [Accessed 20 December 2022].

Ilbert, C. (1908) 'Preface', in J. Redlich, *The Procedure of the House of Commons: A Study of its History and Present Form, Vol 1*, London: Archibald Constable & Co., pp iii–xxii.

Inayatullah, S. (2019) 'Futurology', in H. Paul (ed), *Critical Terms in Futures Studies*, Cham: Palgrave Macmillan/Springer, pp 139–43.

Involve (2018) *Citizens' Assembly on Social Care – How to Fund Social Care*. Available at: https://involve.org.uk/resources/publications/project-reports/citizens-assembly-social-care-how-fund-social-care [Accessed 9 May 2023].

Involve (2022) *Houses of Parliament Restoration and Renewal Programme: Community Conversations, Final Report*. Available at: https://involve.org.uk/sites/default/files/uploads/docuemnt/RR%20Programme%20Community%20Conversations%20-%20Final%20report%20-%20for%20publication_0.pdf [Accessed 13 February 2023].

IPSA (2012) *Reviewing MPs' Pay and Pensions: A Consultation*, London: Independent Parliamentary Standards Authority.

IPU (2022) *Global Parliamentary Report: Public Engagement in the Work of Parliament*, Geneva: Inter-Parliamentary Union.

IPU and UNDP (2022) *The Global Parliamentary Report on Public Engagement*, Geneva: Inter-Parliamentary Union and United Nations Development Programme. Available at: https://www.ipu.org/our-impact/strong-parliaments/setting-standards/global-parliamentary-report/global-parliamentary-report-2022-public-engagement-in-work-parliament [Accessed 12 April 2023].

Jackson, R.M. (1974) 'Politics and futurology', *Futures*, 6(5): 421–3.

Johnson, C. (2018) 'Select committees: powers and functions', in A. Horne and G. Drewry (eds) *Parliament and the Law* (2nd edn), Oxford: Hart Publishing, pp 103–24.

Joint Committee on Human Rights (2023) 'Correspondence from the Home Secretary relating to the Illegal Migration Bill dated 4 April'. Available at: https://committees.parliament.uk/publications/39134/documents/192432/default/ [Accessed 9 May 2023].

Jones, P. (2011) *The Sociology of Architecture: Constructing Identities*, Liverpool: Liverpool University Press.

Judge, D. (2014) *Democratic Incongruities: Representative Democracy in Britain*, Houndmills: Palgrave Macmillan.

Judge, D. (2021) 'Walking the dark side: evading parliamentary scrutiny', *Political Quarterly*, 92(2): 283–92.

Judge, D. and Leston-Bandeira, C. (2018) 'The institutional representation of Parliament', *Political Studies*, 66(1): 154–72.

Judge, D. and Leston-Bandeira, C. (2021) 'Why it matters to keep asking why legislatures matter', *Journal of Legislative Studies*, 27(2): 155–84.

Kahneman, D. (2011) *Thinking, Fast and Slow*, New York: Farrar, Straus and Giroux.

Keane, J. (2011) 'Monitory democracy?', in S. Alonso, J. Keane and W. Merkel (eds), *The Future of Representative Democracy*, Cambridge: Cambridge University Press, pp 212–35.

Kedar, O., Harsgor, L. and Sheinerman, R.A. (2016) 'Are voters equal under proportional representation?', *American Journal of Political Science*, 60(3): 676–91.

Kelly, R. (2014) *Public Reading Stage of Bills*, House of Commons Library Standard Note SN/PC/06406, London: House of Commons.

Kelly, R. (2023) *House of Commons: Services and Facilities*, House of Commons Library Research Briefing 9595, London: House of Commons.

Kelso, A. (2007) 'Parliament and political disengagement: neither waving nor drowning', *Political Quarterly*, 78(3): 364–73.

King, D. (2019) 'Brexit drama gives BBC Parliament TV biggest week on record', *The Scotsman*. Available at: https://www.scotsman.com/news/politics/brexit-drama-gives-bbc-parliament-tv-biggest-week-record-1408168 [Accessed 22 November 2022].

Knight, J. and Johnson, J. (2007) 'The priority of democracy: a pragmatist approach to political-economic institutions and the burden of justification', *American Political Science Review*, 101(1): 47–61.

König, P.D. and Siewert, M.B. (2021) 'Off balance: systematizing deformations of liberal democracy', *International Political Science Review*, 42(5): 690–704.

Koß, M. (2018) *Parliaments in Time: The Evolution of Legislative Democracy in Western Europe. 1866–2015*, Oxford: Oxford University Press.

KPMG (2020) *Reimagining the Future, Rethinking Strategy*. Available at: https://boardleadership.kpmg.us/relevant-topics/articles/2021/reimagining-the-future-rethinking-strategy.html [Accessed 13 March 2023].

Kreppel, A. (2014) 'Typologies and classifications', in S. Martin, T. Saalfeld and K. Strøm (eds), *Oxford Handbook of Legislative Studies*, Oxford: Oxford University Press, pp 82–100.

Lafont, C. (2017) 'Can democracy be deliberative and participatory? The democratic case for political uses of mini-publics', *Dædalus*, 146(3): 85–105.

Landemore, H. (2020) *Open Democracy: Reinventing Popular Rule for the Twenty-First Century*, Princeton: Princeton University Press.

Landemore, H. (2021) 'Open democracy and digital technologies', in L. Bernholz, H. Landemore and R. Reich (eds), *Digital Technology and Democratic Theory*, Chicago: University of Chicago Press, pp 62–89.

Latour, B. (2003) 'What if we talked politics a little', *Contemporary Political Theory*, 2(2): 143–64.

Latour, B. (2010) *Making of Law: An Ethnography of the Conseil d'Etat*, London: Polity.

Lee, C. (2017a) 'May on money: supply proceedings and the functions of a legislature', in P. Evans (ed), *Essays on the History of Parliamentary Procedure: In Honour of Thomas Erskine May*, London: Bloomsbury, pp 171–87.

Lee, C. (2017b) 'A road not taken: select committees and the estimates, 1880–1904', in P. Evans (ed), *Essays on the History of Parliamentary Procedure: In Honour of Thomas Erskine May*, London: Bloomsbury, pp 269–84.

Lee, C. (2020) 'Archibald Milman and the evolution of the closure – part 1: Origins to 1881', *The Table, the Journal of the Society of Clerks at the Table in the Commonwealth*, 88: 5–54.

Lee, C. (2021) 'Archibald Milman and the evolution of the closure – part 2: 1882–1885', *The Table, the Journal of the Society of Clerks at the Table in the Commonwealth*, 89: 5–55.

Lee, C. and Yong, B. (2022) 'Paying for parliament', in A. Horne, L. Thompson and B. Yong (eds), *Parliament and the Law* (3rd edn), Oxford: Hart Publishing, pp 57–86.

Lefebvre, H. (2013) *Rhythmanalysis: Space, Time and Everyday Life*, London: Bloomsbury Academic.

Leston-Bandeira, C. (2014) 'The pursuit of legitimacy as a key driver for public engagement: the European Parliament case', *Parliamentary Affairs*, 67(2): 415–36.

Leston-Bandeira, C. (2016) 'Why symbolic representation frames parliamentary public engagement', *British Journal of Politics and International Relations*, 18(2): 498–516.

Leston-Bandeira, C. (2019) 'Parliamentary petitions and public engagement: an empirical analysis of the role of e-petitions', *Policy & Politics*, 47(3): 415–36.

Leston-Bandeira, C. and Thompson, L. (2017) 'Integrating the view of the public into the formal legislative process: public reading stage in the UK House of Commons', *Journal of Legislative Studies*, 23(4): 508–28.

Leston-Bandeira, C. and Walker, A. (2018) 'Parliament and public engagement', in C. Leston-Bandeira and L. Thompson (eds), *Exploring Parliament*, Oxford: Oxford University Press, pp 308–21.

Leston-Bandeira, C. and Siefken, S. (2023) 'The development of public engagement as a core institutional role for parliaments', *Journal of Legislative Studies*, 29(3): 361–79.

Levi-Faur, D. (2012) 'From "big government" to "big governance"?', in D. Levi-Faur (ed), *The Oxford Handbook of Governance*, Oxford: Oxford University Press, pp 3–18.

Lidington, D. (2021) *Twitter*, 5:36pm, 3 October. Available at: https://twitter.com/DLidington/status/1444703013202022413 [Accessed 12 May 2022].

Loewenberg, G. (2011) *On Legislatures: The Puzzle of Representation*, Boulder: Paradigm Publishers.

Lucas, C. (2015) *Honourable Friends?* London: Portobello.

Lukes, S. (1975) 'Political ritual and social integration', *Sociology*, 9(2): 289–308.

MacKenzie, M.K. (2021) *Future Publics: Democracy, Deliberation, and Future-Regarding Collective Action*, New York: Oxford University Press.

Maer, L. (2019) 'Select committee reform: shifting the balance and pushing the boundaries', *Parliamentary Affairs*, 72(4): 761–78.

Manin, B. (1997) *The Principle of Representative Government*, Cambridge: Cambridge University Press.

Manow, P. (2010) *In the King's Shadow: The Political Anatomy of Democratic Representation*, Cambridge: Polity Press.

Mansbridge, J. (2011) 'Clarifying the concept of representation', *American Political Science Review*, 105(3): 621–30.

Mansbridge, J. (2020) 'The evolution of political representation in liberal democracies: concepts and practices', in R. Rohrschneider and J. Thomassen (eds), *Oxford Handbook of Political Representation in Liberal Democracies*, Oxford: Oxford University Press, pp 16–54.

REFERENCES

Marshall, J., Lilly, A., Thimont Jack, M. and White, H. (2019) *Parliamentary Monitor 2019: Snapshot*, September. Available at: https://www.institutefo rgovernment.org.uk/sites/default/files/publications/parliamentary-moni tor-2019-snapshot-WEB.pdf [Accessed 1 November 2022].

Matthews, F. (2021) 'The value of "between-election" political participation: do parliamentary e-petitions matter to political elites?', *British Journal of Politics and International Relations*, 23(3): 410–29.

May, T.E. (2019) *Treatise on the Law, Privileges, Proceedings and Usage of Parliament* (25th edn). Available at: https://erskinemay.parliament.uk [Accessed 19 April 2023].

McGilchrist, I. (2009) *The Master and His Emissary: The Divided Brain and the Making of the Western World*, New Haven: Yale University Press.

McInnes, R. (2020) *General Election 2019: Turning Votes into Seats*, Insight, House of Commons Library. Available at: https://commonslibrary.par liament.uk/general-election-2019-turning-votes-into-seats/ [Accessed 12 November 2022].

Meakin, A. (2019) *Understanding the Restoration and Renewal of the Palace of Westminster: An Analysis of Institutional Change in the UK Parliament*, Sheffield: Sheffield University.

Meakin, A. (2022) 'Restoration and renewal of the Palace of Westminster: a parliamentary governance challenge', in A. Horne, L. Thompson and B. Yong (eds), *Parliament and the Law* (3rd edn), Oxford: Hart Publishing, pp 87–110.

Mention, A.L., Ferreira, J.J.P. and Torkkeli, M. (2019) 'Moonshot thinking: wishful thinking or business as usual?', *Journal of Innovation Management*, 7(1): 1–6.

Merrick, R. (2020) 'Coronavirus: senior Tory says government is "euthanising" vulnerable MPs as parliament ordered to return in June', *The Independent*, 20 May. Available at: https://www.independent.co.uk/news/ uk/politics/coronavirus-parliament-return-june-mps-robert-halfon-a9523 616.html [Accessed 1 November 2022].

Miller, C.M. (2021) *Gendering the Everyday in the UK House of Commons: Beneath the Spectacle*, Basingstoke: Palgrave Macmillan.

Montoya, C.M., Bejarano, C., Brown, N.E. and Gershon, S.A. (2022) 'The intersectional dynamics of descriptive representation', *Politics & Gender*, 48(2): 483–512.

Mordaunt, P. (2023) *Delivering through Parliament for the British People*. Available at: https://www.gov.uk/government/speeches/delivering-thro ugh-parliament-for-the-british-people [Accessed 30 April 2023].

Morse, A. (2022) *Independent Review of Financial Management in the House of Commons*. Available at: https://www.parliament.uk/contentassets/797ad 54c7ea9440eb5c321da791f6683/7197_go_morse_review_a4_digital_pro of2.pdf [Accessed 18 January 2023].

New Zealand Parliament (2022) *Plain Language Bill*. Available at: https://www.parliament.nz/en/pb/bills-and-laws/bills-proposed-laws/document/BILL_115953/plain-language-bill [Accessed 12 April 2023].

Niessen, C. and Reuchamps, M. (2022) 'Institutionalising citizen deliberation in parliament: the permanent citizens' dialogue in the German-speaking community of Belgium', *Parliamentary Affairs*, 75(1): 135–53.

Norton, P. (2001) 'Playing by the rules: the constraining hand of parliamentary procedure', *Journal of Legislative Studies*, 7(3): 13–33.

Norton, P. (2017) 'Speaking for parliament', *Parliamentary Affairs*, 70(2): 191–206.

Norton, P. (2019) 'Departmental select committees: the reform of the century?', *Parliamentary Affairs*, 72(4): 727–41.

Office of National Statistics (2022) *Trust in Government 2022: Worksheet 1.4*. Available at: https://www.ons.gov.uk/peoplepopulationandcommunity/wellbeing/datasets/trustingovernmentuk [Accessed 21 April 2023].

O'Flynn, I. and Sood, G. (2014) 'What would Dahl say? An appraisal of the democratic credentials of deliberative polls and other mini-publics', in K. Grönlund, A. Bächtiger and M. Setälä (eds), *Deliberative Mini-Publics: Practices, Promises, Pitfalls*, London: ECPR Press, pp 41–58.

Palonen, K. (2019) *Parliamentary Thinking, Rhetoric, Politics and Society*, London: Palgrave Macmillan.

Parkinson, J. (2012) *Democracy and Public Space: The Physical Sites of Democratic Performance*, Oxford: Oxford University Press.

Parkinson, J. (2013) 'How legislatures work – and should work – as public space', *Democratization*, 20(3): 438–55.

Patel, P. and Quilter-Pinner, H. (2022) *Road to Renewal: Elections, Parties and the Case for Renewing Democracy*, London: IPPR.

Pencheva, I., Esteve, M. and Mikhaylov, S.J. (2020) 'Big data and AI: a transformational shift for government: so, what next for research?', *Public Policy and Administration*, 35(1): 24–44.

Peters, G.B. (2012) 'Governance as political theory', in D. Levi-Faur (ed), *The Oxford Handbook of Governance*, Oxford: Oxford University Press, pp 19–32.

Phillips, A. (2020) 'Descriptive representation revisited', in R. Rohrschneider and J. Thomassen (eds), *Oxford Handbook of Political Representation in Liberal Democracies*, Oxford: Oxford University Press, pp 174–91.

Pitkin, H.F. (1967) *The Concept of Representation*, Berkeley: University of California Press.

Policy Institute (2023) *Democracy in Theory and Practice: How UK Attitudes Compare Internationally*, The UK in the World Values Survey, London: Policy Institute King's College. Available at: https://www.kcl.ac.uk/policy-institute/assets/democracy-in-theory-and-practice.pdf [Accessed 21 April 2023].

Prior, A. and Sivashankar, M. (2023) 'Our future in space: the physical and virtual opening-up of parliaments to publics', *Journal of Legislative Studies*, 29(3): 463–81.

Pulver, S. and Vandeveer, S. (2009) 'Thinking about tomorrows: scenarios, global environmental politics, and social science scholarship', *Global Environmental Politics*, 9(2): 1–13.

Puwar, N. (2004) *Space Invaders: Race, Gender and Bodies out of Place*, London: Berg.

Puwar, N. (2021) 'The force of the somatic norm: women as space invaders in the UK parliament', in S. Rai, M. Gluhovic, S. Jestrovic and M. Saward (eds), *The Oxford Handbook of Politics and Performance*, Oxford: Oxford University Press, pp 251–64.

Rai, S.M. (2010) 'Analysing ceremony and ritual in parliament', *The Journal of Legislative Studies*, 16(3): 284–97.

Rai, S.M. (2015) 'Political performance: a framework for analysing democratic politics', *Political Studies*, 63(5): 1179–97.

Rai, S.M. (2017) 'Performance and politics: an approach to symbolic representation', *Politics, Groups, and Identities*, 5(3): 506–11.

Ravenscroft, T. (2021) 'Anne Lacaton and Jean-Philippe Vassal win Pritzker Architectural Prize', *dezeen*. Available at: https://www.dezeen.com. [Accessed 13 February 2023].

Redlich, J. (1908) *The Procedure of the House of Commons: A Study of its History and Present Form, Vol 1*, London: Archibald Constable & Co.

Reingold, B. (2022) 'An intersectional approach to legislative representation', *PS: Political Science & Politics*, 55(2): 294–7.

Restoration and Renewal (2022) *Understanding the Public's View*, London: Houses of Parliament. Available at: https://assets.ctfassets.net/vuylkhqhtihf/1tUxC1EDN0jOgf4nsky2Uy/d95f392c76794915cb4d704484142775/RR_Public_Views_summary_final.pdf [Accessed 13 February 2023].

Roberts, N.S. (2009) 'Grand designs: parliamentary architecture, art, and accessibility', *Political Science*, 61(2): 75–86.

Rogers, R.G. (2015) 'The Welsh Assembly', in Design Commission, *Designing Democracy*, London: Policy Connect, pp 13–14.

Rosa, H. (2013) *Social Acceleration: A New Theory of Modernity*, New York: Columbia University Press.

Rosa, H. (2019) *Resonance: A Sociology of Our Relationship to the World*, Cambridge: Polity.

Rosa, H. (2020) *The Uncontrollability of the World*, Cambridge: Polity.

Runciman, D. (2007) 'The paradox of political representation', *Journal of Political Philosophy*, 15(1): 93–114.

Runciman, D. (2008) *Political Hypocrisy: The Mask of Power, from Hobbes to Orwell and Beyond*, Princeton: Princeton University Press.

Rush, M. and Giddings, P. (2011) *Parliamentary Socialisation: Learning the Ropes or Determining Behaviour?*, Basingstoke: Palgrave Macmillan.

Russell, M. (2011) '"Never allow a crisis to go to waste": The Wright Committee reforms to strengthen the House of Commons', *Parliamentary Affairs*, 64(4): 612–33.

Russell, M. and Gover, D. (2017) *Legislation at Westminster: Parliamentary Actors and Influence in the Making of British Law*, Oxford: Oxford University Press.

Russell, M. and Gover, D. (2021) *Taking Back Control: Why the House of Commons Should Govern Its Own Time*, London: The Constitution Unit.

Russell, M. and James, L. (2023) *The Parliamentary Battle Over Brexit*, Oxford: Oxford University Press.

Salisbury, E. (2021) 'Parliament during the pandemic – a staffer's perspective', in Study of Parliament Group (ed), *Parliaments and the Pandemic*. Available at: https://studyofparliamentgroup.org/wp-content/uploads/2021/01/Parliaments-and-the-Pandemic.pdf [Accessed 12 April 2023].

Sanders, A. and Moles, K. (2013) 'The spatial practice of public engagement: "doing" geography in the south Wales valleys', *Social & Cultural Geography*, 14(1): 23–40.

Saward, M. (2003) 'Enacting democracy', *Political Studies*, 51(1): 161–79.

Saward, M. (2010) *The Representative Claim*, Oxford: Oxford University Press.

Setälä, M. (2017) 'Connecting deliberative mini-publics to representative decision making', *European Journal of Political Research*, 56(4): 846–63.

Shenton, C. (2016) *Mr Barry's War*, Oxford: Oxford University Press.

Shepherd, A., Ville, L., Marren, C., Whitelock-Gibbs, A. and Bazeley, A. (2023) *A House for Everyone. A Case for Modernising Parliament*, London: Fawcett Society. Available at: https://www.fawcettsociety.org.uk/Handlers/Download.ashx?IDMF=0ebb1e86-c3f9-4e41-8bc5-740cee1181cc [Accessed 4 June 2023].

Sortition Foundation (2022) *A House of Citizens for the UK Parliament*, London: Sortition Foundation.

Steffani, W. (1979) *Parlamentarische und präsidentielle Demokratie*, Opladen: Westdeutscher Verlag.

Straw, J. (2012) *Last Man Standing: Memoirs of a Political Survivor*, London: Pan Macmillan.

Street, B.V. (1993) 'Culture is a verb: anthropological aspects of language and cultural process', in D. Graddol, L. Thompson and M. Byram (eds), *Language and Culture*, Clevedon: British Association of Applied Linguistics, pp 23–43.

Study of Parliament Group (2021) *Parliaments and the Pandemic*, London: Study of Parliament Group. Available at: https://studyofparliamentgroup.org/wp-content/uploads/2021/01/Parliaments-and-the-Pandemic.pdf [Accessed 15 May 2023].

Therborn, G. (2014) 'Modern monumentality: European experiences', in J. Osborne (ed), *Approaching Monumentality in Archaeology*, New York: State University of New York Press, pp 333–52.

Thévoz, S. (2022) '18 times Boris Johnson was accused of breaking rules – and got away with it', *OpenDemocracyUK*. Available at: https://www.opendemocracy.net/en/opendemocracyuk/boris-johnson-broke-rules-no-punishment/ [Accessed 28 April 2022].

Thompson, L. (2015) *Making British Law: Committees in Action*, Houndmills: Palgrave Macmillan.

Thompson, L. (2020) *The End of the Small Party? Change UK and the Challenges of Parliamentary Politics*, Manchester: Manchester University Press.

Tritschler, L. (2020) 'Most non-White UK MPs have experienced racism, study', *Politico*, 17 February. Available at: https://www.politico.eu/article/most-non-white-uk-mps-have-experienced-racism-study-itv/ [Accessed 4 June 2023].

UK Parliament (2018) *Assaults on Emergency Workers (Offences) Act 2018*. Available at: https://bills.parliament.uk/bills/2058 [Accessed 12 April 2023].

UK Parliament (2022) *Understanding the Public's View 2020–2022*, House of Parliament Restoration and Renewal. Available at: https://assets.ctfassets.net/vuylkhqhtihf/5JgjzVGBspFldYgthGxAZP/b57e12dc9f95ac7a5447cb9ca73b3e65/RR_Public_Views_summary_final.pdf [Accessed 13 February 2023].

UK Parliament (2023a) *The Story of Parliament*. Available at: https://www.parliament.uk/globalassets/documents/commons-information-office/Publications-2015/THE-STORY-OF-PARLIAMENT-web.pdf. [Accessed 19 April 2023].

UK Parliament (2023b) *Checking the Work of Government*. Available at: https://www.parliament.uk/about/how/role/scrutiny/ [Accessed 19 April 2023].

UK Parliament (2023c) *Conduct in Parliament*. Available at: https://www.parliament.uk/mps-lords-and-offices/standards-and-financial-interests/parliaments-behaviour-code/ [Accessed 19 April 2023].

Urbinati, N. (2006) *Representative Democracy*, Chicago: University of Chicago Press.

Urbinati, N. (2010) 'Unpolitical democracy', *Political Theory*, 38(1): 65–92.

Urbinati, N. (2011) 'Representative democracy and its critics', in S. Alonso, J. Keane and W. Merkel (eds), *The Future of Representative Democracy*, Cambridge: Cambridge University Press, pp 23–49.

Urwin, R. (2022) 'Mothers of Parliament: the challenges of combining parenthood and politics', *The House*. Available at: https://www.politicshome.com/thehouse/article/mothers-of-parliament-the-challenges-of-combining-parenthood-and-politics [Accessed 13 February 2023].

Vale, L.J. (2008) *Architecture, Power and National* Identity (2nd edn), Abingdon: Routledge.

Valsangiacomo, C. (2021) 'Political representation in liquid democracy', *Frontiers in Political Science*, 3(Article 591853): 1–14.

Verge, T. (2022) 'Evoking equality: the gender sensitivity of parliaments through their symbolic function', *Political Studies*, 70(4): 1048–67.

Vieira, R.A. (2015) *Time and Politics: Parliament and the Culture of Modernity in Britain and the British World*, Oxford: Oxford University Press.

Walker, A. (2012) 'A people's parliament?', *Parliamentary Affairs*, 65(1): 270–80.

Walker, A., Jurczak, N., Bochel, C. and Leston-Bandeira, C. (2019) 'How public engagement became a core part of the House of Commons Select Committees', *Parliamentary Affairs*, 72(4): 965–86.

Waylen, G. (2014) 'Space, place and symbols: transforming parliamentary buildings in Germany and South Africa', in S. Rai and R. Johnson (eds), *Democracy in Practice: Ceremony and Ritual in Parliament*, Basingstoke: Palgrave Macmillan, pp 211–33.

White, H. (2022) *Held in Contempt: What's Wrong with the House of Commons?*, Manchester: Manchester University Press.

Wollaston, S. (2019) *The Good Committee*, Michael Ryle Memorial Lecture, delivered 27 June. Available at: https://www.parliament.uk/globalassets/documents/40-years-of-select-committees/Speech-on-27-June-2019-in-praise-of-Select-Committees.pdf [Accessed 9 May 2023].

Wright, A. (1994) *Citizens and Subjects: An Essay on British Politics*, London: Routledge.

Wright, A. (2004) 'Prospects for parliamentary reform', *Parliamentary Affairs*, 57(4): 867–76.

Yong, B. (2018) 'The governance of parliament', in A. Horne and G. Drewry (eds), *Parliament and the Law* (2nd edn), Oxford: Hart Publishing, pp 75–102.

Yong, B. (2022) 'Exposing the hidden wiring of parliament', *UK Constitutional Law Blog*, 10 January. Available at: https://ukconstitutionallaw.org/2022/01/10/ben-yong-exposing-the-hidden-wiring-of-parliament/ [Accessed 1 May 2023].

Index

A

Abizadeh, A. 61
abuse 34, 59
academia, links with 119
accountability
  governance 100, 102, 105
  inter-institutional interaction 9
  Mediator Parliament 66
  representation 49, 50
  responsiveness/reflexivity 146–7
  rhythms, rituals and symbols 34, 40, 45
  see also scrutiny
adjournment debates 117
administration 93, 99–103
Adonis, A. 6
affirmative action 58, 146
Agarwal, P. 34
agenda control 38, 79, 128, 131–2, 140, 152
aggregation of interests 64, 70
AI (artificial intelligence) 62, 150, 154
algorithms 61–2
alienation 33, 37, 39, 126
all-party groups 121
Amess, David 87
annual parliamentary sessions 135
  see also rhythms of parliament
annual reports 40
architecture 5, 6, 143–4
artwork 6, 22, 29, 44
Audit Committees 109
authenticity 46
authorisation of executive actions 8, 49, 50

B

backbench bills 135–6
Backbench Business Committee 131–2
Barr, B. 91
Barrett, V.M. 12
Behaviour Code 88
Belgium 74
belonging 7, 68
Benger, John 24
Bercow, John 88, 140n1
'bicameral issue' 102, 108, 109–10

big data 62, 150, 154
Bills procedures 133, 134–6
Bishop, M. 91
Block, I. 23
Bolsonaro, Jair 46
Bradley, Karen 20
Brazil 73
Brexit 10, 13, 29, 136
Brexit Impact Assessments 114–15
British Sign Language 72, 79, 118
Brito Vieira, M. 54
Bryant, Chris 80
Budget Committee 138, 152
bullying 11, 26, 91, 92, 95, 149

C

call lists 93
Campbell of Surbiton, Baroness 21
candidates for political office 58–9
Castiglione, D. 49, 50
catering facilities 25, 89
'celebrity chairs' 107
Centre for Education 79
ceremonies 33–4
Chamber Engagement Team 79
Childs, S. 22, 43, 90
choirstall layouts 23
citizen assemblies 74, 79, 117, 120
citizen groups' draft laws 135–6
citizen panels 60
citizen-led practices 57
citizen-parliament engagement 65–82
civic spaces 153
civil society 59, 66
class system 42–3, 56–7
clerks 101
Clifton-Brown, Sir Geoffrey 18
club, parliament as akin to 84–5
co-creation 74
codes of conduct 88, 91–2, 107, 151
Coleman, S. 8
collaborative working 26, 108, 109–10, 118–20
collective decision-making 107
collective unity 54–5

173

collectivity, parliament as 48–9, 69, 90
Collignon, S. 59
colonialism 44
Commissions (HoC and HoL) 93, 101–2, 103, 105–9, 151
Committees on Standards and Privileges 45
Commons Procedure Committee 138
communities of practice 73
concerns of electorate, finding out about 72–3, 75–6
conflicts of interest 35
Connecting with the Public (2004) 66
connectivity 4, 7–9, 68, 144
consensus 124
consent 8
consequentiality 76–7
Conservative Party, 1922 Committee 128
constituency-based work 25, 30, 35, 40, 71, 80, 85, 121
constitution, uncodified 2, 90
consultations 79–80
contracts of employment 84
contributors, selection criteria for 3
Cook, Robin 123, 125
Cooper, D. 1
COVID-19
　culture 93–4
　delegated/secondary legislation 136
　government contracts 115
　and physical presence in parliament 19–20, 25
　policy responses 10
　workforce questions 83, 85–6
Cowley, P. 23
Cox, Jo 87
Crewe, E. 22, 33, 35, 36, 40, 42
cross-bench Lords 85
Crown initiative rule 137, 139
culture 36, 45, 84–5, 86, 89–94
Curato, N. 61

D

Dahl, R.A. 55, 58–9
Dávid-Barrett, E. 11
Davis, David 20
debate and deliberation 13, 130
decision-making processes
　collective decision-making 107
　consequentiality 76–7
　cross-party 101
　financial procedures 137
　governance 99–100
　House of Lords 103
　joint HoC/HoL 108, 109–10
　mini-publics 61
　pace of politics 70
　public spending 137–9
decline in standards 35–6
deference 35
delegated/secondary legislation 136

deliberative praxis 61, 74, 79, 114, 128, 130
democracy
　belief in principle of 2
　beyond bounded reimagining 153–4
　crises of 66
　and education 45
　and equality 145–6
　and honesty 46
　legitimation 49
　parliamentary buildings 17–19, 27–30
　public engagement 65–82
　right to participate in democracy 37
Desai, K. 142
descriptive representation 52
devolved nations 57, 63, 91, 106, 120
Dewey, J. 45
digital technologies
　24/7 nature of 34, 35, 65, 70
　access to parliament buildings 29
　AI (artificial intelligence) 62, 150, 154
　algorithms 61–2
　big data 62, 150, 154
　connectivity 8
　culture of leaking 34
　electronic voting 19–20, 22, 25, 93
　e-petitions 23, 79, 80, 117
　information publication 116
　MP-citizen interactions 40
　public engagement 73, 80–1
　screens for news updates 23
disability
　descriptive representation 52
　MPs 20, 21, 56, 89
　Palace of Westminster 29, 90, 95–6, 144
　physical space 21, 22, 29, 71, 144
　virtual participation 20, 21
disruption, as process 45
diversity
　artwork 6, 22, 29, 44
　foundational principles 145–7
　public engagement 68, 74
　rhythms of parliament 37, 39
　unity and the 'presumption of generality' 54–5, 62–3
　virtual participation 20, 21
　workplaces 86, 88–90, 95
division bells 89
domestic committees 102, 107, 109
draft laws 133–4, 135–6, 151
Dryzek, J.S. 61

E

education 45, 79
Elässer, L. 52, 57
election campaigning 40
electoral processes
　inclusiveness 51
　public engagement 69–70
　reform 146, 153

INDEX

representation 8, 49, 50, 55–6
workplaces 89
electronic voting 22, 25, 93
Elizabeth Tower 23
Ellenbogen, N. 26
Ellison, J. 6
employees of parliament 83–5, 89–90
employment rights 88–9
empowerment 67
e-petitions 23, 79, 80, 117
equality
  equality of result 57–8
  foundational principles 145–7
  representation 52–3, 55–9, 63
  workplaces 86, 88–90, 95
Equality Act (2010) 88
equity 37, 146
Eriksen, E.O. 54
Erskine May's Parliamentary Procedure 108, 127
essentialism 52
ethics 35–6, 37, 44–5, 47
ethnic minorities 28, 34, 52, 56, 59, 89–90
European Parliament 106
evaluation 81, 153
Evans, P. 13, 33, 42, 116, 127, 130, 131, 137
evidence, standards of 33, 44, 47, 76, 115–16, 120, 150, 153
exclusion 38–9, 51
  see also inclusiveness
executive/legislature separation 110, 154
exhibitions 44
expenses scandal (2009) 66, 110
experts 34–5, 47, 76, 108, 119, 122, 134, 152
ex-public schoolboys 22

F

families, MPs with 22
Family Room 22
fast-tracking legislation 10
Fawcett Society 90
fear of reprisal 59
feedback loops 76, 80, 116
Finance Committee 102
financial procedures 137–8
first-past-the-post elections 56–7
Fleming, T.G. 13
flexible seating 22
Flinders, M. 2
Fossum, J.E. 54
foundational principles 143–9
framework/skeleton bills 10
franchise, extensions of 8
Freedom of Information Act 116
freedom of speech 44
'fused-powers' relationship 2, 8, 110, 140, 152
future generations 77–8, 148, 150

G

Gardner of Kimble, Lord 17
Garland, J. 56
Geddes, M. 10, 130, 132, 154
gender electoral quotas 58
gender-sensitive parliament 43, 150
general elections 56, 58, 84, 89
geographic/residence-based franchise 49, 50
Germany 18
Giger, N. 57
Goffman, E. 37–8
'gold standard' evidence 33
Goodin, R.E. 61, 77
Gover, D. 10, 130, 132
governance 4, 11–12, 98–111, 147, 148–9, 151
group identities 52–3, 58, 59
guesting 119

H

Halfon, Robert 20
Hansard 118
Hansard Society 30, 113, 114, 120, 124, 136
harassment 11, 26, 59, 88, 91, 92, 149
hate speech 34–5, 45
headshift 3, 15, 143
Health and Safety Executive 87
Health Select Committee 119
Heclo, H. 104
hereditary peers 84
hierarchies 32–47, 69, 74, 95, 96, 150, 151
Holyrood Palace 18
honesty 46, 148
horseshoe shaped layouts 23, 117
House Administrations 93
House Business Committee 131
House of Commons
  governance 11–12, 99–103
  lack of space for all members 22
  procedure 126–41
  public engagement 79
  representation 8
  scrutiny 9, 112–25
  status 42
  symbols and rituals 43
  talking legislature 130
  virtual participation 19–21
House of Commons Commission 93, 101–2, 105–9, 151
House of Commons Staff Handbook 88
House of Lords
  budgetary decision-making 137
  governance 102–3
  internal governance 11–12
  lack of space for all members 22
  partisan politics 105, 128
  primary legislation procedures 134
  procedural rules 129, 140
  public engagement 79

scrutiny 9
select committees 130
Speakers 101
staff 26
status 41–2
symbols and rituals 42–3, 47
virtual participation 21
House of Lords Commission 93, 108
House staff 83–4, 89–90
HR services 11
hybrid bicameralism 60–1
hybrid working in Houses 93

I

IDEA 58
Ilbert, C. 13, 126, 140
impact measurement 123
inattention 126
inclusiveness
  foundational principles 145–7
  future generations 77–8
  House of Commons 43
  peers 43
  physical space 21
  public engagement 68, 69, 71–2
  reimagining representation 55–9
  rhythms of parliament 38
  standard account of democratic
    representation 51
  workplaces 86, 88–90, 95
Independent Complaints and Grievance
  Scheme 88
Independent Parliamentary Standards
  Authority (IPSA) 87, 89, 91, 93
individualism 39, 44–5, 107, 110
Independent Expert Panel 92
inequalities 33, 43–4, 52
  see also minority groups
informal interactions 21, 34, 41
informal modes of representation 59
information provision 114–16, 118
inquiries 79, 80, 117, 120
Institute for Government 97n3
institutional roles, taking on 106
institutional unwellness 32–6
integrity 37, 44, 46
interaction 5, 9–14
interconnectivity 118–20, 144
interest groups 51, 52–3, 59, 63, 70
intergenerational injustice 77
inter-institutional interaction 9–10, 144, 154
Inter-Parliamentary Union (IPU) 66, 67, 153
intersectionality 2, 53, 58, 150
intra-institutional interaction 10–14, 144, 154

J

James, L. 10, 13, 132
jargon, reducing 71–2
Johnson, Boris 11, 35, 46, 115

Johnson, C. 107
Johnson, J. 62
Joint Committee on Human Rights 115
joint working 118–19, 135
  see also collaborative working
Judge, D. 18, 49, 61, 62, 148

K

Kahneman, D. 131
Keane, J. 3
Kedar, O. 57
Kelly, R. 12
Knight, J. 62
knowledge, hierarchies of 33, 36–7, 44,
  150, 153
König, P.D. 54, 62
Koß, M. 130, 131, 139
Kreppel, A. 152

L

Lafont, C. 61
Landemore, H. 60
language usage 71–2, 118, 146
Latour, B. 33, 40
lay members of parliamentary
  Commissions 108, 109, 151
Leader of the House 101, 104, 106, 109
leaking of information 34
Lebedev, Evgeny Alexandrovich 115
Lee, C. 102, 108
Lefebvre, H. 38
legislation procedures 128
legislative procedures 10, 130, 132–6
legislative space, parliamentary buildings
  as 19–24
legitimation
  alternative forms of non-electoral
    representation 60
  and equality 55–9
  'fused-powers' relationship 8
  governance 100, 106
  hybrid bicameralism 61
  mini-publics 61
  'presumption of generality' 54
  procedure 126, 127, 128, 129, 146
  representation 49, 50
  symbols and rituals 69
Leigh, Sir Edward 20
Leston-Bandeira, C. 8, 18, 28, 49, 66, 69,
  72, 79, 80, 133, 144, 148
Levi-Faur, D. 99
Liaison Committee 115, 117, 118–19, 121
liberal democracy 4, 39, 147
Lidington, David 26
liquid democracy 60
listed building status 6, 25
listening 24, 68, 76–7, 117
lived experience 8, 66, 79
lobbying 84

INDEX

local communities, parliament in 71, 73, 85, 96, 150
London-centricity 25, 29, 73
Lords Spiritual 84
Loughton, Tim 18
Lucas, Caroline 18
Lukes, S. 38
lying 46

M

Maer, L. 10, 113, 121, 130, 144, 147, 154
majority will 70
Manin, B. 54, 63
Manow, P. 17
Mansbridge, J. 51
'masks of virtue' 46
mass meeting spaces 30
maternity leave 88–9
Matthews, F. 80
May, E. 13
May, Theresa 17
McGilchrist, I. 131
McKinnell, Catherine 23–4
Meakin, A. 6, 18, 103, 143, 144
media scrutiny 121
media training 46
Mediator Parliament 66, 81
meritocracy 43
Merrick, R. 20
'Messages' 134–5
#MeToo 88
mini-publics 60, 61, 74, 117, 120
ministerial office 91, 106, 115, 121–2
minority groups
  attacks on 34
  descriptive representation 52
  MPs 56
  public engagement 70
  quota systems 58
  representation of 6, 7, 8, 22, 150
  rhythms of parliament 38–9
  symbols and rituals 44
misleading the House 114
mixed parliamentary committees 74
monitoring bodies 119
Mordaunt, Penny 12
Morse, A. 102
Moss, G. 8
MPs
  career paths 121–2
  consultations with constituents 80
  dyadic versus systematic representation 51, 53
  as employers 91–2, 95
  governance 12, 104
  insecurity of role 89
  MP-citizen interactions 35, 38–40
  'post bags' 73
  professional development 91, 94–5

relatability 75–6
rhythms of parliament 37–41
sanctions for misconduct 11
scrutiny 121
self-regulation 10–11
as staff of parliament 83–4
multidirectionality of responsiveness 53

N

narratives, negotiation of 44
National Audit Office 112, 122, 137
nationalism 44
neo-corporatism 59–60
Netherlands 18
network governance 60
networked parliamentary offices 73
neuropsychology 131
new buildings, proposals for 18
New Zealand 71
NGOs (nongovernmental organisations) 59
non-electoral models of representation 59–62
Northern Ireland Assembly 120
Norton, P. 13, 103, 130

O

Office for National Statistics 2, 8
office spaces 26, 86
open democracy 60
open government 116
openness, as principle 143–4
Ostbelgien model 61
outreach 71, 73, 79
over-promising 40

P

pace of politics 70
Palace of Westminster
  decanting 96, 103, 104
  dilapidation of 6, 25, 27, 87, 103–4
  disability 29, 90, 95–6, 144
  governance history 100–3
  legislative space 19–24
  as public democratic space 27–30
  Restoration and Renewal programme 6, 27, 87, 96, 103–4, 109
  rhythms of parliament 39–40
  suitability of 16
  as a symbol of democracy 17–19
  symbolic intent 5
  as workplace 24–6, 85, 86–94
Palmer, Keith 87
Palonen, K. 13
parallel debating chambers 23
Parkinson, J. 5, 6, 17
Parliament Square 30
Parliamentary Digital Service 84
Parliamentary Heritage Collections 6
parliamentary officers 73
parliamentary privilege 91, 114, 118

participation does not equal engagement 67
Participation Team 79
partisan politics
  and the Commissions 110–11
  governance 101, 104, 105, 110–11
  public engagement 69
  representation 54, 56
  scrutiny 128–9
  workplaces 85, 92–3
partnership working 118–20
party quotas 58
Patel, P. 8
pay, pensions and allowances 91
peers 38, 41, 43, 83–4
performance 6–7
persons papers and records (PPR) 114–15
Peters, G. 99, 100, 102, 103, 105
petitions 23, 24
  see also e-petitions
Petitions Committee 23, 79
Phillips, A. 52, 58
physical presence in parliament 19–22
physical space 5–6, 16–31, 71–2, 117–18, 149–50
Pidcock, Laura 18
Pitkin, H. 17, 48, 49, 50, 62
plain language 71–2, 140
plenaries 22, 131, 132, 133, 134, 138, 139, 152
pluralism 59–60
podcasts 118
Policy Institute 2
'political nation,' connections with 8
political speeches 46
polling 117, 120
populism 44
Portcullis House 38, 85
portfolios 106
'post bags' 73
postmodernism 35
post-truth society 34–5
power differentials
  intra-institutional interaction 13
  mini-publics 61
  minority groups 6
  peerages 41–2
  rhythms of parliament 38
  rituals 42
  scrutiny 115
presence/non-presence 19–22, 25, 93
present, as starting point 4–5
'presumption of generality' 54–5, 62–3
primary legislation procedures 132–4
Prime Minister's Questions 24, 79, 114, 118, 124
principal-agent relationships 50, 51, 53
principles 4, 143–9
prioritisation of MPs time towards quality 41
prioritising the institution 98, 104–5, 107, 110, 148, 151

Private Member Bills 80, 135–6
'problem of unity' 50
procedure 12–13, 42, 49, 126–41, 145, 151, 154
processes of reimagining 2–4, 142–55
process-legitimacy 129
professional development 91, 92, 94–5
promises, under-deliverance of 40
proportional representation 57–8
protest spaces 30
proxy voting 60
Public Accounts Committee 112, 119–20, 122, 137
public engagement
  citizen-parliament engagement 65–82, 150
  continuous nature of 72–3
  core principles 67–8
  meaning of 67
  openness, as principle 144
  parallel debating chambers 23–4
  parliamentary buildings as public democratic spaces 27–30
  scrutiny 113, 116–18
  welcoming and inclusive 71–2
public galleries 29
public inquiries 120
public policies
  algorithms 62
  future generations 78
  joint working 119
  and MP 'post bags' 73
  public engagement 76–7
  responsiveness/reflexivity 53
  scrutiny 122
  standard account of democratic representation 49
public reading stages of primary legislation 133
public schoolboys, parliament configured for 22, 42–3
public spaces 6–7, 16, 27–30, 153
Puwar, N. 7, 27, 43, 69

Q

quality of participation 39
questions in parliament 114
Quilter-Pinner, H. 8
quota systems 58, 150

R

racism 90
Rai, S.M. 6–7, 17
rapporteur systems 122
Ravenscroft, T. 17
Redlich, J. 13
re-election, as goal 101, 105, 107
Rees-Mogg, Jacob 11, 19, 20
reflexivity 53–4, 62–3, 146–7
reform versus reimagining 3

refurbishment of physical estate 6
regions 63
Reichstag building, Berlin 18
Reingold, B. 53
relatability 75–6, 145
relevance 68, 74–5, 145
remote access to parliament 19–20, 21, 93, 96, 117, 151
remote working for parliamentary staff 25, 86, 87
renovation projects 16, 95
reporting back to citizens 76, 116, 118, 119–20, 124
representation
  access to parliament buildings 28–9
  artifacts 6
  descriptive representation 52
  disability 21
  dyadic versus systematic representation 51, 53
  electoral versus non-electoral 48, 49, 51, 59–62, 150
  equality 146
  governance 105, 111
  House of Commons 8
  local level 40
  not the same as engagement 68–9
  partisan politics 54–5
  priority over participation 8
  proportional representation 57–8
  reimagining 48–64
  representative chains 50
  standard account of 49–50
  symbolic representation 17
  theory of 48
resonant connections 39
responsiveness/reflexivity 53–4, 62–3, 145–7
Restoration and Renewal programme 6, 27, 87, 96, 103–4, 109
restorative architecture 16–17
'rewrite authority' 130, 138
rhythms of parliament 37–41, 47, 147–8, 150
right to participate in democracy 37
rituals 32–47, 69, 150
robes 42, 43
Rodgers of Riverside, Lord 18
Rosa, H. 37, 39
round-table events 117, 118
Royal Commissions 120
Rüdig, W. 59
'rule of Crown initiative' 137, 139
rules, procedural 13, 35–6, 42, 49, 126–41
Runciman, D. 46, 54, 63
Russell, M. 10, 13, 109, 123, 130, 132

S

safe workplaces, need for 26, 85, 86–8, 94
Saward, M. 17, 59, 63, 145–6
Schäfer, A. 52, 57

Scotland 18, 120
scrutiny
  agenda control 132
  delegated/secondary legislation 136
  domestic committees 107
  effective 113
  governance 102, 108
  interaction 9–10
  openness, as principle 144
  parallel debating chambers 23
  procedural rules 128–9
  public engagement 66, 80
  reimagining 112–25, 147, 151
  reimagining parliamentary government 154
  rhythms, rituals and symbols 34
  secondary legislation 10, 136
  security 23, 26, 27–8, 86–8, 89–90, 143–4
select committees
  financial procedures 138
  governance 102, 106
  impact measurement 123
  language, parliamentary 118
  listening role 117
  procedure 130–1, 152
  public engagement 73, 79
  rhythms 38–9
  scrutiny 9–10, 113, 115, 117, 121
  soft power 124
  unopposed return 115
  workplaces 93, 96
Select Committees Engagement Team 79
self-authorised representation 59, 63
self-exclusion 51, 59
self-regulation 102
Senedd building, Cardiff 18
Setälä, M. 74
sexual misconduct 11, 88, 149
Shadow Leader 101, 106
shared workspaces 26
Shenton, C. 5
Siefken, S. 66, 79
Siewert, M.B. 54, 62
size of chambers 22
slavery 44
social class 42–3, 56–7
social distancing 19, 85, 93
social hierarchies 6
social movements 59
social parliament 63
social proximity 52, 56
Social Shorthand formats 118
soft power 124
sortition 60–1, 74
South Africa 73
space 4, 5–7, 16–31, 43
Speaker 13, 45, 71, 101, 105–6, 114
spin doctors 46

staff *see* workplaces
Standards Committees 91–2
Standing Orders 12–13, 107, 126, 138, 151
State Opening of Parliament 33, 42
status 33, 41–2
Steeper, Zoe and Lewis 23
Steffani, W. 130
Straw, J. 13
Straw Review 102
Street, B. 36
structural inequalities 52, 58
summoning witnesses 114–15
surveys 8, 33, 74, 75, 79, 90, 117
sustainability 68, 77, 78, 148
symbols and rituals 5, 17–19, 41–6, 69, 146, 150

T

Teacher Ambassadors 79
tenure of staff 84, 89
territorial diversity 63
terrorism risks 86–7
Therborn, G. 5
Thevoz, S. 36
Thompson, L. 72, 133
tradition versus principle 20
translations 72, 79, 118
transparency 9, 18, 78, 102, 106, 108–9, 110, 143–4
tribalism 34
Trump, Donald 46
trust 2, 8, 29, 35, 37, 78, 148
truth 34–5, 40
Twitter 34, 117

U

unborn citizens 77–8, 150
UNESCO World Heritage status 6, 18, 25
unity 54–5, 62–3
universality 49
unopposed return 114–15
unwellness 32–6, 147–8
Urbinati, N. 51, 54
urgent questions 114, 124–5
Urwin, R. 22

V

Valsangiacomo, C. 60
Verge, T. 43
video-conferencing facilities 117
violence, risk to staff of 86–7
virtual participation *see* remote access to parliament
'votable agendas' 132
voting rights 50, 55

W

Wales 18, 120
Walker, A. 8, 23, 27, 79
Warren, M.E. 49, 50
wellness, enhancing 37, 147–8, 150
Westminster Hall 23–4, 79, 117
'Westminster system' 2
wheelchair users 22
White, Gemma 92
White, H. 10, 21, 27, 36, 87, 123, 128
white men, dominance of 42–3, 92
Whitehall 85
Wollaston, Sarah 121
women
  abuse 34, 59, 87
  all-women shortlists 58
  challenges to legitimacy of 89–90
  descriptive representation 52
  exclusion from participation 39, 59
  gender-sensitive parliament 43–4
  MPs 56, 59
  representation 22
working classes 56–7
working versus talking parliaments 130–1, 136
workplaces 24–6, 83–97, 146, 150–1
World Heritage Sites 6, 18, 25, 103–4
World Values Survey 2
Wright, A. 7, 104, 107
Wright reforms 107, 121, 132
written participation 20–1

Y

Yong, B. 12, 101, 102, 103, 108
youth engagement 77–8
youth quotas 58
Youth Select Committee 79–80